Betrayal and Survival and Beyond

A Memoir

Betrayal and Survival and Beyond

A Memoir

by Mathis Szykowski

DORRANCE PUBLISHING CO., INC.
PITTSBURGH, PENNSYLVANIA 15222

The events, people, and places herein are depicted to the best recollection of the author, who assumes complete and sole responsibility for the accuracy of this narrative.

ISBN: 978-1-4349-0144-6
Library of Congress Control Number: 2008931923

Printed in the United States of America

First Printing

For more information or to order additional books, please contact:
Dorrance Publishing Co., Inc.
701 Smithfield Street
Pittsburgh, Pennsylvania 15222
U.S.A.
1-800-788-7654
www.dorrancebookstore.com

For my parents,
Ichok Szykowski and Pepi Pincu Szykowski,
who were assassinated at Auschwitz. For my children,
Monique Celia Mojica, RaphaÎl Anthony Szykowski,
Sebastian Conway Collett, and Catherine Brooker Collett.
Also for my grandson, Ehren "Bear" Thomas.

Acknowledgments

I wish to thank the friends who labored and read this memoir during more than a decade that it took to be written and revised. In particular I want to thank my friend and former colleague Raymonde Carroll who never lost faith in the validity of this memoir, and who spent countless hours making insightful suggestions. I also want to thank David Young and Michael Dirda for their encouragement. Many thanks go to Betty and Marvin Mandell who took risks in publishing two chapters in New Politics, and for the immense contributions they made in changing my life. Thanks to all the friends, too many to mention, who read or heard me read parts of this memoir.

And above all, thanks to my wife Carol Graham, who sustained my efforts to write about the events of my life with an unfailing sense of humor and perspective.

Introduction by Michael Dirda

All lives are interesting, but some lives are more interesting than others. Mathis Szykowski—perhaps the most brilliant teacher of literature I have ever known—never talked about his own past in the classroom. Whether a course was devoted to Flaubert or French stylistics, Szykowski would patiently elicit critical remarks from his class about that day's assignment. But eventually he would surrender to the force of his own thought and begin to point out distinctive elements in a paragraph from Stendhal or a student composition, gradually teasing out the implications of the diction and imagery or even of the syntax of the sentences. By the time the bell rang, you knew that passage inside and out, top to bottom, and you knew it would never need to be interpreted again. Szykowski had seen everything there was to be seen in it.

While there were many superb teachers at Oberlin College at the end of the 1960s, this professor of French alone possessed what one might call the authority of lived experience. When Szykowski spoke of politics and war and human aspiration, of love and dashed dreams, of work and art and ideas, you knew he wasn't just lecturing. These were matters about which he felt passionately; they were real, immediate, vitally important. He would glance around a seminar table and those eyes—huge behind their thick black spectacles—would peer into your soul. To some students, his classes were distinctly unsettling, but to others they provided an intellectual exhilaration that has never been forgotten or gotten over.

Back then I used to wonder about Szykowski's past. I knew he was a Polish-Romanian Jew from France and he didn't come to teaching until his late thirties. But what was his life like before he started graduate study at Stanford, before Oberlin hired him on a tenure track contract, eventually granting him tenure even though he hadn't yet received his Ph.D.? How did this extraordinary man become himself?

That life story is told in Betrayal and Survival and Beyond, one man's often harrowing experience of the twentieth century. Just tracing the basic outline of Mathis Szykowski's early life is humbling. A traumatic childhood in Paris during the 1930s as the son of unhappily married working-class Jews. An adolescence spent largely on the run during the German occupation of France. An orphan at sixteen because of the war and the Holocaust—and then a refugee to the United States.

Only in 1946 did the young Szykowski, who had already experienced a full lifetime of suffering and loss, travel by Liberty ship to New York, where he stayed briefly with an uncle before crossing the country by train to California. He had other relatives on the West Coast, and there he hoped to continue his education. But before long, he was drafted, so he really started to learn English among soldiers in Louisiana.

During his military service he was stationed in Japan, where he passed through the ruins of Hiroshima. After his discharge, he took up one minimum-wage job after another—working on a conveyor belt in a bread factory, constructing prefabricated showers, selling tickets in an amusement park, and operating mimeo machines and presses in a print shop.

Of course, much of his real life went on elsewhere. Szykowski joined socialist groups and the Workers Party, espoused Wilhelm Reich's unorthodox ideas about the relationship between the body and mind, went to the movies constantly, listened to music, and read book after book.

In New York City, he lived a hand-to-mouth bohemian existence, yearned for friendship and love, eventually married and divorced and married again, and had children. Hoping for financial security, he ended up heavily in debt for years after a friend's business scheme failed.

Yet when this memoir closes, Szykowski is thirty-six years old, the proud possessor of a bachelor's degree, and about to move his family to Stanford University. He has managed to survive, but as he says, "I did not do it by myself; I had help along the way. I also had incredible luck. Surely this luck was abetted by my own will to act, but I owe immense debts of gratitude to the many people who were there to help me up when I was down. Through them, I learned to heal and celebrate life."

It has been my privilege to know Mathis Szykowski for more than forty years. Long ago he was my teacher at Oberlin College, and he remains my teacher still, though now I also count him as a friend. As anybody who knows him would expect, *Betrayal and Survial and Beyond* tells a remarkable, sometimes heartbreaking story. But then, as any reader of this memoir will soon realize, Mathis Szykowski is a remarkable human being, as courteous to others as he is curious about the world, both inspiringly intelligent and deeply kind.

Michael Dirda, a longtime columnist for the Washington Post Book World, received the 1993 Pulitzer Prize for criticism. He is the author of the memoir *An Open Book* and of four collections of essays: *Readings, Bound to Please, Book by Book,* and *Classics for Pleasure.*

Preface

I was sixteen years old when most of my family, including my father and mother, died in the Holocaust. Born in Paris, the only child of immigrant parents from Poland and Romania, I embraced wholeheartedly French culture as it was taught in the French school system. I resisted my parents' reservations about the trustworthiness of the Gentiles: "All anti-Semites! The best of them!" And I ignored expressions of anti-Semitism. I always claimed to be French, first and foremost. I was determined to become the best of citizens. My world and my dreams crumbled in the years that followed the defeat of France in 1940.

When some thirteen thousand Jews were arrested in the early dawn of July, 1942, I realized that Jews of all ages, gender, and national origin were destined to spend the war in concentration camps. There were already a few camps in France then where men were detained by the French or German authorities. I was frightened by the prospect of winding up in one of these camps. I turned to my mother and urged her to flee Paris with me into the non-occupied zone of France. She refused but provided the funds for my escape. I spent the next twenty-seven months living as best I could, and I survived the war.

I want to stress that no one survives solely by one's efforts and will to live. Survivors of the concentration camps, such as David Rousset, Elie Weisel, Primo Levi, and many others, have testified that their survival was due to help received at a critical moment, when their lives were in the balance. During those twenty-seven months of exile, there were many occasions where my life was in danger. I was helped by people who had nothing to gain by helping me, and who risked their own lives in the process. They were ordinary people acting in extraordinary ways in a time when it was safest for them to close their eyes and acquiesce.

When I returned to Paris after the Liberation, my life was safe, but my future was precarious. My formal education had stopped in 1941, and outside of being a passable farmhand, I had no marketable skills. When my father's older brother, who had immigrated to the United States before World War I, opened his home to me. The promise of a new family and future was irresistible. I left France on June 1, 1946, and became an immigrant. I did not see my native land again until the summer of 1969.

I have tried to understand the meaning and consequences of the events that played havoc with my early life. I have revisited the trajectory which took me from Paris to a college campus where for 30 years, I taught French and French literature.

Chapter One

Lodz was still a part of Russia when my father was born there in 1898. It was an industrial city and, I imagine, it was still feeling the growing pains of industrialization with crowded, unsanitary living conditions and foul air. The Jewish neighborhood where he grew up had unpaved streets, which turned into rivers of mud during the rainy season. Chickens and ducks in the streets, goats, cows, and delivery men with horse-drawn carriages rounded up the teeming life of the neighborhood. My father was the youngest of eight children, seven boys and a girl. He and two of his brothers survived an outbreak of diphtheria at the turn of the century. He reported that his mother had doted on him. His family was traditional, orthodox, and of modest means. A photograph of my grandmother and grandfather, which my father received in Paris in the 1920's, reflects the faces of two worn out people. My grandmother's eyes are sad, and a faint smile crosses her face; my father had her eyes. Grandfather's eyes are half closed. His white beard is short; the mouth set. Grandfather worked in a factory producing seltzer water, while my grandmother owned a small vegetable and fruit store. My father recalled getting up in the wee hours to help her carry her merchandise into the store. My grandparents were not assimilated Jews, nor did they aspired to be anything but Jews left to live in peace. They lived in fear of the Poles and the Russian police; my father called them Cossacks. Despite these hardships, my father always spoke of a happy childhood, the happiest time of his life. He had a mother he adored and who spoiled him and an older brother he admired and wanted to emulate. I loved listening to him tell and retell the tall tales of his childhood.

His older brother, Yossel, was something of a hooligan, a rebel who brought the outside world into his orthodox household. My father recalled with great delight the time his brother sat down at a Passover dinner and took out a bagel from his pocket, bit into it, and watched his father have an apoplectic fit. My father's face would light up with a malicious grin, and he would cackle at the end of his story. Yossel's rebellion triggered my father's own rebellion at Hebrew school. His favorite example was of the time the rabbi was teaching the story of Abraham and Sarah and of their sorrow about being childless. Abraham and Sarah prayed very hard and very long, each in solitude, and soon after Sarah was with child. "Impossible! That's not the way it happens," blurted my father. That outburst earned him a severe spanking. That rabbi had a very long beard and a heavy hand. My father did not grow up to be a religious man. He went to the synagogue on important holidays and lit a candle in remembrance of his mother's death.

Yossel not only rebelled against family and religion, he rebelled against societal norms. He was a member of the Jewish Bund, a Marxist party associated with the Second International. When Yossel joined the Bund, new ideas and a social consciousness entered the house. He spoke of the coming of a better world, especially for Jews. He spoke of a world where men would live freely, as equals. My father, in awe of his older, and in his view, glamorous brother, soaked up these ideas of progress and socialism and carried them for the rest of his life. He was not a theoretician; he could not have explained any aspect of socialist doctrine. But he had a strong sense of what was morally just, which carried him as he worked for his union and his community.

I began to hear these stories from my father in 1936. I was ten years old. My parents had separated for the final time. My mother had left home without me, and I discovered a father I never really knew. In France that spring, a Popular Front government had been elected and my father, after more than four years of unemployment, hoped to regain his right to work and find a job. On weekends, when I saw him, he told me stories about his childhood, stories about his brother's misadventures, and stories about how he and his friends had thrown stones at the Cossacks. Unfortunately, he also told me about the misdeeds of my mother and her family, stories that would poison my mind against her. That spring, the Spanish Civil War had started and despite the fact that fascism had triumphed in Italy and Germany, there was hope for a new and more just world, a promise that was held out to us by the example of the Soviet Union. The trials of the old Bolsheviks were brushed aside; we did not talk about the Nuremberg racial laws or the persecution of German Jews. We thought it would soon all go away. The Revolution was coming. I listened to my father's friend Favich recount his adventures during the October Revolution in Petrograd. I listened to tales about Uncle Yossel being thrown in jail during some riots and about how my grandmother had bribed the police to let him go. I listened to promises of abundance and equality and how talent would be recognized and rewarded. Six years later, both Favich and my father were murdered in Auschwitz.

There is one event in my father's life of which he spoke very little, but which I wish he had spoken of in greater detail because it foreshadowed his future in France and illuminated one of the few known aspects of World War I. Lodz was Russian territory when the German troops occupied it in 1915. My father was taken, at the age of seventeen, to a forced labor camp in Germany. He told of being starved, beaten at times, and worked for long hours. As a Russian civilian, he was not protected by the Geneva Convention; he never saw a member of the Red Cross. When my father told of being shipped to Germany with other young men and forced to work under dire conditions, I accepted it with a sense of horror and awe. Among all his incredible adventures, the one that was not told in any detail was how he was arrested or taken into custody. He never spoke about how he felt at the time or what it meant to be uprooted from his family, his language, and his culture. I have thought quite often about the culture of silence among Holocaust survivors. Many did not speak out until many years had passed, or until the Eichmann trial in Jerusalem shed new light on that period. Some survivors refused outright to evoke any part of their experience; they lived within their nightmares. My father had survived the Great War, relatively safe in a German camp, while others had lived and died in the trenches. He had not suffered as much as some, and when he told stories of his internment, he avoided melodramatic tones. He was not a hero in his own eyes.

He never went home. I wish now that he had spoken of his decision to go to Paris rather than to return to Lodz. I never knew whether his decision was conscious, well reasoned, or if it was the result of an impulse to reward himself after four years of confinement. As a child, it did not occur to me to ask him, my mother, or any member of my family, under what circumstances they decided to emigrate to France; it was something we did not talk about. Later on, I accepted without questioning that economic reasons had been the overwhelming motivation for leaving their native land. I had to become an immigrant myself to understand that there were other reasons to emigrate.

In 1919, at the age of twenty-one, my father arrived in Paris. I have a sepia photograph of him at age twenty-six that shows a mane of dark curly hair crowning a very serious mien. The photo was taken a few months before his wedding. He had a broad, crooked smile, which he hid in photographs in order to hide his missing teeth. He was wearing a bow tie, as he did in his wedding picture. I never saw him wear a bow tie again. I have inherited his waddling walk, but not his blue eyes.

My father was without identification papers and had no marketable skills. World War I had wreaked havoc on the French population. France needed to be rebuilt, so immigrants were welcomed to perform all sorts of tasks. Many immigrants arrived in France with work contracts to work on large industrial farms, in mines, or in construction. My father could read and write in four languages: Polish, Russian, Hebrew, and Yiddish. He also had a working knowledge of German. All that was useless in France. He found a job in a tannery where he learned to prepare expensive pelts for the furrier trade. This was not a traditional skill among Jews in Paris, and it would not help him to establish his own business. It would be a source of conflict between him and my mother, whose entire family aspired to the affluence and respectability of small business owners. My father was a gregarious man who liked people. He enjoyed the companionship of his coworkers and the activities of his union. Of his early years in the tannery there is one incident that he used to illustrate his naiveté. On the day of his first paycheck, some of his coworkers, following the custom in France, invited him to have a drink at the local bistro. In 1919, absinthe was still served, and a round of that deadly brew was ordered. His companions mixed their drink with water, but my father, like any self-respecting Eastern European with a taste for strong vodka, could not be persuaded to pour water in his glass. If he could drink vodka, absinthe would not present him a challenge. Each worker paid for a round in turn. After an hour, my father was not feeling well, and he decided that dinner was the needed cure. He ordered his food with the usual carafe of wine, but soon after the bistro began to swirl around him. He had to be carried to his room, where he lay sick for three days. That was the only time in his life that he was drunk.

He made a choice that was to have drastic consequences in later years. After the Versailles treaty was signed, Poland became a national entity once again. My father had come to France as a Russian refugee; all Russians who came to France after 1917 or who did not return to the Soviet Union could claim refugee status. Although he could have claimed his Polish citizenship by applying for it at the Polish consulate in Paris, he did not. I doubt that his inaction stemmed from political conviction. I believe that he saw no reason to reclaim his Polish identity. He never expressed any love or nostalgia for Poland. Life in France was far more pleasant than it had been in Poland, especially in 1919. Paris was a lot more exciting than Lodz, so why worry about being a citizen of any country? Or perhaps he thought he was better off the fewer dealings he had with the authorities. I understand that feeling quite well; I still have pangs of anxiety when I cross the Canadian border to visit my daughter and have to explain why I am entering Canada. But, being a Russian refugee did not seem to bother my father. Under Nazi rule, being a Polish Jew was not any safer than a Russian Jew. I can't help thinking that if he had claimed his Polish nationality, my father might have spared himself fourteen months of captivity in Compiègne.

I know much less about my mother's childhood and adolescence. I have recently acquired a photograph of her from when she was a young woman in Romania. In it, she wears a folkloric dress, and she sits sideways on a round table, one of her legs dangling, her hair sporting a bandana which hides her blondish curls. Over her gray eyes, she wore rimless glasses, which she could not prevent from sliding down her nose while she worked. Her most striking features were her lips, thin and hard-set.

According to her papers, she was born in 1895, in the town of Roman. According to her family, she was born in 1892. She would thus have been six years older than my father. My grandmother had married a widower who brought a son with him. I was never told what my grandfather did for a living, nor what kind of life they shared in Roman. When my grandfather died, my mother was nine years old. He left my grandmother with four children to raise. Severe poverty soon befell the family. My mother, Pepi, who later called herself Pauline, was placed as an apprentice with a family where she was housed and fed in return for being a domestic servant and learning to be a dressmaker. She rarely spoke of that period of her life. During the ten years that she raised me, there were only a few hints about her early life in a family of strangers, accompanied by reminders of my very privileged life. She envied her brothers, Avram, or Adolph, who later became a watchmaker, and the youngest, Lazare, or Paul, who became a tailor, who were not sent away. My grandmother kept the family together by caning chairs. I was told that she would walk miles from farm to farm, carrying her tools, her materials, and sometimes even chairs on her back. She was a small woman with an indomitable will who had received an education uncommon for girls in her time. Unlike most of her family, she could read Hebrew books and understand what she read. My mother never learned to read. Living conditions were harsher for my mother than they were for my father. When my family and I visited Roman in 1993, it was obvious that life was still tough.

Because of her family's poverty, and because she was a girl, my mother was not sent to school. By the time I realized that she could not read or write, I was used to her way of counting metro stops or searching familiar landscapes to navigate the streets of Paris. After I learned to read, I could help her find her way around Paris. Later on in my life, I realized that the Romanian side of my family was practically illiterate, save for my uncle Adolph. By contrast, the members of my father's family had received the equivalent of an eighth grade education. Paradoxically, the Romanian side of my family became much more successful than the Polish side. However, vanity played a large role in my mother's life. She was quick to adopt the latest fashions and was always in fierce competition with her siblings, and especially her sisters-in-law, about the goods each of them had acquired and flaunted. As a child, I witnessed bitter fights between my parents that were caused by my mother's petty jealousies and what she perceived to be my father's inability to provide for his family.

As in my father's case, World War I played a part in my mother's immigration to France in 1922. During the war, her brother Adolph was drafted and sent to the Hungarian front. For a non-assimilated Jew in Eastern Europe or in the Balkans, ideas such as " patriotism," "defense of country," "or ultimate sacrifice" were not very meaningful. Adolph managed to become a prisoner of war as soon as possible. His life as a prisoner of war was far from comfortable, but it was humane and he lived through it, just as my father had lived through his internment in Germany.

Economic conditions in Romania in 1919 were poor. My grandmother had a half sister who had emigrated to France at the turn of the century. My great-aunt Jeannette and her husband, Maurice Leizer, were well established as tailors in the Latin quarter of Paris. The couple proceeded to encourage members of their family to join them in France, which was paradise in comparison to Romania. In France you could work hard and build up a good business, you could live anywhere you wanted because French society was a model of tolerance. There were no laws against Jews. Jewish children attended school with other children. Jews were accepted at the university, and in time a Jew could become a French citizen, a registered voter, and become more French than the French.

Uncle Adolph immigrated to France in 1919, practiced his trade, and sent money home. He eventually brought his mother, sister, and youngest brother to Paris where they practiced the trades they had learned in Romania. Whenever I conjure up an image of my mother from that time, I see a woman bent over with a needle in her hand. I can still hear her sigh, laugh, or complain about an ache, but her needle kept going until the task was done. In 1940, I read and heard that Jews were either parasites, plutocrats, or Bolsheviks.

Adolph installed his mother and sister in a *mansarde* in the Saint-Paul quarter, near the Marais, where there was a large community of Jews and all the necessary shops to maintain an orthodox household. Both my grandmother and my mother were very observant Jews who followed faithfully the rituals of Judaism. They lived with no heat, no hot water, and a Turkish-style bathroom in the hall. But there was still room for numerous dish sets, so they could observe important holidays. Although we always gathered in my grandmother's apartment for the first night of Sėder, it's a mystery to me how she managed to cook on a small gas burner. Our own apartment was also quite small, but it too contained the requisite set of dishes for an orthodox home.

My mother was not her mother's favorite child. As she approached her late twenties, she was considered an old maid and a disgrace to her family. Since my grandmother could read her Hebrew prayer books, my mother's illiteracy added to the contempt her mother felt. Nothing my mother did found favor in her mother's eyes, whether it was a dress she had sewn for a client or a meal she had cooked. Granted, she was a terrible cook; so terrible in fact, that when I visited her at the age of fourteen, I would often cook for myself. She was often too busy working from early morning until late at night to bother with cooking. However, she was not a forerunner of modern feminism. She worked because she had to; it was an absolute economic necessity. Had she married well, she would have been content to manage her home and enjoy the amenities she felt she deserved, and that she deserved because of the deprivations of her childhood. Most of the people I knew were poor, and in the Jewish community all feared the effects of the evil eye in all aspects of their lives. My mother would sigh and complain about her hard life, and, on occasion, show off the riches she had acquired through her hard work. On the other hand, if a friend or relative pointed out one of her prized possessions or her good health, she would spit three times to counteract the "evil eye." I remember how embarrassed I was when she insisted we both spit three times each time we passed a Catholic church.

My parents were introduced to each other in 1924 by a matchmaker. In that way, they followed a tradition of Jewish life from their native lands. My grandmother was pleased with her prospective son-in-law because he could read and understand Aramaic Hebrew, which meant they could discuss the Torah. My mother's family promised to provide a substantial dowry to get the couple started. I never heard a single anecdote about their courtship or their wedding day, but I heard a lot of recriminations from my father about the undelivered dowry. He'd been deceived, he had said, and had married an old maid whose family had left their promises unfulfilled. "What could you expect from Romanians?" he asked. "They were all thieves and liars."

Yes, in my home, both Poles and Romanians had nothing but derogatory remarks to make about each other. Neither ethnic group displayed an abundance of tolerance and generosity.

My parents were married in November of 1924, and they rented a two-room apartment on rue des Bois, in a neighborhood that was essentially home to working-class families and a substantial number of low-income housing developments. Our building had probably been built in the nineteenth century, when the neighborhood still bordered the edge of the countryside. Between our house and the Porte des Lilas, there were a lot of unbuilt and uncultivated hills. From time to time, we would walk to a small dairy farm to get fresh milk. Once a week or so, a man would appear with his goats, and he would fill a cup or a container for a very modest sum. My mother believed that drinking fresh goat's milk would prevent all sorts of diseases, particularly tuberculosis. My mother and grandmother had all sorts of theories about food. My grandmother always reeked of garlic; she would rub raw garlic on the crust of French bread for a snack. When I tried to imitate her, the garlic burned my mouth. As soon as one of her friends or relatives would tell my mother about the benefit of some new food, she would rush out to buy it for me. That is how I came to suck on raw eggs, eat ham and horse steaks, and drink cod liver oil. Since some of these things were not kosher, I was not given a plate, knife, or fork to eat my meals. I discovered how my ancestors ate their food long ago. My mother's obsession with food unintentionally started me on the road to atheism. I ate that *treif* food, and despite the fact that God saw all and knew all, I survived.

Our apartment had only one bedroom and a dining room. The kitchen was a small alcove that could only accommodate one person. It contained a stone sink with cold running water, a gas burner, and a small working table. The alcove was crammed with pots and pans and cleaning supplies. We washed everything in the kitchen, including our food and faces. Brushing my teeth began in the home of my foster parents when I was ten years old. I was bathed once a week in the dining room, and when I grew a bit older, I was taken to the municipal showers where I had precisely twenty minutes to wash up. We washed our laundry in the kitchen sink in a large basin and dried it on strings we hung across the ceiling. Next to the kitchen, there was a small room housing a sit-down toilet, which was also used as a storage space. I slept in the same bedroom as my parents until I was ten when they separated. The dining room was also my mother's work room and contained a table with chairs, two buffets, a sewing machine, and a coal stove that heated, in a manner of speaking, the house in winter. I can still see the gas chandelier, which provided us with light, and hear the hissing of the flames. When we got electricity, we had long discussions about whether it represented a greater danger to our lives than gas.

My parents brought me back to the place where I was born in 1926. I was a large baby, and my mother had a difficult delivery. But because I was born with swirling hair, my mother's friend predicted that I would be a lucky person. That is why my mother, in very trying circumstances, never appeared to panic: she knew I would be fine. Early in my short life, this prediction was proven true. I was sick with a high fever and began having convulsions. Rather than calling a doctor, my mother summoned a neighbor who saved me by putting a set of cold keys behind my neck. That was the beginning of my mother's unshakable faith that nothing tragic would ever befall me.

My parents were not suited for each other. They had traits that could only cause misunderstandings and eventual separation. For example, my mother was a hardworking woman with a desire to become affluent. Money, she thought, would solve all her problems. It would buy her the clothes, furs, and jewelry that signaled success and would show her mother that she was as wealthy as her brothers. Throughout her life, my mother sought the approval of my grandmother. But my grandmother, as devoutly religious as she was, was neither loving nor lovable. I remember one of my aunts telling me in 1978 that thirty-six years after my grandmother disappeared in Auschwitz, she was still frightened of her mother-in-law, and that she shivered whenever she thought about her. My aunt also thought that her mother-in-law had the powers of a sorceress and said she could feel knives going through her heart when she looked at her. I was not frightened of my grandmother, but I knew that she did not like me because I was my mother's son. In my family, sparing the children from adult quarrels was an unknown concept, and hitting someone below the belt was quite common. I was quite aware that my grandmother's favorite grandchild was Adolph's son, Maurice, who was the first grandchild born into the family. I always envied Maurice's position, but recently I discovered that he did not really feel that favored. "I rarely saw our grandmother even though she lived a few blocks away" he told me. To my father, money and success meant very little even though he worked hard at his job. Tanning furs is an occupation where you are in constant contact with foul odors. When we recently visited a leather-tanning compound in Morocco, I was reminded of the horrible stench of my father's workplace. He brought home with him the smells of the factory. This was not the husband my mother had dreamed about as a young girl. He was satisfied to bring home a paycheck and would have been happy to eat food prepared with care, read his newspaper aloud, and discuss the state of the world. I remember listening to him read the serial novels and the romance biographies that his Yiddish newspaper carried daily. That's how I first learned about the evil monk Rasputin and King Karol's mistress. He expected my mother to show the same devotion to her family as his mother had to hers, along with the same generosity of spirit. My mother had never experienced devotion or generosity. It would take the threat of death at the hands of the Nazis for her to save my life.

In the first years of my parents' marriage, however, the economic situation was good, and they began to save money to build a house in what is now a suburb of Paris but was then farm country. I never understood why they undertook such a project, one no one else in the family imitated. The house my parents built—a very modest one—was located in an offshoot of Villepinte called the Clos-Montceleux. There were a few families who lived there the entire year, but most residents came only during the summer months. The air in Paris, polluted by coal dust and industry, was reputed to be very bad. During my childhood, tuberculosis was a feared disease. Whenever one of us became sick or looked pale, fresh air was the prescribed tonic. In the winter, we were swathed in clothes, with scarves hiding the lower half of our faces. To this day, like most French people, I fear drafts. When our house was finished in 1929, we began to spend our summers there.

The house was built with bricks covered by stucco. It had three small rooms and an alcove kitchen. Here too, we washed in the kitchen, but we also had an outhouse. There was enough ground for my father to cultivate a vegetable garden and plant a few fruit trees. One summer we even raised a few chickens. The predominant language in our new neighborhood was Yiddish; occasionally, you could hear all the languages of Eastern and Central Europe, as well as the Balkans, being spoken. French was definitely a minority language, and it was poorly spoken by the vacationers. The whole neighborhood, extending five or six blocks, was full of women and children who deserted Paris for the fresh air. Sometimes the men would come home in the evening, but the majority of them would arrive on

Friday afternoon and leave Monday morning. There was a broken-down old bus that would go to the local train station twice a day. If you missed the bus, you had to walk three kilometers. There were few local stores in those years: a couple of bars, a bakery, a grocery store, and a weekly outdoor market. During the week, milk and milk products, eggs, and fruits were sold door-to-door from horse-drawn carriages. However, since kosher food and cooking were a must in our neighborhood, the men would arrive from Paris with purchases from the Marais or Belleville. Even live fowls were brought home to be butchered ritualistically by the resident summer *shohet.* My mother always sent me to have the chickens killed. I can still recall the animal's neck being plucked while a prayer was said, the razor blade sliding against its throat, and the fowl running around the shed as it bled to death. Years later I witnessed the killing of chickens with an ax; the fear I felt in my stomach did not make a vegetarian of me. Instead, I felt both repulsion and fascination. It is remarkable how, as children, our sensibilities can coexist with our cruelty. Our humanity hovers between the expression of our sensibility and our propensity to kill.

Chapter Two

My earliest memory is of hanging out our apartment window on the rue des Bois, yelling, "Maman! Papa!" and running frantically from the bedroom to the front door. I was two and a half years old, and I had been alone for several hours. My parents, for once, had gone to a movie, relying on the fact that I was a sound sleeper. I believe now that I was a sound sleeper precisely because I had become accustomed to the familiar noises of the house. When all was perfectly quiet, I felt threatened and woke to seek the comfort and protection of an adult. Panic seized me that day when I discovered I was alone. I tried to open the front door, but it was locked. I did succeed in opening a window and pushing the steel shutters open. As I began to cry out, windows opened, and our neighbors tried in vain to calm me down. It was not the comical scene that Truffaut portrayed in *Small Change*. In fact my parents were quite displeased to find me awake and crying. I most likely got a lecture on my stupidity, a lecture I received numerous times in the future. The following morning I woke up with an excruciating earache. In my mother's mind, anything that happened was either to be blamed on her enemies, real or imagined, or by the will of God. Either she had been cursed by a jealous person, or God was punishing her for having gone to the movies without her most precious possession, her son. That day I was wrapped in a blanket and cuddled to my mother's bosom. The all-too-brief warmth I experienced that day left me with a longing for affection that has never left me. I think it is also the source of my feeling that even in times of pain and distress, happiness is close at hand.

At about the same time, I was enrolled in the local kindergarten which faced the elementary school I later attended. My mother sent me there because she worked at home and could not have me interfering with her work schedule. Not only did I go to kindergarten all day, but I was taken to an after-school nursery at the end of the day. My memories of these years have become somewhat blurred—a few incidents, but mostly feelings. Attending a French kindergarten and nursery contributed in no small part to my becoming a French boy—a boy who began to reject the culture his parents were trying to instill in him. I think, however, that my parents wanted to raise me as a French child to insure my success and happiness in life. They were happier and wealthier than in their native land, and they wanted the very best for me. For my parents, the French culture and its language were the key to a successful future. But at the same time, they insisted that I conform to Jewish ways, and be a good student of Hebrew, and be a good Jew. They did not understand the contradictions of conforming to a multiplicity of cultural behaviors. And if in their daily encounters they met with misunderstandings or even hostility, it was always blamed on the gentiles' anti-Semitism. They often blamed Jews for provoking that anti-Semitism.

When I was seven years old, I refused to learn Hebrew. My parents were bitterly disappointed, but still they brought

Yeshiva students to the house as tutors. I remember that one student would draw letters of the Hebrew alphabet on pieces of cardboard. "That's an aleph, Mathis," he said.

"What's an aleph?" I asked.

He replied, "An aleph is an aleph. Look, see, remember! Here, you draw it. No, no! Not like that!"

My eyes were already damaged, but no one in my family or at school realized it. Although I was cross-eyed, no one had thought to have my eyes examined. It was not until second grade that I was sent home with a note informing my parents of the problem. This meant that I could not draw an aleph, nor could I recognize any of the other strange signs that were drawn for me. Because I was not learning, I began to understand what it meant when the teacher pulled on my sideburns so hard tears flooded my eyes. Pride and stupidity kept me from crying out. My early years in the French school system taught me that it was forbidden for a boy to cry out or sob; the punishment would last until he had regained his self-control. Physical punishment in the thirties was still administered as long as it did not leave any visible marks. Hair pulling or arm twisting were safe ways for teachers to punish unruly boys. It was a system that bred rebels and/or child beaters. Despite the punishment I endured, I was brave enough to tell my parents that I was too busy learning French to assimilate another language. My Hebrew teachers did not speak French to me; they had recently immigrated to France and spoke only Yiddish to me. I was sent to Hebrew school on Thursdays, but I did not make any more progress there. Instead, I played games and once had a role in a Hanukkah play. My refusal to learn Hebrew signaled to my parents that I was not a genius; my parents were certain that I would never be a rabbi, doctor, or lawyer. Since my bad eyes affected my coordination and dexterity, God only knew what would become of me, or how I would make a living. Of course my parents blamed each other for my failures. Whether I took after the Romanians or the Poles, I was a catastrophe.

My kindergarten memories border on the magical. I remember sitting on the floor in the refectory, listening to the teacher reading a fairy tale as images pass by on a screen. In one image, the fairy-tale queen is sewing. She sits by a window, looking happy and serene. In the next frame, the snow is spotted by what seems like a pool of blood. Long after the queen dies, the blood haunts my dreams. I can make the blood appear before I fall asleep, but I can't make it go away. So I hide under my blankets. A few years later I will see the previews for a film about vampires, and after that, I will fear having my blood sucked out of me as I sleep. During this time, I also like to whirl around and around until the whole earth is whirling with me. The school's courtyard is covered with cement; the outside latrines smell no matter what the season.

The after-school nursery is my favorite place to be as a child. In French the nursery is called a *dispensaire,* which means it is a local infirmary, or a place in my working class neighborhood where health and recreation are supervised. At four P.M., the children were greeted by a gate opening to a wooded garden leading to what must have once been a mansion. Behind the mansion there is a hilly yard dotted with a few swings, parallel bars, and some rings. All the children at the nursery come from working-class families. There were no fees to pay. I remember coming through the gate and singing a folk song. A young woman stopped me and asked me to sing the song all over again. To this day, I still know the song. The young woman smiled, fussed over me, and gave me a kiss. I have forgotten her face but not her smile. Before we were sent out to play, we were given a snack of bread and butter and sometimes a piece of chocolate. When it was discovered that I had poor vision and a lazy eye, I was given vitamins which were rubbed into each of my arms. My eyes did not improve, but the attention made me feel important. Our hygiene was also a concern. Once a week we were given a shower, and brushes were distributed so that we could scrub our knees, ankles, and elbows. During one spring, each child was given a small plot of land to grow a garden. I decided to grow beans. I came home excited, but my parents laughed at me. Although I watered my garden daily, the beans did not sprout. I most likely drowned them. I remember being very happy in that place.

Because I had failed as a Hebrew scholar, it was often stated that I would not amount to anything. I was nonetheless expected to make my parents proud. The least I could do was to be a good student with good grades they could brag about within the family and to their Jewish friends. Other people's geniuses—their prizes—were always held up to me as examples and goals, but the underlying message was that it would be surprising if I ever achieved anything. That's how I came to think that all people are essentially flawed and that egalitarianism was the answer to all my problems. It's hard for an only child to withstand his parents' criticisms and their ensuing disappointments, but an awful lot of moral victories are begging to be achieved. I did become a good student once glasses were fitted onto my nose, but not to please my parents. I did it to defy their dire predictions.

In these early years, my mother, albeit with good intentions, found a way to wound me. Eastern Europe and Russia had produced a number of Jewish musical prodigies so many mothers dreamed that their sons would grace the concert halls of the world. My mother's cousin was a first-prize violinist at the Paris Conservatory of Music. My mother, ever envious, told me that she had bought a violin from a violinist friend whose son was a certified genius in school. I was to be taught by this master teacher. At six years old, the prospect was exciting. At my first lesson, I received a music notebook where I was to write down an octave of the scale twenty times. I was shown the violin that was to be mine, but I was not allowed to touch it. It was years later that I learned that children must have two years of learning *solfège* before touching an instrument. First the theory, then the practice. In France, training the intellect and instilling discipline is at the core of music education; making music is, at first, secondary.

I traced my octave twenty times, which earned me praises from my teacher. I sang my notes and was held up as a model of seriousness to the violinist's son who was present at the time. Unfortunately, my first musical lesson was also my last. I never saw my teacher again. Instead, I learned my music theory in school. I questioned my mother for years, but she could no more admit that I probably had no musical talent than she could tell me that she could not afford the lessons. Nor could she admit that she had never bought the violin. For years I begged her to go retrieve the violin for me. She promised me each time that she would, but she never did. I could not admit that she had lied to me. Yet, it took a long time before I learned to distrust what I was told.

I entered first grade in October of 1932. I had learned to read and write in the kindergarten I had attended for nearly four years and had been trained to behave according to a well-planned code. I remember a teacher from that period who taught me to write. My eyes, as I have said, were poor. My hand-eye coordination reflected this condition. I can still see myself, bent over the teacher's desk as she is guiding my hand to form a good *m*. The pressure of her hand on mine is heavy, and she is dissatisfied, frustrated by my failure to perform as she orders. She pulls on my hair, and tears well up in my eyes. But I do not cry because boys do not cry in front of a class. If they do, it enrages the teacher and provokes laughter and mockery from the other boys. A boy must be brave—stoic. He must become tough. I don't always succeed, and I suffer the consequences: taunting in the school yard or in the street on the way to and from school. Home is the place I let go, but I only do mischievous things or things that I am forbidden to do. My favorite revenge on my mother is to cut the belt on her sewing machine, making her waste time by repairing it. Sometimes I jumble up her bobbins of thread or throw her pins on the floor. I throw tantrums and refuse to eat the food I am served. In desperation, my mother has bought a *martinet*, a stick of wood with thin leather straps attached at the end. She can now whip my bare legs while I howl and become hysterical. At home I am not brave, and no one laughs at me.

My first grade teacher always sits behind her desk. She never walks in the aisles. She is severe. Her hair is gray, and she wears it in a chignon. She never smiles, and she disciplines us with the long stick she keeps near her desk. The stick is used to open and close the transoms on the windows. The stick has a metal hook on its end, and when she hits you on the head, your whole skull resonates. I am a talkative child so I often go home with headaches. At the end of each week, she distributes medals and good conduct certificates. If I don't bring home a certificate, my mother refuses to give me dessert for a week. That, however, can be a double- edged sword; when I am entitled to a fruit for dessert, I can complain that the dessert she offered is not the one I wanted.

During the first six years of my life, my father appears to have left no trace of his presence. I was told many years after his death by members of my surviving family that he was an affectionate, indulgent father. However, my memories of him are quite dim. I remember a sort of perverse laughter as he read some story in his Yiddish newspaper or as he retold an anecdote that highlighted either my gullibility or my unintended candor. On some afternoons, usually Saturdays or Sundays, I would visit my grandmother or go to the Place des Fêtes or the Buttes Chaumont to play. Once, my mother decided that we should go to a matinee movie but admonished me not tell my father. This would be a secret between us. My father was home when we returned from the movies, and he greeted me with a question about where I had been and what I had done. I was three years old then so I blurted out, "I am not going to tell you that we went to a movie." Later, I was told that my father made a guessing game of my reply. Stubbornly, I stuck to my guns. He always had that perverse laughter as he retold that story. To this day, I hate secrets and can't keep them. Another anecdote about me which delighted him left me with a wound so deep that it took years to heal. Next to our house in Villepinte lived a family with three girls. The girls were born in France, but the parents hailed from Romania. As neighbors we used to get together in the summertime to eat homemade ice cream or watermelon. On one such occasion, my father started to tease the youngest of the three girls by asking her if she would marry me when she grew up. We were both six or seven years old at the time. Marthe answered that she wanted to have beautiful children and that since she thought I was ugly, marrying me would never happen. I might have forgotten the pain that her answer caused, but my father kept that anecdote in his repertoire forever after. He had no idea how it hurt me when he told that story. To him it was just a funny story. Even if I had complained, he would not have understood. In those days, people were not trained to articulate their feelings.

I remember a morning in the spring of 1933 when my father was packing a trunk with his belongings. The house was very quiet then, quite unlike the previous day when I had witnessed my father grab a heavy glass saltcellar and throw it at my mother's head. The saltcellar missed her but shattered the glass door of our dining room. They had, most likely, been fighting about money or about my grandmother's meddling. I think that the violence of his act frightened my father. He was not by nature a violent man. He had a temper and would occasionally yell and raise his hand, but he never struck me. This act of violence led to a decision to separate himself from his wife. In 1933, in a Jewish family, that solution shamed the entire family. It was a major sin.

Years later my father told me that he came to see me every day when school let out. It sounded plausible to me since he was out of a job at that time and because I was his fierce ally against my mother. But I don't remember seeing him that often or during the school week. I remember some weekends with him—the dingy hotel room that he could rent by the week or the month. The room had a bad bed, a broken down armoire, a sink, and a table on which rested a wash basin and pitcher. There was no heat in the room, but we had lots of blankets on the bed. The pitcher was filled at night so that we could wash in the morning with room-temperature water. The water was not even tepid; I used to wash my face pretty much in the way that a cat does. Two scenes have stuck in my mind from that period. One Saturday afternoon, my father and I were walking on the steep long street that leads from Place des Fêtes to Place de la République. It's springtime, and one of the first five and dime stores has just opened on the street. The store is full of toys, clothing, and snacks. I tell my father that I am hungry. I am offered a ham sandwich in a *petit pain* that cost one franc. To my father's astonishment, I devour three or four of these. When asked why I was so hungry, I reply that I have had no lunch that day and that my mother has told me that since I was going out with my father, he could feed me. While I have a very clear image of myself standing at the counter, biting into the sandwiches, I have no visual memory of the discussion I had with my mother about who was going to feed me that day. All that remains is that feeling of hunger and the taste of the *petit pain* stuffed with ham. I doubt that I told my father a lie that day, for the pattern of my parents playing emotional football with me is one of my most painful memories of my childhood and adolescence. The second memory from this time is somewhat more traumatic. One weekend my father failed to meet me at our usual meeting place. He never came to the house or brought me back to my mother. Instead, we would meet and part in front of the school. One day, however, he did not show up. I waited and waited, but he did not come. I was not angry, but I was panic-stricken, and I felt as abandoned as the day I discovered I was all alone in our apartment. But I could not yell, and I did not dare move away from the spot because I was afraid that he might show up and not see me. Forlorn, I went home and wondered how my mother would react. To my surprise, she was not home. I later learned that she had made plans to go to the theater with one of her friends and spend the night in a steam bathhouse, something she used to do almost every month. Not knowing when she would return, I sat down on the stairs to wait for her, feeling sorry for myself while preparing a long list of grievances I would throw in her face when she came back. It got darker and darker in the stairwell of our apartment building, and I became bored of pushing the *minuterie*. Besides, I was getting very hungry.

In the tenement building in which we lived, I had befriended two families and the concierge. I would often spend time in the concierge's lodge. The lodge was quite small, but it contained cages with canaries that whistled fantastic tunes when Monsieur and Madame Dritter whistled to them or even just sang when you did not expect it. The canaries were an endless subject of conversation. Madame Dritter also had books in her lodge that she read to me. One was *The Adventures of Robinson Crusoe*. I was particularly delighted with the way the main character went about building a house that was just big enough for him and cultivating a garden that just enough food for him. At night when I was unhappy, I'd go to sleep fantasizing I had run far away from home and had my own little room with my own little kitchen and that I was very happy in them. When I saw Madame Dritter again in 1969, she recalled an incident in which she and I had locked horns when I was a child. At about age three or four, I was given a tricycle that I was allowed to ride unsupervised in the courtyard. The courtyard pavement was uneven, and my tricycle squeaked a lot; no one in my family would think of oiling the pedals. Madame Dritter complained about the noise I was making, to which I replied with unconscious effrontery: "Go back to your dirty country!" I was, of course, only repeating what I had heard French people tell my parents when they complained about the way they were treated. A native of Alsace, Madame Dritter was smart enough to recognize the source of my impudent remark. In 1930, her accent, which was reminiscent of the German dialect she spoke at home, could still arouse hostility from the Parisian populace in my neighborhood. But that evening, Madame Dritter was not in her lodge. I was also too ashamed to tell anyone that my mother was not home and that I was hungry and had nowhere to go. I didn't have any friends my age when we lived on the rue des Bois; I was not allowed to invite friends to our house. It was a small dwelling, and we would have disturbed my mother as she worked. Besides, a non-Jewish boy would not be welcome in my home. There was a time on the playground, at Place des Fêtes, when my mother gave me strict orders not to play with an African boy in the sandbox. One of our neighbors, Madame Hertel, kept a lot of cats in her apartments. She made lots of toys for the cats with whom I enjoyed playing. Whenever she got a new kitten, she would hang a cork on a string from a door handle. The kitten's losing battle with the cork would make me laugh until I almost lost my breath. Madame Hertel was very kind to me and was always very patient. She spoke to me as if I were a grown-up, and she even showed me how to sauté new potatoes without peeling them. I was impressed. Monsieur Hertel was a conductor on a Paris bus line who distributed and canceled bus tickets on a very intriguing gray metal box that had a turning handle. He carried the contraption around his waist and pulled the chain that signaled to the driver that the bus could go forward. Monsieur Hertel wore a uniform with a smart cap. He looked more important than the man who pushed the buttons to close the doors and signal the engineer on the metro. I held both Monsieur and Madame Hertel in the highest esteem. But on the day my father failed to meet me, the Hertels were not home. I sat on the stairs and cried. Another neighbor, Madame Roland, rescued me. She took me in, fed me, and put me to bed all the while expressing a great deal of surprise at my mother's absence. I never forgot Madame Roland's kindness, and although I visited her often, I do not recall much about her and her life. I do not recall a Monsieur Roland, but I am sure that she was married. When my mother returned home, she was angry at my father's irresponsibility; my father's reaction was identical to that of my mother. Between them, I was often left to my own devices. Still I had survived without them: I had been found, fed, and sheltered. The world could still be a kind place where boys who felt abandoned were rescued.

That summer my parents, having separated, did not go to Villepinte. Fresh air was deemed essential for their only son, so I was taken in by an elderly French couple in Villepinte who supplemented their income by boarding children from Paris during the summer months. They had room for as many as nine children in the summer and kept two or three in the off-season. That summer I began to discover a brand of French cooking quite different from the food I was served in the school canteen and far more tasty than my mother's recipes. Madame Charbonnat, or *Mémère* as she liked to be called, had been before a *cordon bleu* cook in for several aristocratic families, before World War I. One of the families she claimed to have served was the Dreyfus family; I was to hear a lot about them a few years later. Her husband, whom the children called *Pépère,* had been a chauffeur for these same families and had driven an ambulance during the Great War. Now, he serviced Otis Elevators in the fancy sections of Paris. Years later I accompanied him on a day's work and was absolutely thrilled to ride up and down on the most beautiful elevators I had ever seen or have seen since, except in old movies.

Mémère was born and raised in the Vosges region of eastern France. She was quite round, energetic, and her cheeks always smelled like freshly dried laundry. In my eyes, she did everything to perfection; even her shouting fits had a theatrical grandeur. I found her again as Françoise in Proust's *A la Recherche du Temps Perdu.* Like Françoise, *Mémère* could coldly kill a chicken, or rabbit, drown squabs, and deftly turn out a mayonnaise or a sumptuous cake. Her loyalties and dislikes were fierce. It was not hard to fall in love with *Mémère,* and I did. My poor mother had to endure unfavorable comparisons to *Mémère* that fall. *Pépère* was born in the Berry, a region of central France. His face was hollow and ruddy, and he suffered terrible backaches from his sciatica. *Pépère* worked constantly when he was home, repairing, building, or tending to his large garden and his fruit trees. To me he seemed a magician with his hands; there was nothing he could not do. His war stories always fascinated me: so many bullets, so many pieces of shrapnel, so many grenades had missed him that I came to believe that he was indestructible. All his tales were told in a low, calm voice, without theatrical gesticulations, facial contortions, or flashing eyes. He told each tale in the most sincere voice. I was in awe of him.

In the fall of 1933, I entered second grade. I also became insufferable, criticizing everything my mother cooked. *Mémère's* cooking set the standard for my gastronomical wants; she had spoiled my taste buds forever. Had I spent only that summer with her, I may have forgotten the smells of her kitchen. But I was to live with her three more years. In second grade, it was discovered that I could not see very well. At that time, doctors used to come at least once a year, and all the children were lined up to be examined. This was particularly helpful in poor neighborhoods where the money for regular checkups was not available. In these poor quarters many children suffered from the alcoholism of past generations. Poor nutrition had left them with rickets, and their lungs and hearts were often affected by the coal dust and soot from the chimneys. Paris in the early part of the century was not a healthy place to live. Fresh air was often recommended by the doctors as a cure. Once it was discovered that I had a vision problem, I was taken to an eye clinic founded by the Rothchild family, near the beautiful park of Buttes-Chaumont.

After months of being separated and being pressured from the family, my parents reconciled for my sake. They never allowed me to forget this. My father came home, but he did not bring peace and harmony with him. The depression was hurting France, and laws were being passed to limit the working capacities of foreign workers. The Laval government, I believe, decreed that only one foreigner could be employed for every ten French citizens. My father's work permit was revoked, and he firmly believed that his misfortune was the result of a plot organized by my mother and her family to have him deported as an undesirable alien. I heard him tell the story over and over for years with such intensity and sincerity that I embraced it as the absolute truth. After the war, I came to believe that it had been an episode of total insanity on my father's part. Losing his right to work had unhinged him. He was sane, kind, and generous in all other aspects of his life, but the subject of his wife's family and their evil intentions was too much for him to bear. The story of his sickness is bizarre enough to be told.

My father believed that his wife and her family plotted against him shortly after they were married. The reasons for their enmity were never quite clear; they were based on some vague perception that Romanian Jews were not to be trusted, that they hated Polish Jews, and that my father's lack of ambition made him unacceptable to my mother's family. The Romanian side of my family was always well dressed in the latest fashions with shining shoes. They bragged loudly about the restaurants and night clubs they visited and the very important people they knew. My mother's aunt and her husband were excellent tailors and had developed a clientele among some well-to-do bourgeois and among high functionaries in the Paris Prefecture. I remember a man named Chiappe who was the prefect of Paris, the equivalent of a state governor in the United States. My mother's relatives were supposed to have had enough influence with him to have my father arrested, stripped of his papers, and slated for almost immediate deportation. My father claimed that he was not deported because his child was a French citizen and that his deportation would bring undue hardship upon me. However, his working papers were never returned; the French police must have thought more about my psychological welfare than my physical well being. My mother and her family always denied my father's accusations. My mother's family, through Chiappe, had tried to help my father so if my father did not have working papers, that was entirely his fault, not theirs. My father, they reasoned, must have done something or said something that aroused suspicion of him as a subversive character. France, they opined, would be well rid of a man without ambition, and who did not appreciate fully, as they did, the wonderful opportunities for success that France offered. That there was a worldwide depression and laws discriminating against aliens did not matter to my mother's family. My father was guilty of incompetence and judged unworthy of the family. My father stuck stubbornly to his story of victimization because there was no way of explaining his misfortune. He was not able to obtain working papers again until 1936, when a Popular Front government was elected.

Second grade brought glasses and the first incidents of persecution at school. In 1934, glasses were unusual and earned those of us who wore them a great deal of scorn from our schoolmates on the playgrounds and in the streets. I felt both the sting of humiliation and relief. Now that I was able to focus in class, my grades improved. Wearing glasses paled in comparison to a political event that shook French society and made me aware that I was a Jew and a stranger in a foreign country. On February 6, my birthday, we were supposed to go to my grandmother's house for dinner. But my father came home that evening and announced we could not go out because there was rioting in the city. He said people were being beaten, particularly those who looked foreign or Jewish and that heads had been split open and cars and busses were burning. In short, a revolution was going on. This was the aftermath of the Stavisky affair.

In my home, the Stavisky affair was talked about daily as my father read aloud from his Yiddish newspaper. Stavisky was a foreign Jew who had been mysteriously shot in his luxurious apartment. That alone was enough to arouse my parents' fears. In my home, as in many Jewish homes, if a Jew made the headlines, it was a cause for great concern. Back then, there was an overwhelming feeling that what one Jew did affected all Jews. When it became clear that Stavisky had managed to corrupt many government officials with his shady stock speculations, the royalists, the radical nationalists, and the native fascists resolved that the Third Republic had run its course and that it was time to bring in a strong anti-democratic form of government to restore law and order. It was time, they shouted, to give France back to real Frenchmen with true French values and traditions. The French rightists took to the streets. Law and order parties don't mind the use of organized violence.

As it has been observed by many French writers, children can be cruel, especially when they act out the prejudices they learn from their parents. My last name was quickly transformed into Stavisky-the-dirty-Jew, which led to fights in the school courtyard. During that time, I had a recurring dream that I was fighting my schoolmates and giving a good account of myself. Suddenly, a sword would appear, and I would be stabbed in the heart. I always woke up at this point in the dream with a pain through my breast. Being called a dirty Jew or the equivalent of a dirty kike was my first encounter with anti-Semitism. However, each morning I would eagerly go to school and do my best to be a good little Frenchman. I still felt that I belonged; I did not adopt my parents' feelings toward the Gentiles. In school, I was treated like everyone else. My teachers were dedicated to the ideal that we were the future citizens of the greatest country in the world. The Stavisky affair was not allowed to die; it would be pointed out in 1940 along with the Dreyfus affair as a significant example of the way in which Jews corrupted the moral fiber of France in their eternal quest to conquer the world.

My father was unable to work in a tannery because of the reactionary laws so he got papers that allowed him to buy and sell goods. In 1934, he became involved with two stores which were in fact the properties of my mother's brother Adolph. How this came about is a story rich in ironies. Adolph had become quite successful over the years, so successful that he no longer repaired watches but only sold expensive jewelry. He had also a partner whose name I never knew and of whose existence I am not certain. I suppose the depression hit the jewelry business hard because the two partners devised a fraudulent scheme. They hid a large amount of jewels and Adolph fled to the United States. His partner declared bankruptcy. The hidden jewels had not been paid to the wholesalers and would bring them a tidy fortune after a few years. In short, they were thieves. When Adolph returned one or two years later and asked his partner about the jewels, the partner looked quite surprised and feigned total ignorance of the situation. I have recently seen my cousin Maurice, Adolph's eldest son, who gave me a totally different version of the fiasco. Maurice told me that his father and his brother Paul, had buried the jewels in the basement of the rue Charles V, where Paul and their mother lived. When Adolph returned from the States, his brother claimed that there had been a flood in the cellar and that the plumber had found the jewels and stolen them. Nothing could be done to recover the jewels from the plumber since the jewels were in fact stolen property. Adolph was known for his fits of anger, but not even that could help him find the stolen goods. He went back to the United States. Not long after, Paul acquired a store where he sold custom-made suits for men. He also bought a beautiful apartment and fathered a second daughter. Even now, the story of the missing jewels remains a mystery. But the biggest scandal in the family was the impending divorce between Adolph and his wife, Marcelle. With a broken heart, Adolph left to make a new life for himself in America, far away from the woman he had loved so much. My father claimed that the divorce was engineered by my grandmother who did not like that Marcelle was of Polish descent. Marcelle was born in Poland but had come to France as an infant, and that, in my grandmother's eyes, made her an inadequate Jewish wife. In my grandmother's eyes, Marcelle was not a kosher cook and was not well versed in the secrets of Romanian gastronomy. As far as I could tell, my aunt Marcelle was a better cook than my mother and certainly the equal of my grandmother. However, Marcelle introduced her husband to French cooking, thus committing a great sin. Grandmother did not approve of Marcelle's lifestyle. She liked to go dancing, eat at good restaurants, and wear fancy clothes and jewelry. She enjoyed the roaring twenties, so my grandmother accused her of being adulterous. Years later, my mother echoed these accusations. Grandmother appears to have been at the center of a viper's nest. She was a religious fanatic who could not understand the ways of the French people and desperately fought to preserve traditional Jewish ways in a society where religion was losing its influence. She could not accept the pressures to become assimilated, which meant that a Jew was to be French first and foremost and that Jewishness was to be exercised as a religion. One was not a Jew, but an Israelite. Before the war, assimilated Jews did not live in the Marais, Belleville, or the Eleventh Arrondissement in Paris. These quarters were reserved for immigrants who had kept to their old ways and persisted in their quaint customs. This concentration of Jews made the raids of 1941 and 1942 much easier for the French police.

With Adolph's departure for the United States, my father formed an informal partnership with Marcelle. They transformed the jewelry stores, located rue de Flandre and rue Mazarine, into fur shops that sold ready-made coats, jackets, and stoles. In the middle of the depression, that business venture was an utter failure. My aunt Marcelle was distracted by her divorce, and my father had very little experience when it came to running a business. My mother's envy toward her sister-in-law did not help matters. Within three months, the two shops were closed. My parents could no longer afford their modest flat in Paris and moved to the house they had built in Villepinte. There my mother continued to work at home, lining fur clothing. My father would carry the work back and forth to the city, and on weekends, he would travel to markets in the provinces and try to sell fur clothing. A completely new life began for me at the end of that school year. Villepinte was to be my home base between 1934 and 1942.

Chapter Three

In 1934, Villepinte was mainly an old agricultural town. The center of the town had streets unevenly paved with cobblestones. The architecture harked back to the seventeenth and eighteenth centuries. Some of the farm buildings had thatched roofs. The church was of Roman-style and was probably much older than the rest of the buildings. The town hosted a sanatorium run by nuns. My childhood landscape had constituted of densely populated buildings erected on steep hills and narrow streets. Villepinte was built on entirely flat land crisscrossed by roads bordered occasionally by hedges. There were, for a city boy, few things to capture the eye. All there was to see were immense fields of wheat, oats, barley, and potatoes. The sound of a working tractor, Belgian work horses pulling enormous loads of farm products, or the solitary flight of a biplane heading for the airport of Le Bourget were the greatest source of excitement. Amazingly, Villepinte was located only ten miles from Paris and derived its wealth from three or four large industrial farms worked by an immigrant population that had arrived in France with work contracts after the Great War. These laborers lived largely in the old part of Villepinte in housing provided by the owners of the farms. Some who had other trades and had managed to save some money lived in the new part of Villepinte, the Clos-Montceleux, where the Jews came in the summertime, and which had an Italian population, too. It was a sort of melting pot with the usual frictions. These ethnic groups disliked each other heartily, with the greatest hostility in evidence between the Jews and the Poles. However, there was no violence between these groups, except in the school yard. Most of the abuse that I remember was of a domestic nature: drunks beating their wives on a Saturday night or quarrels resulting from petty jealousies between neighbors. Today, the Clos-Montceleux and old Villepinte have been preserved, but the farms have disappeared and high-rise apartments have replaced them.

We moved to Villepinte during the summer of 1934. My father began to bring my mother her work from Paris and to take it back to the city a few days later day. Working at home was not unusual in the trades associated with clothing. Many manufacturers subcontracted parts of their products. For instance, my great-uncle and aunt, the Leizers, and my uncle Paul, sewed men's coats in a room above their stores. They started with the cloth the client had chosen. Typically at the Leizers, my great-uncle would cut the cloth according to the measurements he had taken and my great-aunt Jeannette would do all the sewing that had to be done by hand. During the high season, there was another tailor to sew by hand as well as someone to do the sewing on the sewing machine. There was also a pressman, but my great-uncle often did the pressing with heavy irons that had been heated on specially made gas stoves. At the Leizers, by working twelve-hour days, a coat and a half could be sewn in a week. The pants and the waistcoats were contracted out to other specialists. In the fur trade, the linings of coats and other fur pieces were often done outside the fur shops. Fur shops were always full of flying hair, often quite dirty, so the finishing was often contracted out. It was sound business practice since most businesses tended to be small. My mother was an early riser and worked very late every day, often until midnight. She did not have much time to cook or clean the house. The shopping was easily done since most things came to the neighborhood via local merchants or local farms in lorries drawn by horses. It was my job to fetch the daily baguette of bread and buy the supplies not delivered to our door at the local stores. My father brought kosher meat from Paris. In the summer, chickens and ducks could be bought from the farmers and killed ritualistically. That summer my father grew enough potatoes, carrots, and onions for most of the winter. He also raised three or four chickens, but that was the only year he did that. He tried to recruit me to work in the garden with him, but I soon complained that it was too hard. He did not insist, and I now wish that he had. On the weekends, he would take a bundle of furs and take it to the farmers markets around Paris and as far as Chartres. Once he exchanged a neck fur piece for a goose; during the depression there was very little money available, especially to farm people. In fact, we all had very little money. We were very fortunate that my mother continued to have work; we never lacked for food in our home. World War II taught me what hunger is, and how it can torture you.

My parents' reconciliation did not bring peace between them, nor even a brief truce. The hatred and hurtful words did not let up. I fled the house as often as possible, and I would not come home until it was absolutely necessary. During that summer and in the following year, I spent most of my time at my friend Paul's house. Paul Manoutsis's home was even more modest than ours. It was a wooden house with only two rooms and a narrow kitchen. His parents slept in the room that served as a dining room. Paul shared the second room with his older sister Jeannette. They had an outhouse, but in addition they had a small cabin where Mr. Manoutsis made shoes for a manufacturer in Paris. In 1942, when he was sick and his children were working, I delivered his bundle of shoes to a small shop in Belleville and brought back the raw materials. Mr. Manoutsis was of Greek descent, but he was a Greek who had been born in Turkey. There was a large minority of Greeks living in Turkey before World War I, as well as a large minority of Turks living in Greece. Greece had been occupied by the Turks for centuries and then had regained its independence in the first half of the nineteenth century. Mr. Manoutsis came to France with one of his brothers at the end of World War I before the Turkish government invited the Greeks to return to their country of origin. The two brothers married French women, two sisters, which made their children double cousins. Paul, Jeannette, and I shared a foreign origin as well as our exotic names and looks. We were not quite French, although we did not recognize it at the time. A few years ago when I saw Jeannette and asked her how she felt about being the child of an immigrant, she said that she had always felt French. I was surprised, given that most of her childhood was spent amid foreigners. I felt French too, but I knew that I was different. My family always referred to the Manoutsis family as the "Greeks;" everyone seemed to identify his or her neighbors by national and religious origins. Polacks were Christians, but the Litvacks and Galicianers were Jewish. During the Stavisky scandal, I realized that as a Jew I was not like other children. At Villepinte I was much more conscious, especially in the summers, of the un-Frenchness of the Jewish community. But all of the children born and raised in France affirmed their French nationality. Paul and Jeannette had a French mother, but they had their father's beautiful olive skins and dark large eyes. Still, they spoke French like their mother and identified with her way of life, especially her French cuisine.

Except for the previous summer that I had spent at the Charbonnat, Jewish-Romanian cooking was my daily lot.

Paul Manoutsis was almost two years older than I, but we were both crazy about comic books. We did not have a radio, and we seldom went to the movies. But when a small circus arrived, short silent films were always shown under a tent lit by hissing acetylene lamps. Paul and I would incorporate all the characters in our games, especially those whose adventures were heroic, magical, or intergalactic. There were lots of empty lots covered with tall grass through which we crawled, looking out for savage beasts to fight with our wooden rifles or wooden swords. We were always the undaunted and the unconquered, the perfect heroes of our times. Paul was my first real friend. As an only child, I was starved for the companionship of children my own age, of the brothers and sisters I did not have. I was also jealous of the love that Madame Manoutsis lavished on her children, just as I envied the affection that Paul and Jeannette showed to one another. Brother and sister were uninhibited about hugging and kissing one another. I could not picture myself in that situation so I would turn away in order not to see them. My parents loved me, yet my memories do not include gestures of affection and I would swear on a stack of Bibles that I never saw any signs of affection between them. For years I experienced discomfort when someone touched me or when I had to express myself emotionally in a physical or verbal manner. Somehow I learned to understand my feelings intellectually, but my physical self was always unsure, distrustful, and quite afraid of emotions. My mother is not to blame for her coldness. Her own childhood had been stolen from her when she was hired out at age nine by her widowed mother in one of the poorest countries of Europe. My grandmother never knew how to show affection, but both she and my mother were very good at finding fault in others. In my early years, my father was a rather shadowy figure. My close relationship to him grew only after my parents had separated and he had to parent me. As a child, I could tolerate rough and tumble play, but gestures of affection or displays of tenderness made me turn my head away. In fact, I kept everybody at arm's length. I did not know how to make myself accessible or lovable.

The elementary school that I attended in Villepinte was very different from the school in Paris. Its seven grades were housed in three classrooms, and its student body was diversified by class and nationality. First and second grades were taught together, so were the third and fourth grades and the fifth, sixth, and seventh grades. However, very few of the students made it to seventh grade. Since a diploma was necessary to graduate from sixth grade, only the best students from the sixth grade were allowed to present themselves at the countywide examination which lasted a whole day. In the fall of 1934, I started third grade. My teacher, Madame Violle, was married to the school's principal. Monsieur Violle also taught the upper grades. The couple lived on the school grounds. Under the Third Republic, teachers were often provided with housing by the state.

Madame Violle was the gentlest person I had met in my short existence. Her face was round and open, and her hair was cut just long enough to cover her ears, She was the only teacher whom I dared to contradict, and who let me get away with it. In a French school, children were severely reprimanded or punished for misbehaving. I had never heard of a pupil challenging a teacher's knowledge. Even in high school, where asking impossible questions was often a tactic to distract a teacher from the subject at hand, students expected a full elucidation of the impossible question. If we did not agree or were not satisfied with the answer, the teacher was not challenged in class but was thoroughly attacked and reviled in the courtyard. In general, a teacher's word was law—not only in school but at home as well. None of us would ever tell our parents that we had in some way incurred our teacher's displeasure because severe penalties would have been imposed.

In the fall of 1934, I challenged Madame Violle on the results of a particular long division problem. She called me to the blackboard and made me demonstrate in front of my sniggering classmates how I had arrived at my answer. In France, being called up to the blackboard was more often than not an occasion for humiliation. Madame Violle shushed the laughter and allowed me to complete the entire exercise. To my surprise, she announced that I was right and that she had made an error. That was a momentous event in my life. In that moment, it was as though I was cured of my stupidity. My parents were wrong; I could do things well. I might not be able to learn Hebrew, but I could do long divisions better and faster than anybody in the entire third grade. That day, Madame Violle did not punish me. She patted my cheek and sent me back gently to my seat. After that my whole attitude toward schoolwork changed. I went from being somewhat indifferent, to wanting to excel, and to always having the right answers. In midyear, I was skipped to the fourth grade, and although I did well, Madame Violle and her husband decided to keep me in fourth grade for one more year. Had I been a child of affluent, middle-class parents, I would have been promoted to the fifth grade. After the sixth grade, I would have been enrolled in a *Lycée* in Paris where I would have received the classical education of a French bourgeois child. But most of us in Villepinte did not go to school beyond the age of fourteen, after which we were placed as apprentices in a trade. My parents had also planned this for me. They believed that a trade coupled with my knowledge of Yiddish would allow me to live anywhere in the world. They knew about exile, but I did not, and could not imagine living anywhere but France.

Madame Violle came to my rescue on one other occasion, rescuing me from certain humiliation as I began to sob in front of my classmates. In the spring of 1936, just a few short weeks after my mother left my father and me, she sewed for me a school-length smock of black satin. It was shiny, soft, and fragile; usually school clothing was made of sturdy material and hid very well what we wore underneath. That kind of uniformity was supposed to hide our class differences too; we still knew who was from a rich family. In those days, a well-decorated pencil box, an elegant pen knife, or fancy glass marbles would identify the wealthy among us. But within a few weeks, the satin smock my mother had sewn began to unravel at the hem and develop holes around the pockets. By then I was living with the Charbonnats because my father worked on the other side of Paris and came home only on weekends. My mother had taken all my clothes when she left Villepinte, so my scant wardrobe had become even scantier. Still, I was required to go to school wearing a smock. In desperation, I rolled my smock up to my waist and tied it in a knot behind my back, hoping all the while that no one would notice the infraction of the dress code. I told myself that no one would pay any attention to me if I kept very still behind my desk. Either the gods were against me that day, or they were determined to expose my disgraceful state for, lo and behold, Madame Violle called me to the blackboard to solve an arithmetic problem involving the division of a fraction by a fraction. Just as I solved the problem and began to recite the rule of division, my smock fell down, revealing, for all to see, the miserable state of my smock. The class burst out laughing. Suddenly, I went from being important to being ridiculously pitiful. Madame Violle rose from her seat and took me in her arms, saying to the other students, "When you have acquired as much intelligence as Mathis, you will also have acquired the luxury to laugh at him." From then on, I felt very special, and Madame Violle remains for me a model teacher.

My parents' marriage continued to deteriorate during my fourth-grade year. My mother increasingly resented my father's inability to earn a steady income. Her resentment was also fueled by my grandmother's interference in her marriage and the envy she felt toward the rest of her family. The fights between them grew more frequent and more bitter; it did not seem to matter whether I was present or not. It all culminated during a shouting match in which my mother threw herself at my father, and as she struck him, they both fell over a storage trunk and into an armchair. My father pushed her off him brutally, and her glasses flew across the room. When they both got up my mother's nose was skinned, and my father's face was scratched. I remember screaming; it all happened so fast that I was paralyzed and unable to understand what I was seeing. My father left the house with the sound of banging doors.

That day, my mother decided to leave Villepinte and return to Paris. She halfheartedly asked me to go with her, but I was vying for first prize in school and was reluctant to leave my fourth grade to go live in my grandmother's quasi hovel with her. Since it was a Thursday and there was no school, I was given a franc to go to see a movie. When I returned home, my mother, most of the furniture, and all of my clothes were gone. When my father returned that evening, he wanted to know why I had not gone with my mother and what I had been doing while she was packing. I said I had gone to see a movie but did not mention that my mother had asked me to go with her to Paris. I did not understand what was happening to us—what was happening to me. Despite my parents' previous separation, I could not imagine what it meant to have only one parent at home, or what it meant to lose contact with my mother. Except for my cousin Maurice, I did not know anyone whose parents were either divorced or separated. I did not know what to expect, or how I was going to live. Still I felt relieved that the fights were over. I learned later that my mother lodged a complaint with the police before leaving Villepinte, alleging that my father had beaten her. He was later called in to answer her claim, but nothing came of it. In 1936, battered women from the working class, or immigrant populations did not concern the law. Wife beating was a subject for jokes and comedy.

After my mother left, my father's financial situation seemed to improve. The Popular Front had won the elections, and the restrictions against foreign workers became more relaxed. My father was able to get his working papers and found employment in the tanning industry near Paris on the opposite side of Villepinte. He moved out and rented a room in a hotel that catered to migrant workers. It was a miserable room with a creaky bed and a mattress shaped like a boat. It seemed like all French beds had boat shapes; you always rolled into the middle of them. That room was not significantly different from the one he had rented in Belleville a few years earlier. Its rent was cheap, and it was close to his place of work, as well as to the bistro where he took his meals.

I went to live with the Charbonnats and was to stay with them for more than three years until October 1939, when my father took me to a boarding school in Versailles. He then reported with other volunteers and draftees to the French garrison in Le Mans, where he was supposed to train to fight against the German army. The time I spent with the Charbonnats brought about a total change in my life. I had a roof over my head, good meals, and clean clothing, yet I was afraid. I did not know what was expected of me. My education began with my table manners: I learned how to hold my spoon, fork, and knife, how to hold my elbows by my side while I ate, how to sit and how not to sit, when to speak and when to be quiet. The mastering of these rules would guarantee that I would become a civilized French boy. I tried my best to please my hosts, but somehow I did not always remember how to behave, especially during or after my mother's infrequent visits.

When my parents separated for the first time, nothing had changed for me. I lived in a familiar place with my mother and, except on rare occasions, my life continued the way it had. Despite our battles, the most important person in my life was my mother. I never asked myself whether she loved me or I loved her. She was my mother, and though I might disobey her or act like a brat, I was bonded to her with a blind love that is customary to all children. Although I refused to go with her when she left me, I soon began to feel sorry for myself. I slowly realized that I had been abandoned, and that caused me to react in unfamiliar and unexpected ways. I became resentful and angry, so much so that when she came to visit, I could hardly look at her, while mean words came out of both our mouths. During that time, we always separated in anger, and I was left to wonder what was wrong with me. As a result, I grew closer to my father. I was deadly afraid that he would leave me too.

After my mother left home, three weeks passed before she came to visit. I didn't hear from her. Telephones were rare, and she did not know how to write. I had not written to her either. When she did visit, she came in to the Charbonnats' house dressed as if it were a festive occasion. She looked so elegant to me, and I was so self-conscious about my appearance that I greeted her quite awkwardly. "So! Mathis, you're not happy to see me? Maybe I should not have come?" She spoke to me in Yiddish, which further embarrassed me in front of *Mémère*. We had always spoken Yiddish at home or with our Jewish friends but never before the *goyim*, lest we provoke an angry comment that we should speak French or go back from where we came. We walked out into the courtyard, but she did not ask how I was, what I felt, or what I was doing in school. I began to shout about my clothes and, why was she wearing her best outfit while I had nothing to wear? We did not touch each other; we simply yelled at each other until tears began to run down our cheeks and our voices to choke. "I am keeping your clothes," she said. "Someday you'll come and live with me."

"I have no clothes now!" I yelled.

"Let your father worry about that."

"I want my clothes now!" I yelled again.

"No! When you come to live with me."

We left each other without as much as a good-bye. On her way out, she could not resist telling me that I was just like my father, and she could not expect anything good from Polish blood. I did not see her again for six weeks, not until school was out.

That year I won first prize, which meant I had obtained the highest grades in my class for the entire year. In the French school system, that was a big deal. At the end of each school year, around the fourteenth of July, there was always a ceremony held to mark the students' achievements. The first-prize winner would receive either a richly bound book or a modest sum of money that was put in a savings account at the post office. We learned new songs and listened to the mayor of Villepinte make a speech. Parents and children were dressed in their Sunday clothes, and the municipal band performed in perfect cacophony. How proud I was when my name was called to receive a very heavy book decorated with gold letters and then to shake the mayor's hand. My father was there, as were the Charbonnats, but my mother was not there. She was too angry and too busy. She had found a new way to hurt me—to punish me. Her absences set a pattern: I would accuse her of something, and she would respond by punishing me. On the one occasion that I put my arms around her neck and kissed her. She pulled away and rebuffed me.

For the first time in my life, I had a room of my own in what seemed to me an enormous house with an enormous garden. Since I was the only ward in the house during the school year, I had the undivided attention of my foster parents. I spent the weekend with my father, learning more about his childhood and my mother's conspiracy against him. I was fiercely loyal to him. When he took up with another woman, I felt totally betrayed.

Chapter Four

Although I had won first prize in school that July of 1936, I did not have a happy summer. I hardly saw my mother, and my anger against her grew more vocal. True, I had refused to go with her to Paris, but I could not abandon the possibility of winning first prize in school. Still I felt she had agreed with my decision much too quickly. There had been no discussion, no yelling, no tears, no attempt to exercise her authority. At ten years old, it suddenly became my responsibility to choose which parent I wanted to live with. Of course she thought that I would join her later; that's why she had taken my clothes. That embarrassed my father, who had to borrow money from a friend so I could have a change of clothing.

She never brought my clothes back. That summer I shamed her into buying me a bicycle—my first two-wheeler. If I wanted a sign of love from my mother I had to shame her into it by reciting a long list of the terrible things she had done. I would blame her for her selfishness: "Look, Mama, look! You have six pairs of shoes and a fur coat. Last year you took a trip to Romania, and you did not even bring me a bar of chocolate."

Often her answers were meaner than my hurtful accusations. Once I complained to her that she never came to see me, and she replied that the only reason she was there that day was to keep her "enemies" in the family quiet. I later learned that she had been severely criticized by her family for leaving me behind when she left my father. What she had done was unheard of in Jewish families, Leaving your husband was understandable, but leaving your only child was unforgivable. My mother was so obsessed with what her family thought, she did not realize she had hurt me. The damage she did that day would haunt me for years.

Having a bicycle allowed me a measure of freedom. At the end of July, eight girls had arrived from Paris to enjoy the countryside's fresh air. As a rule, *Mémère* kept us all busy at play in the courtyard. We either played in a pile of sand, or we played house. *Mémère* understood that I needed time with boys my own age, and she would grant me time off with my shiny new red bicycle. I would go riding with Paul Manoutsis all over the Clos Montceleux. But often, I also got into trouble for forgetting the time I was supposed to be back. My relationship with the eight girls was at times quite painful. I did not get along with two older girls. Nana, whose parents ran a clothing business at the Saint-Ouen market on the edge of Paris, had all the airs of a child of *nouveau riche*. She delighted in humiliating me by making disparaging remarks about my clothes. Nana was the sophisticated miss from Paris, the rest of us were to serve as her loyal vassals. She knew how to find our weak spots and was adept at bringing tears to my eyes. I feared her but could never find the right words to avenge my humiliations. Paulette was the Charbonnats' only granddaughter. Her parents worried about her progress in school, and I was given the task of tutoring her that summer. In exchange I could have any book I wanted as a present. My ignorance of books was boundless, but Madame Violle had read some anthologized pieces of Hector

Malot's *Sans Famille* and Victor Hugo's *Les Misérables* to us that year. In my situation, these titles had an immediate, irresistible appeal. Unfortunately, my tutoring was not a success. Paulette could not master the formulas for finding either the perimeter or the area of a square. I would cajole and yell, but nothing helped. Paulette much preferred to play than solve mathematical problems. During the three years I spent with the Charbonnats, I was assured that these books would be bought for me. That promise was never kept. It was also difficult for me when the parents of the girls would show up, and I was not spending the day with my father. I could hardly stand the kisses, the hugs, and the laughter, not to mention the toys, candies, and the fruits. I would often hide when the candy was passed around so that I could nurse my grudges and feel that I had been deliberately slighted. I once confided to my father the injustices that were visited upon me during these visits, but he did not understand. I did not need the candy anyway he said; therefore my feelings of persecution were totally unfounded.

That summer, I became fascinated with the Spanish Civil War. War, I thought, was the ultimate adventure. My head was filled with the glorious history of France: the epic battles fought, the heroes killed both in victory and defeat. I had no idea that anyone real could die, nor did I have the slightest inkling what death meant to anyone. No one had ever suggested or described the horrors of war to me. My father had told me about being beaten in a German camp, but that was just a story, and the beatings seemed no more damaging or painful than a spanking was to me. At school, we cheered when Joe Louis had beaten Max Schmelling and broken some of his ribs. When the Italians attacked Abyssinia, we made racist jokes in the school yard. And when *Pépère* spoke about his experiences as an ambulance driver in the Great War, it all seemed like a fantastic adventure. Alas, I thought I had been born too late and nothing like that would ever happen to me. The Spanish Civil War started out as an adventure from which I would be absent.

In the house there was a radio, and *Pépère* brought home a newspaper every day. I read the news from the Spanish front. Many years later, I discovered the inanities of press releases written about war. Villepinte had elected a Popular Front mayor and municipality, and on some Sundays there were often parades with banners proclaiming solidarity with the Spanish Republicans and an outstretched red flag held in which money was collected to provide aid to the embattled anti-Franco fighters. A few young men even left for Spain to join the International Brigades. As a child. I had always been ill at ease in a crowd, but these demonstrations stirred up my imagination. Franco, Mussolini, and Hitler were laughable clowns, and the subjects of bad jokes. The newspaper that was brought home by *Pépère* had a right-wing orientation and splashed the front pages with stories of churches, monasteries, and convents being burned to the ground and of nuns being raped. While the Charbonnats believed these stories, my father and his friends dismissed them as just another example of fascist propaganda and yet another proof of anti-Semitic machinations. Their hopes were pinned on the Soviet Union, which would soon make short shrift of all these bandits. Many years later, I discovered that both sides had committed unspeakable acts during this conflict, but by then the realities of war, the German occupation, and the opening of the concentration camps had punctured my notions of glory.

Toward the end of September, a traveling carnival came to Villepinte. I took a ride on a fast, whirling merry-go-round, becoming dizzy and nauseous. The next day, I was ill with a sore throat and high fever during a visit with my father. It was one of those childhood illnesses that one forgets rather quickly, except that this one took on a rather dramatic turn. I began to bleed from my nose, and no one was able to stop it. The doctor came and stuffed my nose with gauze and cotton; neighbors put cold keys down my back. I can still recall the taste of blood as I swallowed it. This lasted for about ten days; my father thought that I was going to die. He contacted my mother. She came a few days later as I once again was bleeding, and she sat on the couch opposite my bed, wringing her hands. She had not kissed me, nor was she holding my hand. She sat wringing her hands, silent. My father came into the room and suggested that I should be taken to a specialist. Since he did not have enough money to do so by himself, he appealed to her for help. She sat there, considering how much money a specialist might cost. My mother complained that she worked hard to earn her money which caused my father to fly into a rage and chase her out of the house. I witnessed that scene in total silence, too weak to cry or to protest. By early October, I had stopped bleeding on a daily basis and was taken by my father at the Lariboisière Hospital in Paris. Daily salt water rinsing was prescribed to strengthen the inner walls of my nose. From then on, my nose bleeds became occasional episodes that occurred when I was particularly upset. Since the doctors could find nothing wrong with me, I believe that I had become so unhappy, I unconsciously tried to die.

School began October one. I reported to school three weeks late for Mr. Violle's class. He had a well-deserved reputation for severity and was feared by all the students. Mr. Violle had a corpulent frame. He was definitely obese besides having a deep voice that could send shivers through us when he became angry. He was the total opposite of his wife, but he was also a superb teacher who could do and teach anything. The first few months of the school year, I was totally disoriented. I could not catch up with my lessons and could not understand what was going on in the classroom. It was as if my brains had run out of my nose. Soon I began having excruciating stomach pains that would bend me over and paralyze me. During the attacks, *Mémère* would put me to bed with a hot water bottle, and in a couple of hours, the pains subsided. These attacks occurred in the midst of our noon meal, so several afternoon classes were missed. A few times *Mémère* called a doctor, and he diagnosed me with gastritis. The doctor prescribed a granulated medicine that tasted like charcoal, and I was given a potion to fortify my constitution. *Mémère* did her best to make special meals that would pacify my stomach. Nothing seemed to help, and no one appeared to have any solutions. I was a mess.

In the three years I spent at the Charbonnats, I became quite ill a few times with bronchitis and the flu. Although I did not like being sick, I enjoyed the care I received. *Mémère* was very attentive. She would apply a mustard seed cataplasm to my chest and leave it on for a long time, no matter how hard I cried that my skin was falling off. But she was also gentle, picking the mustard seeds off my chest or back when the treatment was finished. *Mémère* made infusions from leaves and herbs gathered from her garden so when I was ill, there was always a thermos bottle of these potions next to my bed. When I began to feel better, *Mémère* would bring me a book or magazine, and I would be allowed to come down to the kitchen to sit in a soft chair with a hot brick under my feet and watch her prepare a meal.

I did not see my mother until late January of that year. She arrived, regally dressed in a fur coat with silver foxes around her neck, as my eleventh birthday approached to announce that her cousin Paul Loeb was getting engaged, and there was to be a huge celebration in a rented hall in Paris. Paul was the only son of my grandmother's half sister, Ethel, who was married to a shoemaker. Ethel and her husband ran a small store in Bagnolet, which I often visited as a child on Sundays with my mother. I liked the smell of the various leathers and of the glue even though it made me feel nauseated. I did not know Paul very well; to me he was a grown-up. But there was a lot of speculation in the family as to his plans or prospects of getting married. Paul was said to be of delicate health and had an ulcerous stomach, so his engagement was a major event for the Romanian side of my family. However, this event was on the same day as my birthday. My mother offered me a new suit of clothes and new shoes if I would come to the celebration. I asked my father for his permission to attend the party, but he refused.

When my mother came to fetch me that day I told her that I could not go with her, but I eventually decided to disobey my father and followed her into Paris. We spent the whole day buying an outfit for me to wear to the party. The possible consequences of my action did not enter my head; I refused to think about the reaction my father would have to my disobedience. I was too excited to be back in the city with my mother and sporting brand-new clothes. The reception that evening was sumptuous. There was food, music, speeches, and dancing. I was dazzled. It was during this time that I approached my mother to give her a hug and was pushed away. Unfortunately, Paul did not get married. He was deported to Auschwitz in 1942, where he later died. His parents survived the war.

The next morning I was awaken by a terrible ruckus in the courtyard of my grandmother's house. My father was shrieking that he wanted to see his son, but the concierge and my uncle were barring his way. He could not come up to see me, and my mother kept me from going down to see him. It seemed that the yelling went on forever, and the threats my father and uncle made were escalating. Eventually, my father left without me. I was in tears. I did not want to stay with my mother and even less so with my grandmother. The next day, I was sent back to Villepinte by myself. I took the metro to the Gare du Nord, the train to

Sevran, and walked the three kilometers to the Charbonnats' house. I cried all the way.

When I arrived, *Mémère* greeted me in tragic tones. My father had arrived on my birthday loaded with presents: a bottle of champagne, a camera, and all sorts of other goodies. He had come prepared for a grand time. He wanted to spoil me and wished to make up for having denied my request to attend a bethrosal in Paris in the company of my mother. However, the guest of honor was missing. Not only had I disobeyed him, I had betrayed him. He had left very angry, and *Mémère* could not begin to tell me what was in store for me. I hoped that my father had gone back to Paris and that he would forget about my crime. Although his choleric fits fell as fast as they arose, I was out of luck that time. My father arrived after dinner and asked in a cold voice why I had returned. He did not ask for an explanation or make reproaches. He simply told me to go back to my mother. He walked out, leaving me to my sobs. No one tried to console me or to reassure me. *Mémère* worried aloud how my room and board was going to be paid and by whom; she was not prepared to keep me free of charge. *Mémère* suggested that I go back to Paris, which only caused me to sob louder. I was thoroughly humiliated, and I was desperate. My father had turned away from me, and my mother did not want me. I did not want to live with her because that would be further proof of betrayal of my father. I thought of running away and disappearing forever. I had been orphaned and had nowhere to turn. I could do nothing but wallow in self-pity.

The next day, I wrote an angry letter to my mother, blaming her for all that had happened to me. She did not come to fetch me or to see me. I did not see her again until late August when my father took me to the hospital to see her. A hysterectomy had been performed, and she was in pain. In 1937, surgery and aftercare frightened patients and their families. My mother was in a big ward with bad smells and hardly any privacy. Her face was pale, and she moaned a lot, I thought. My presence did not cheer her up; she was not glad to see me. I had fought my father about going to see her. In those days I was very good at carrying grudges. I kept track of all the injustices and slights visited upon my long suffering person. My mother that day blamed me for her illness. She held me responsible for her illness and told me she would have been a happier woman if she had given birth to a stone instead of me. I should have cried, but I had done all my crying on my eleventh birthday. I had become so angry with my mother that her mean words were simply added to the long list of my grievances. I did not cry again until my late twenties. I wanted, even needed to cry many times, but the tears would not come. No one could hurt me again; I had become a tough kid.

I did not have a brilliant academic year. I woke up before the preparatory examinations in June that signified a student had successfully completed six grades of school. As bad as that school year was, I did make a new friend, David. We were the only two Jewish kids in a school where many students were the children of Polish or Ukrainian immigrants. We were often subjected to insults that we did not understand although the tones, taunts, and snarls of our classmates were unmistakable. Often during recess, we would stand with our backs against the schoolhouse wall while our enemies hurled themselves at us. We were two valiant knights, David and I, pushing back the savage hordes. Sometimes we would also look at each other and begin laughing uncontrollably until we ran out of breath. If we were asked what we were laughing about, we could not answer, we did not know. David and his family survived the war. They emigrated to Israel.

On weekends, my father and I would often visit the Gelblum family. They were addicted to playing dominoes and enjoyed drinking tea. Their daughter, Fanny, was about my age, and she made no secret about the fact that she liked me. But because I was eleven and she was fat, I did not return her affection. I did not want to be made fun of at school by being seen with her, so I rejected her offers of friendship. The conversation at the Gelblums' house revolved mainly about two subjects: romantic adventures or misadventures in Petrograd during the Revolution or Mr. Gelblum's knack at buying old objects from people in Paris to resell at the flea market in Clignancourt. I loved listening to the tales of the Revolutionaries and the White Guards, even though they had caused the Gelblums to fear for their lives. Still they praised the Great Stalin and the marvelous new society that he was building. Were I to live in the USSR, I would have a great future. But that was also the time of the Moscow Trials, and it just so happened that I was being taught about the era of the Terror during the French Revolution. During a discussion about the Moscow trials, I innocently blurted out that Stalin, like Danton and Robespierre, would lose his head. My elders were shocked and wisely opined that I did not know what I was talking about but that I would know better in time. As it turned out, we were all wrong. But in 1937, no one understood that the counterrevolution had already occurred. Worse, no one understood the peril Hitler represented and how many lives he would annihilate. All of the Gelblums, except Fanny, perished in Auschwitz.

That fall I began sixth grade with great anticipation. I was going to earn my certificate and take my place among the successful students despite stomach cramps that would periodically bend me over in pain. I made no connection between the pressures and expectations I put on myself, and the pains I suffered. No one else did either. I simply had a weak stomach. A regulated diet would cure my digestive woes.

The news of the Spanish Civil War, the rumblings in Austria, and the International Fair kept me glued to the radio. The Charbonnats complained bitterly about the destruction of the old Trocadero in Paris and the ultramodern building that replaced it. In school, Monsieur Violle sang the praises of the new scientific museum. I had not yet gone to see the fair, but my father had promised to take me. Some of my schoolmates had gone, and they regaled us with exotic descriptions of the African pavilions and the fabulous fruits and foods served there. When I finally went to the fair in the spring of 1938, I was disappointed by the smallness of the Spanish exhibition. On the walls of the exhibition, there were appeals for help, proclamations about the values of freedom, and cries for revolution. By that time, France and England had adopted a policy of nonintervention; the Popular Front government had closed the border between France and Spain. It was rumored that the USSR was helping the Republic, while Hitler and Mussolini were sending thousands of "volunteers," and equipment of modern warfare to Franco to help in his crusade against Bolshevism and godlessness. Many years later, I came to believe that if Hitler and Mussolini had been defeated during the Spanish Civil War, World War II, the Holocaust, and Hiroshima could have been avoided. I still feel that way.

The pavilions that impressed and frightened me the most housed the Russian and the German exhibitions. I don't remember whether the pavilions stood next to one another, but I am inclined to believe they faced each other. This satisfies my aesthetic sense of the monstrous and absurd. The Russian building was dominated by two giant statues of a man and a woman holding a hammer and sickle. The German pavilion sported huge statues of naked men, women, and gods. Each displayed the wonder of its industries and strengths by graphs and pictures depicting the achievements of its people. The section on Siberia mentioned gold mines. The floor was occupied by all kinds of tractors. There were pictures of Marx, Angels, Lenin, and Stalin. The German exhibit was somewhat more warlike, with lots of Nazi leaders in uniform, particularly Hitler. Anti-Semitic propaganda did not grace the walls, and it would have been hard to imagine that in a few years, extermination camps would appear in Eastern Europe. There was also an American pavilion, but I don't recall seeing it. That day we concentrated on the French provinces, where we watched the dances and tasted the food. Austria had been reunited with Germany, and the people around me who, after years of hard struggles, had earned the right to a paid vacation, talked about that first paid vacation in the history of France.

To recover from her operation, my mother went to a winter resort in the Swiss Alps. I had not seen her since I had visited her in the hospital. I was still smarting from her cold reception and had not expressed any desire to see her. My father did not mention her name, which was just as well; anytime he spoke about her, whether I was present or not, bitter words would come out of his mouth. Only many years later did I realize that he had used me as a weapon against her. My mother was far from perfect, but I wish now that my father had kept me out of his quarrels with her. But in those days, people did not read manuals on how to raise children; we had to rely on the wisdom of our parents. I saw my mother at the Charbonnats a few weeks after her return from the mountains. She brought me some Swiss chocolate and a souvenir trinket from the resort: a little wooden man on skis. Either she had remembered my earlier complaints, or she was trying to make peace with me. I ate the chocolate, but our private war did not abate.

Soon, another family scandal reached me via my mother on one of the rare occasions that she came to Villepinte. It seemed that my cousin Maurice was to go live with his father in the

United States. His mother had consented to let him go, his visa had been approved, and the tickets for the *De Grasse* bought. He was taken to Le Havre. His baggage and he were put aboard the ship, and tearful good-byes were exchanged. The next morning, I was told, Maurice knocked at his mother's door. He had jumped ship at the last moment and managed to return to Paris. I can well imagine his father's shock and anger as he recovered his son's luggage at the New York pier. I should have found this event amusing, just as I should have empathized with my cousin's situation, but I could not understand why anyone would pass up an opportunity to live in New York City. Moreover, I could not understand why he had waited until the last minute to jump ship and run away in his pajamas. All the money his father had spent for his departure had been wasted. I was outraged. In my view, he should have refused to go in the first place, or he should have honored his commitment to his father. At twelve years old, I was not experienced enough to perceive gray zones; black or white was easier to see. Had I been able to read some of the classic romantic novels of the nineteenth century or even some of the pulp magazines, I would have discovered the importance of emotional impulses.

That July I passed the state's examination and completed sixth grade. As a reward, the school took us on a daytrip to the resort town of Le Tréport in Normandy. It was the first time that any of the students, including myself, had seen the sea. We left by bus at five A.M. and returned at midnight. Our time by the seashore was short, but we wet our feet and pants, climbed a cliff, and visited the souvenirs shops. I came home with such glowing tales that my father decided to take his first paid vacation in a pension at Le Tréport. He and I spent a wondrous week together on the beach, walking up and down the top of the cliffs. Two things have remained vividly in my memory from that summer vacation: the extraordinary freshness of the food, and how at low tide, the sea would withdraw an enormous distance so that I could walk for quite a while before I came to water. Neither of us knew how to swim so I just waded in up to my neck, and my father baked in the sun claiming that it did wonders for his rheumatism. He was only forty years old that summer. A photograph taken at the beach shows a man with a sad expression on his face. He still has a mop of hair, but his beard is graying, and he has gained a lot of weight.

At the end of summer, we were convinced that war with Germany was imminent. Hitler was demanding the return of the Sudentenland from Czechoslovakia, which had a treaty of mutual defense with France as well as the Soviet Union. We believed that if Germany used force, war would be declared on the spot. When the French began to call up some of its military reserves, the inevitability of war was obvious to all of us. There was jubilation when Chamberlain and Daladier acceded to Hitler's demands under the proviso that, now that Germany was reunited to Austria as well as to the Sudenten, there would be no more territorial demands from Germany. The dissenting voices came from the Czechs and from the Communists who denounced the Munich pact because the Soviet Union had not been consulted. The Daladier government began a systematic policy of repression against the Communists, and the Popular Front in France was destroyed. Politics took a turn to the right.

On November 7, 1938, Hershel Grynzpan, a seventeen-year-old Polish Jew, walked into the German embassy in Paris intending to kill the German ambassador. Instead, he killed Ernst von Rath, a third secretary. That murder precipitated what has become known as *Kristalnacht*. Upon hearing of the murder of von Rath, it was felt that Jews would pay dearly for this act. No one thought that Hershel's gesture, as foolish as it may have been, pointed to a resistance of the Jews to Nazi persecution. Years later, when I read accounts of the Warsaw

Ghetto uprising, I was struck by the cry of the first SS officers who fell under the bullets of the Jewish fighters: "Jews have arms! They are fighting back!" In 1938, we did not think of organizing, of fighting back. And yet, I remember photographs in *Paris Match* showing Dachau and the harsh treatment of its inmates at the hands of the camp guards. Of course we did not know that within a year special squads would gun down Jews in trenches all over Poland and Lithuania. But after *Kristalnacht*, no one, and especially no one in Germany, could claim ignorance of the progressively more repressive policies toward Jews. The other thing that struck me that year was the attitude adopted toward German Jews who managed to escape from Germany—a mixture of pity and resentment. Surely the German Jews were suffering just as the eastern Jews had suffered in years past. They deserved to be helped with money or food or any way that one could help. But on the other hand, they were still arrogant Germans who had not always welcomed the poorer Jews from the east. Now that the shoe was on the other foot, there was some poetic justice to their plight. By being refugees, they were calling attention to themselves and to the Jews who already lived in France, and there was enough anti-Semitism without their help. When I read *The Last of the Just* by André Schwartz-Bart, I did not recognize the welcoming German Jewish community of which he wrote. These were not the German Jews my family had known.

There was hardly a ripple of protest when Nazi Germany invaded Czechoslovakia in March 1939. Earlier that year, Franco had crushed what was left of the Spanish Republic. Thousands of Spanish refugees crossed the Pyrénées into France. Many found themselves in camps such as Gurs and Rivésaltes and later were deported to Hitler's extermination camps. Still, Chamberlain and his umbrella were the heroic symbols of a heroic peace.

The next fall, four of us started seventh grade with Monsieur Violle and were introduced to algebra. Those who had not succeeded in passing the state examination were left in sixth grade, but those who were fourteen years old started an apprenticeship. My friend Paul Manoutsis became an apprentice at Renault's in Billancourt. During the course of that year, Monsieur Violle called my father in to talk. In France, a teacher only called a parent when a child was in trouble. In a way, I was in trouble; if events ran their expected course, I would shortly start as an apprentice in the clothing industry. Monsieur Violle urged my father not to let that happen. He pointed out to my father that with my poor vision, I would not become a very skilled worker. My manual and artistic skills were poor; I would never be able to draw a straight line. I would have a better chance in life he said, if a way could be found to further my education. He promised my father that he would find a good secondary school for me and that he would write the necessary recommendations if my father would agree to his plan. My father thought that education was reserved for the children of the elite bourgeoisie. I did not fit this category, and besides, there was no possibility that the financial burden could be sustained. In our social class, the way to success was to have the kind of skills that could help a shrewd individual build up a business.

Monsieur Violle had almost convinced my father of his plan, but the final arguments were left to me. I had to reaffirm that I had no taste for a manual trade and predictably that I would be a failure as an apprentice in a furrier shop. All I wanted to do was to become a teacher just like Monsieur Violle, and I concocted a plan that would only require my father to support me until I reached the age of sixteen. After that I would pass an exam, and the French republic would take me in charge. Several days later, my father agreed to let me attend school beyond the seventh grade. Monsieur Violle found a reputable school in Versailles, wrote several letters of recommendation, and arranged for me to take the entrance examination. He even sent me off with several notebooks and other supplies belonging to the school so that I would be prepared no matter what happened.

Chapter Five

During the summer of 1939, rumors of war began to be heard again. Despite the promises that Hitler had made at Munich a year earlier, he was demanding the return of Danzig to Germany. Although the subject of war pervaded conversations as well as the newspaper headlines, no one seemed to believe that war was imminent. The Munich pact and the occupation of the Czech Republic in March of 1939 had fostered a climate of cynicism. France and England had sold out the Czechs to avoid war, and it was barely twenty years since the Great War had ended. A generation of men had been slaughtered, and now their sons would be sacrificed so that the Poles could have access to the Baltic Sea. In the opinions of my family and their friends, anything bad that happened to the Poles and their anti-Semitic government was to be applauded. Who had defended the Polish Jews during the pogroms of 1938? Who had protested the restrictive measures against Jews in Poland? Soon, political posters began to appear on the streets of Paris, denouncing the parties who wanted to go to war over Danzig. The political right favored peace and reconciliation with Germany, and denounced the left and the antifascists as war mongers and tools of Moscow. It now seems ironic that many members of my family agreed with the French right and native fascists that it was not worth fighting with Germany over a small port city. After the Hitler-Stalin pact, the political situation reversed itself. The Communist Party embraced pacifism, and my family and their friends resorted to Machiavellian explanations to understand the alliance. "Good old Stalin," they said, "was not selling out to Hitler, He was paying back France and England for having shunted him at Munich. He was biding his time, and eventually you'd see the Big Bear crush that evil Hitler, may his name perish forever." Just the same there would be no war, and if there was to be one, it would not occur about Danzig. Hitler must have read our minds and not been overly disturbed by the ultimatums Paris and London sent him. He attacked Poland, and we were shocked when France and England actually declared war on Germany.

During my last year of elementary school I had seen a tremendous amount of antiwar movies. The best known film from this time is Renoir's *La Grande Illusion* which has for me some troubling aspects. It shows, through the tragic friendship of an aristocratic German commandant of the Stalag and his equally aristocratic French prisoner, the end of the old order. There is a love story between an escaped French officer and a beautiful German farmer's wife that holds the promise of peace. What is shocking, however, is the presence of a stereotypical Jewish officer named Rosenthal, who is very rich and quite vulgar in his tastes. Rosenthal is not quite as brave as his Christian counterpart and tolerates derogatory language. There is no beautiful woman to reward him or console him for the sufferings the war has also inflicted on him. Two other films from this period stick in my mind. The first one, *Ultimatum*, takes place around the time that the Archduke of Austria was assassinated in Sarajevo and is about the lengths two officers go to avoid the inevitable. Their failure to stop the war makes them very conscious of the absurdity and horror of the situation. The second film, *J'Accuse*, shows the carnage of Verdun in all of its atrocity and meaninglessness. Twenty years after the horror, the world is again threatened. The star of the film, a survivor of Verdun, appeals to those who died on all battlefields to rise from their graves and protest the war by opening their war wounds and exposing their crippled limbs.

The war was declared during one of my rare visits to my mother. She had recently moved out of her mother's apartment and was living above her brother's store on the rue du Faubourg Saint Martin. For the first time in her life, she was living by herself although her brother was still available if she needed him. Her apartment was accessible from the outside and was connected to the store below by a flight of stairs. She did not have the whole apartment to herself; her brother kept a part of it for the shop. But she had a large room with an alcove kitchenette and a Turkish-style toilet down in the hall.

The first few days of war were feverish with activities. I expected the German planes to fly over Paris at any moment, meeting the French air force in an epic battle. Instead we spent our first days together painting my mother's window panes blue so no lights could be seen from the outside and gluing newspaper strips across the panes so she would not be hurt if they were shattered by exploding bombs. We also spent time at city hall looking at gas masks, which we were now required to carry at all times. We had to locate the nearest metro station; it would be a shelter in the event of an aerial attack. After a few days, life in Paris returned to normal. Except for the gas masks and the blued windows, we went about our business as usual, and I busied myself buying school books and going to the local movie theater to see dubbed American films.

Poland fell quickly after the German and Soviet invasions. My father's friends claimed that the Soviet invasion of Poland was ordered to protect the Poles from the Germans, because the Soviet Union could not possibly have territorial ambitions. Thus, on October 1, my father took me to the Ecole Primaire Supérieure Jules Ferry in Versailles and deposited my luggage and me in the school dormitory. My father had volunteered to join the French army, so on my first week end off, I joined him in Villepinte for a meal with the Gelblums. The next day he said good-bye to his friends; his eyes were full of tears. I felt like crying but could not. Our good-bye was short. We kissed and took leave of each other. Then he left for the garrison of Le Mans. After three years of living with the Charbonnats, I was inured to departures. Instead I was proud my father had volunteered to fight. At the age of forty-two, my father seemed very old to me, and I was afraid that he would never come back. What would happen to me then?

I wrote to my father every day. Since he could not write that well in French, somebody wrote his letters for him. I always felt that between the dictation and the writing, his voice was lost. I did not recognize his words, his way of constructing a sentence. His substitute always corrected his grammar, so at least I would get letters that were written in decent French. My life at Jules Ferry was not as easy as I had imagined it would be. For the first time in my life, I had a variety of classes to choose from, each with its own teacher. Relations between teacher and students were impersonal, the grading was severe, and for that first semester I felt disoriented and uncomfortable in a system where discipline was harsh. Dorm life was not easy either. The first part of the semester I slept in a quad, but then I was moved to a large room that resembled a hospital ward. Each student slept on a steel bed, with a single shelf to hold our toiletries and a footlocker to store our personal effects. We followed a strict schedule: up at seven-thirty A.M., a quick wash in the common bathroom, and breakfast in the refectory, classes from eight-thirty A.M. to eleven-thirty A.M., lunch, classes from one-thirty P.M. to four-thirty P.M., study hall from five P.M. to six-thirty P.M., dinner, study hall from seven-thirty P.M. to nine-thirty P.M. and lights out at ten P.M. On Thursday afternoons, we would go for an afternoon walk in town to see the castle's gardens or to take in a movie. It was a spartan sort of existence punctuated by punishments if we broke the rules of the dormitory. The punishments consisted of copying pages and pages of the dictionary. In Monsieur Violle's classroom, we had conjugated verbs in all their modes and tenses. But at Jules Ferry, we had access to a larger portion of the lexicon. Still as boarders, we were closely supervised, often by graduate students eking out a living so they could pursue their studies. They were supervised in turn by an officer of the school whom we derisively called the "adjutant." An adjutant in the French army was a high- ranking noncommissioned officer.

My mother came to visit me once in the fall of 1939. Her cousin, Paul Leizer, had been gunned down in the streets of Paris. She did not relate what this tragedy meant to the rest the family; instead she told me that there was justice in the world and that she felt avenged for the pains that the Leizers had inflicted on her. Why Paul Leizer was gunned down in Paris, I will never know. But I have heard two versions for his death. According to some in my mother's family, Paul had been trafficking in gold and had gotten mixed up with some unsavory characters. He was a victim of gang warfare. The story that I heard from his parents in 1945 was quite different. They maintained that Paul had been secretly working for the French Intelligence service and had been executed by French Fascists. His father tried to have the newly installed liberation government declare Paul a national hero. I suspect both versions of the story are lies, but Alfred Leizer grew up with the myth of his brother's heroism and became a true hero in the *maquis* of the Vercors on August 1, 1944, when he was killed in an ambush along with the novelist and literary critic, Jean Prévost.

In my quad there was a boy named Dupuy who quickly became my friend. He was a committed Catholic, and a political right-winger. We disagreed on practically every subject, but that did not stop us from being friends. We shared the same quarters, and the administration was our common enemy. He even took it upon himself to convert me. One Sunday he convinced me to accompany him to church. The only time that I had ever been in a church was to attend a baptism for a relative of the Charbonnat family. I still remember the fear I felt as I entered that modest church with its crucifixes and the stations of the cross. To voluntarily go to mass represented an act of heroism; I always expected something terrible to happen to me in a church. Although I had lived with Gentiles and had eaten their food, the temple roof had never collapsed on my head. At that time, I considered the ubiquitous presence of God pure quackery. My father had insisted that I do my bar mitzvah so he would not be shamed in front of his friends and neighbors. But I had not learned Hebrew, nor did I understand what I was supposed to read in the Torah. That did not faze my father who set about dictating what I was supposed to say. I proceeded to memorize what I had transcribed, rehearsed how it should be said, and thus acquitted myself fairly well during the ceremony. But being blasphemous to please my father was child's play compared to attending mass to placate a friend. I was terribly shaken when Dupuy grabbed my hand and dipped it in the holy water. I was petrified—It was as if I had become conscious that I had committed treason.

The war was going nowhere, and the military bulletins reporting activity in the no man's land between the Maginot and the Siegfried lines were dull and predictable. But the patriotic fervor among the students was high. We sang the martial songs of Maurice Chevalier, including the *Madelon* and one that promised we would soon be hanging our laundry on the Siegfried line. The French called it *la drôle de guerre*, but in the States it was called the phony war. It was the war that was not. But we soon had something to cheer about: Soviet troops invaded Finland and the heroic rhetoric that ensued lifted us out of the doldrums. There were not enough adjectives in the whole French dictionary to praise the bravery of the Finns as they resisted the Soviet Army.

Despite the nation's patriotic fervor, we did not feel that there was a war going on. We became more aware of the situation after Germany invaded Norway and more air raid drills were organized. We welcomed these drills as a diversion from our classes and a chance to make idiotic comments that we thought were very smart. Only once did we really become frightened as the bombs fell near the Renault factories in Billancourt. We could hear the explosions and feel the vibrations in our shelter. For once we were quiet.

Norway was no match for the German army, but we still did not realize that when Holland and Belgium were invaded by the Germans. The Maginot line proved useless; it only extended from the Swiss border to the Belgium border. Many years later, I learned that the Maginot line had been constructed in such a fashion that its guns could only face Germany. If the soldiers stationed there were attacked from behind, it became a useless line of defense. The impregnability of the Maginot line was a myth that kept the French defense establishment from modernizing its armies. The military bulletins assured us that our valiant troops were retreating to positions "well prepared in advance." We still did not realize the gravity of the situation and expected the Germans to falter long before they reached

Paris. Although the refugees were streaming in from the north of France, we thought that was normal. There was no reason to panic; the same thing happened in 1914. All would soon be well.

That June I went to see my mother. I had planned to spend a day with her in Paris and then to spend the next day in Villepinte to see that everything was in order at our house as my father had asked me to do. When I told her about my plans, she insisted that she would go with me. Although they were not divorced, I had strict orders from my father not to allow my mother on "his" property. Once again I was caught in the middle of their conflict; international wars do not abolish private ones. However, I was not willing to take her to Villepinte. My father's orders were not to be disobeyed. I still remembered the consequences of having disobeyed him on my eleventh birthday. But I was not brave enough to tell her that I would not take her with me or that I would not give her the keys so that she might go there by herself at another time. So I made up an excuse to sneak out of her apartment and took the train to Villepinte. I didn't feel any remorse about betraying my mother; loyalty to my father was much more important. On Sunday I returned to Versailles after spending a marvelous sunny day with Paul Manoutsis. It was the last time he and I played our childish games together. We did not know it then, but we were saying adieu to the joys and cares of our childhood. We would soon have to face a different reality.

When I got back to Versailles, Jules Ferry was in utter chaos. Panic had struck the administration. The school was closing on June 10. We had to pack our belongings and leave. I had two suitcases that I filled with my books and notebooks. I took the train to Paris to ask my mother for shelter. I had very little money and nowhere to go. I could not have fed myself in Villepinte, and I did not intend to live without food. I showed up at my mother's, dragging my two suitcases. She was unaware of the military situation; she was very angry with me for having betrayed her. She did not want to ever see me again. I had no other choice but to join my father in Le Mans, if he was still there.

The train station was mobbed with people trying to get out of Paris. Everyone spoke to everyone. The Parisians had suddenly lost their sense of privacy, and rumors flew back and forth at amazing speeds. I was hungry, thirsty, exhausted, and confused. At around eight P.M., I heard that a train was leaving for Le Mans. I followed a crowd of people, and managed to climb aboard the train, and stationed myself near an exit door where I could breathe. That exit door was kept open all night so that passengers could travel on the steps. We were packed into the train like sardines, but no fights broke out. There was a feeling of comradeship, occasional good humor, and concern for one another. I was asked several times where I intended to go and why I was all alone. I was able to answer freely about my father's whereabouts but could only hint about my mother having decided to stay in Paris. The passengers shook their heads in disapproval. No one had bothered to buy a ticket for the train ride, and there were no controllers on the train. The railroad employees were in full solidarity with the passengers; there were no longer any schedules or any routes. We were simply fleeing the advancing Germans. I was just a fourteen-year-old boy hoping to find his father in Le Mans. Today you can take the TGV and be in Le Mans in less than one hour, but on June 10, 1940, the train took twelve hours to travel the same distance. The train traveled slowly and stopped frequently, as if forward motion were painful. We were strafed once during the night, but I don't think that anyone was hurt.

I arrived in Le Mans sometime the next morning and found my way to the army barracks to see my father. He was surprised to see me and quite embarrassed about my sudden appearance. He was given the rest of the day off to try to dispose of me. He took me to a family in town, distant relatives of his, about whom he had never spoken and whose name I have forgotten. We were served a lunch, which I devoured, having not eaten for more than twenty-four hours. My father was advised to take me to city hall where someone would be able to help us. There were many children from Paris who had been evacuated and were living in children's centers. That evening I was put on a local train to Sillé-le-Guillaume with traveling orders and a letter for the director of the children's center. My father and I parted once again. We would not see each other for almost four months.

It was late in the evening when I arrived at the center, which was located in the upper story of a grammar school. Two classrooms had been cleared and served as dormitories; they were crammed with a hodgepodge of cots and bunk beds. There was a large kitchen and a narrow oblong dining room. I was assigned a cot in the big boy's room where boys ages eleven to fourteen were staying. The usual paperwork was to be done in the morning; I was exhausted, emotionally in a fog. During the next four years, I would frequently cloak myself in emotional numbness while going through the motions of day-to-day survival. For the moment I had shelter, and that was enough.

The next morning I told the directress of the shelter the biggest lie I have ever told in my whole life—a lie that would haunt me for many years to come. I told where my father was and relayed his army address, but when it came to identifying my mother, I blurted out that she was dead. This brought me immediate sympathy, but it also spared me from having to communicate with her. I was very angry with her; she had in effect thrown me out into the streets of Paris—penniless, with nowhere to turn. The years that I had lived with the Charbonnats had isolated me from the rest of my family, and I did not know them well enough to knock on their doors and ask to be taken in. In a way, my mother had ceased to be my mother. She had been so hurtful during these last years that I did not think I loved her anymore. I did not want her to know where I was, and if that caused her any pain, I felt she had earned it. So I said that she had died, and I have lived to regret it.

School was still in session in Sillé-le-Guillaume. I went to class in a building across from the center that looked like a castle. I remember crossing a moat to enter the building, which is why I thought the school resembled a castle. The school closed a couple of days later. Paris had fallen, and the German Army was racing southward. We kept busy taking long walks through the countryside. There I met British soldiers who were breaking up camp and fleeing toward the coast hoping, no doubt, that they would not be cut off by the Germans. They gave us cigarettes, but I became nauseated after smoking them. Having these perfumed English cigarettes, however, was a thrill. On another afternoon, we were playing soccer in a stadium when a couple of planes flew over our heads and started shooting at us. No one was hurt, and we claimed the planes had been Italian. We had not seen any identification on the planes, but rumors had it that only Italian planes strafed civilians. Italy had recently joined Hitler in the war, hoping to get a share of the spoils. That strafing kept us talking all evening.

On June 18, German motorcycles with sidecars appeared in the town. The German army was arriving, and we were told by the staff to stay in the dormitories. When we heard that the ground-floor classrooms and the courtyard of our school would be occupied by German troops, we descended to the lower level and looted its closets of notebooks, pens, and pencils—anything that would be of use to enemies. The Germans were here, but they would not get any of the supplies. We were all severely reprimanded for our petty thievery, lack of discipline, and disrespect toward public property. We were not, after all, sabotaging the German army. And we were no longer at war. France had surrendered.

German troops were bivouacked in the courtyard. We watched them, curious and frightened by the green uniforms moving about, shouting an idiom we did not understand and which we had always mocked. We were ordered to stay clear of these soldiers; incidents had to be avoided at all costs. The behavior of the German soldiers was spotless; they were very polite in the streets and in the shops and bought anything that could be sent home with Occupation Reich marks. The people had expected to suffer humiliations and violence so they were astonished by the discipline and courtesy of the invaders. Of course, we disobeyed our guardians by sneaking down to the courtyard. We wanted to get a closer look at these victorious warriors. We were welcomed with smiles as we formed a group around them, gesturing and exchanging a few stock words in French and German. One of the soldiers, a short stocky man—a far cry from the blond giants we had been promised—took out his wallet and showed us pictures of his wife and four daughters. The word "daughter" is the same in German and Yiddish, but I was smart or frightened enough not to speak any Yiddish to him. In the blink of an eye, our enemies were suddenly transformed into people with wives and children. We reminded him, I think, that he had another life, that he was more than a soldier. He may have been a farmer or a factory worker with the same daily cares and joys our parents had felt. Now his unit was recuperating before it raced toward the Atlantic Ocean or the Spanish border. His war in France was over: he had dreams of invading England. "Ya England kaput." I should have hated him, but I could not find in myself any evil in that soldier. I wondered about him many times over the years; had he made it home to his family, or had he been killed?

I made friends with a Jewish boy from Paris who was a few months older than myself. Nathan Mannker had a bunk next to my cot; he had recently lost his father and missed his mother and his three sisters quite a lot. He had a chronic toothache and moaned a great deal about it, but no one seemed to care. Nathan was much more aware of his sexual feelings than I. In fact I was still quite innocent, especially in my thoughts. In the Versailles dormitory, the boys smirked about whores and whorehouses, claiming that the older students who looked haggard in the morning had participated in these nocturnal revels. At that time, sex was considered a forbidden fruit, dirty, and absolutely debilitating. Anyone who engaged in sexual activity was in the process of destroying his mind and body. Nathan was the first to talk to me about masturbation. He wondered if the activity in which he engaged in would make him blind or insane. He told me he suffered from asthma, but I never saw him having an attack that summer. The first time I went to his house in Paris; however, he was lying in bed, struggling for breath. I was not in any position to pontificate on the subject of masturbation or sex; it both repulsed and frightened me. The notion that sexuality bred dreadful diseases was commonplace, so I could not understand what was so fascinating about it. Neither of us knew anything about girls, but we deemed them to be both inferior and mysterious creatures. We also considered those who engaged in the act of sex outside of matrimony as immoral people with weak character. However, that did not stop us from singing bawdy songs or telling salacious jokes; we were unable to make a connection between fantasy and reality. Nathan and I talked at great length without ever coming to any sort of resolution or becoming bored of our unanswerable dilemmas. We became inseparable. Toward the middle of August, his sister Dora appeared and took him back to Paris. At that time, many children were being returned to their parents.

Only a handful of students whose parents could not afford the train fare remained in the center, along with myself, who had no home to return to.

The center finally closed down at the end of August. The staff members accompanied us to Paris on the train, but there was no one to meet me at the train station. I was taken to the Lycée Jean-Baptiste Say in the Sixteenth Arrondissement. Cots had been set up in the classrooms, and students ate in the refectory. At the lycée, we were minimally supervised. There was little to do and no materials available for arts and crafts, but we were taught a lot of songs. The children were waiting for a parent to pick them up. Some had become separated in the initial exodus from Paris, others were orphaned. After ten days of living boredom, I decided to write to the mayor of Villepinte inquiring if anyone had heard from my father. A few days later my father appeared at Jean-Baptiste Say. The mayor had dispatched my letter to my father's house. He had come home from Toulouse in the nonoccupied zone and had been feverishly trying to locate me. There was no mail service between the two zones in the early days of the Occupation. He had gone to ask my mother if she had heard anything about my whereabouts. She had answered that I was fine. She had consulted a chiromancer who had assured her that I was safe; therefore, her mind was at peace. I had never seen that side of my mother. When I questioned her about it, she admitted that she often went to see a woman who consulted her tarot or cards for a fee. I believe now that my father should have spared me that story, or at the very least, his opinion about my mother's behavior. He did not realize that by lowering her in my esteem, he was also telling me that I was not important enough, to warrant any thought beyond the professional words of a soothsayer.

I wanted to know what had happened to my father after I left him in Le Mans and how he had managed to get to

Toulouse. It turned out that a day after seeing me, he became ill with the measles and was running a high fever. At his age, measles were considered very dangerous, possibly life threatening. He had been evacuated by ambulance to a hospital in Toulouse. I asked him if he had been trained to fight, but he had only done some guard duty with an unloaded carbine. He told me that his stint in the army was laughable, that there was no real or efficient organization, and no real will to fight or understand why there was a war in the first place. He had come back to his home to find me. Had he stayed in Toulouse, he may have survived the war. I say may, because a man without a country would have been an easy target for the police of the Vichy government, which could have delivered him to the Germans. But in 1940, I was happy and proud that he had come back for me.

Chapter Six

The first few days in Villepinte brought anxiety rather than the joy I thought I would feel as well as sadness about my former schoolmates who had been killed running away from the advancing German troops. I was also apprehensive about the kind of existence we would soon lead as Jews under the German Occupation. My father had his share of grief; a few weeks after our reunion, a postcard from his brother in Lodz announced that their father had died from starvation. There were no details about his death, so we could not imagine what was happening to the Jews in Poland. I was alarmed by articles I read in the newspapers as well as the commentaries I was hearing on the radio. The media focused on the reasons behind France's staggering defeat and finding the responsible parties.

The media claimed that France had been defeated because its fundamental values had been perverted by foreign elements and foreign ideas. Because France had been too open a society, welcoming riffraff from other nations, subversive ideas had become the norm. France had lost its moral fiber—its inherently heroic national character. The Third Republic had been too self-indulgent and greedy; the people had become lazy and godless. They had hosted all kinds of "undesirables"—Jews, Gypsies, and other people of impure blood who injected unsavory mores into traditional culture. Too many of these undesirables advocated the doctrines of Karl Marx and the Bolshevik movement he spawned. Communists, Freemasons, and Freethinkers were the grave diggers of the Christian faith. Moreover, all these subversive activities were financed by an international conspiracy of Jewish bankers. But the Jew was by far the most dangerous of these enemies. The Dreyfus and Stavisky affairs were brought up, and the Popular Front was reviled along with its Jewish prime minister, Léon Blum. The irrefutable proof of the Jews' evilness was the publication of the *Protocols of the Elders of Zion,* a fake document invented by the tzar's police, which supposedly revealed that the ultimate goal of the Jew was to conquer the whole world by corruption and to destroy Christianity and Western civilization. This propaganda frightened me, but it was so absurd that I used to laugh at it too. Little did I realize then that the demonization of the Jew was necessary for what was to come. Later when I visited Paris, I was shaken by the virulence of the propaganda. The walls were plastered with posters denouncing the "evil Jew as the hydra of international Jewish plutocracy, the vanguard of International Bolshevism." The posters denounced the sufferings and killings experienced by Russian workers in the Soviet Union and praised the advent of a national revolution in a new Europe. There was an exhibition depicting the satanic Jew as well as a German-made movie called the *Jew Süss* that played repeatedly in local movie theaters.

The schools reopened late that fall. In October the decrees of the Vichy government, which legislated the status of the Jews in France, were made public. I was still in Villepinte then, and my father did not want me to return to Versailles. He did not understand, nor did he approve of, my continuing interest in education. Perhaps he was more worried about the future than he let on. I was almost fifteen years old, and he could not pay the room and board at Jules Ferry. I vehemently pointed out that given my poor vision and my clumsiness, school was really my only option. He suggested that I go live with my mother and commute to Versailles from her house. That meant that I had to go see my mother and negotiate some kind of peace with her. Our meeting was difficult, but we were able to come to an agreement about the subjects that were acceptable and those that were not. Subjects that were absolutely taboo included my father's character, his life, and her desire to reconcile with him. I did not want to be put in a position where I would have to defend him or act as an intermediary between them. On the other hand, my mother had no strong wishes to resume married life with him; she was simply responding to her family's pressure to attempt a reconciliation for my sake. They had done that before with disastrous results. In the past when she had approached me about the idea of a reconciliation, I had not been very receptive. I liked my peaceful life at the Charbonnats and the intimacy that had grown between my father and me. I did not want to have any part of that life disturbed again.

When I arrived at my mother's home, I noticed that on my uncle Paul's store a poster was displayed in his window informing the public that this was a Jewish-owned store and that, by law, it was now operated by an "Aryan" manager. Eventually, that manager would own the store and my mother's flat. My aunt Raymonde, who survived the war by hiding in a convent, had to call on the French authorities to recover her property. I had read the decrees affecting the status of Jews in the newspapers but seeing these measures in real life was a shock. Nor was the running of Jewish enterprises by all-too-willing gentiles the only repressive step taken by the government. All Jews working for the government or for government agencies and who were by that very fact French citizens, were dismissed. Jews who had been naturalized after 1927 saw their citizenship abrogated. All Jews had to register with the police and have their identification papers and ration cards stamped with the word, "Jew." A Jew was not allowed to change his place of residence without the expressed consent of the police. These repressive measures were taken by the French government in Vichy; German measures would come later in the course of the war.

In the fall of 1940, food was scarce in Paris. The war had interrupted the harvest, and the German Army was fed on French goods. Many French people had ties to the countryside and were able to get supplies, but soon everything became rationed, from bread to clothing. Even potatoes were difficult to obtain. We could, however, get plenty of rutabagas, turnips, and Jerusalem artichokes—vegetables that used to be fodder for animals. The black market was the most common source of foodstuffs not available in stores; my mother availed herself of it even before I came to live with her. In those days, I was always hungry, and my hunger knew no bounds. I could have eaten all day long.

The schools were reopened, so every morning I took the metro to the Gare Saint-Lazare and the train to Versailles. I deposited my lunch pail in a bistro near the school where it could be warmed up at lunchtime for one franc. Once in a while, my mother would give me money to eat in the bistro. I did a lot of my reading on the train, as well as my homework. However, the peace between my mother and me did not last more than six weeks. We had a horrible fight, triggered, no doubt, by the volatility of adolescence. We called each other names and yelled words so hurtful that my uncle Paul grabbed me by the throat and threatened to kill me the next time I showed such a lack of respect for my mother. The next day, my mother ordered me out of the house.

I rejoined my father who was renting a room in a hotel near Clignancourt, not far away from the Gelblum's new apartment. I swore to my father that I would never see my mother again. This time our breakup was definitive. I had been wrong in fighting with her, but that did not stop me from feeling totally justified and outraged that I had been sent packing again. My father did not help matters either; he was only too glad to take my side and condemn my mother's action.

During that fall semester, I renewed my friendship with Nathan. I called on him one Sunday at his home rue Rochechouart and met his mother and his three sisters. After that I visited them almost every Sunday, and his family became a second family to me. My father had become involved with a woman named Anna. He had asked me whether it was acceptable that he live with her. He was, after all, a young man who had been separated from my mother for nearly five years. I had no objections, for I thought he should have a chance at having a better life. The first time I met Anna, she reached out to me and tried to kiss me. I recoiled sharply. It was not a gesture I had expected, and it was the wrong kind of gesture. In her eagerness to please my father, she had acted too fast. I was incapable of accepting affection as a matter of course. I had once been made to kiss Madame Charbonnat's granddaughter during her birthday celebration and had blushed from head to toe. My meeting with Anna had an inauspicious beginning, and our relationship only went downhill from there. My father was obviously taken with her. I was not. Unfortunately for both of us, Anna spoke but a few words of French. She had recently arrived from Poland after a pogrom that had occurred in Lodz. She was thirty-four years old, and I was barely fifteen. We could communicate in Yiddish, but that was not an idiom I favored, particularly not while walking in the streets or dining in a restaurant. The French, in general, did not appreciate a foreign language being spoken in their presence. As Jews we were already sufficiently despised without further attracting hostile comments because of our language.

Nathan and I resumed the intense conversations that we had started in Sillé-le-Guillaume, but this time we were joined by his two older sisters and sometimes by his mother. Dora was seventeen and Suzanne, nineteen. Suzanne was engaged to a young Frenchman from a bourgeois family in Le Havre. They had met while he was on leave from the army, but he was now a prisoner in Germany. Suzanne talked about her fiancé, Bernard, almost constantly. She also talked about her ideas of marriage and love and all she expected from their life. We talked about our hopes for the future, completely oblivious to the possibility that we might not have any future. We were aware of the German presence, the repressive laws, and the shortage of food. We were cold and hungry, but we could not imagine that extermination might be our lot. We often took long walks along the Paris boulevards or went to a movie. Sometimes we bought nonrationed crepes made from dark flour that tasted awful but temporarily quieted our pangs of hunger.

In January my father sent me back to the boarding school at Versailles. There the main dishes—often the only dish—consisted of rutabagas boiled in water and occasionally cod fish that had been dried and rehydrated. The fish was served in some sort of white sauce with a floating potato. I hated the very smell of that cod fish and never touched it; even the potato tasted awful, but I ate it anyway. I used to fall asleep counting the loaves of peasant bread I was going to devour each day after the war. The prospect of eating good French bread held such a promise of happiness and had such a soporific effect.

In the early part of 1941, I became conscious of feelings of jealousy and resentment toward my father. He and Anna had moved into a small hotel room near the rue Montorgueil, and for the first time in his life, he was doing well for himself. He was using his connections in the tanning trade to buy and sell furs that were not readily available to furriers. He was earning a healthy profit on the black market, and could afford to eat at restaurants that still served good foods. He was gaining weight while I was in effect starving in Versailles. My father now paid scant attention to me; he was too busy being happy. I complained to him of being hungry all the time, but he made no effort to provide me with food at school. I had to watch my schoolmates eat the supplies they brought or received from home. I did not have money or anything to trade for food, and I felt that he had abandoned me to my own devices. I must have let my feelings show because he took me aside to reassure me that he still loved me as much as ever—even if he was now involved in a new relationship. I did not believe him. The only other time that he had talked to me seriously was in Anna's presence to express the opinion that I should leave Versailles, my book world, and find an apprenticeship somewhere in Paris where I could learn a solid, respectable trade. At that moment, I saw them both as my enemies. Yet I never wavered in my loyalty toward him, even when I visited my aunt Raymonde and complained about the quality of the menu at Jules Ferry.

A week later, my mother showed up in Versailles with two shopping bags full of food. My aunt, I learned from her later, had complained to my uncle Paul about the shameful way in which I was being treated. He, in turn, had pressured my mother to bring me supplies. I can still picture her in the courtyard of Jules Ferry, facing me from far away. I did not greet her, nor did I approach her. And I refused the food that she had brought me. I was not interested in making peace with her, and

I was not to be bought off with groceries. I did not have not any reason to forgive her and told myself I did not love her. To accept food under these circumstances would deprive me of my pride and would betray my father by admitting to her that I was not properly provided for. I was angry at my father, but he was still the most important person in my life at the time. I heroically refused the food, and my mother went back to Paris with her two bags. Childish victories are made of such absurd actions.

Anna and my father moved to Villepinte in April, and on one of my weekend visits, I learned that some of the Jewish men I had known during our summers at Villepinte had been arrested and were in French internment camps. These arrests had occurred in an orderly, almost civilized fashion. The police had summoned the men, mostly of Polish origin, by letter and ordered them to report to the police station with a suitcase containing clothes, a blanket, and food for three days. Being law-abiding men, they reported and were taken to Beaune-la-Rolande and Pithiviers. Later, there were roundups in the streets and at the entrances of the subway, too. It's possible that my father and Anna had moved to Villepinte because they were tired of living in a hotel, but it seems more likely that my father thought that Anna, as a newcomer, would be safer in the suburbs.

At that time, the internment camps in both zones were under the supervision of the French police. The prisoners were allowed to receive mail and packages and were even allowed some visitations from their families. There were some tales of escape that circulated. The Jews in Villepinte were all fearful, but there was not yet a sense of the impending tragedy that was unfolding. We had no inkling of the killings that had taken place in Poland and in the Baltic countries; the wall of silence had not been broken yet. One morning I even found a leaflet in our mailbox that had been distributed by the underground

Communist Party urging us not to participate in the imperialist war between England and Germany and to welcome the German proletariat in uniform. I could not believe what I was reading since the daily propaganda on the radio and in the newspapers always denounced the Communists and sang the praises of the national revolution and a New Europe. The Communists who had accepted the Soviet-Hitler pact were caught in an ironic and damning situation. When Germany attacked the Soviet Union, we felt the war would soon be over. Hitler had finally made the same mistake as Napoleon, the Russians and the Russian winter would crush him. It did not enter my mind that anyone in my family was going to be directly affected by these events. So on this particular weekend, I took the train to the Gare Saint Lazare, the metro to Jean-Jaures, and caught the bus to Villepinte. At the bus station, a neighbor, Monsieur Mandell, stopped me and blurted out that my father had been arrested. For a few seconds I became paralyzed, numb, unable to understand what had happened. I was going to Villepinte, but my father would not be there. I could not imagine it.

This is what Anna told me. My father was on friendly terms with one of the policemen who had come to arrest him. The evening before, he had gone out to have a drink with his friend. If the policeman was aware of my father's impending arrest, he did not let on. Or if he did, it was probably in such a way that my father did not understand him. I know that I have not always understood the oblique ways in which officials or even those in positions of authority convey information. My father was not quite assimilated and adept in manipulating the French language, so it is possible that he missed some hidden meanings. It is also possible that the policeman was afraid to compromise himself and did not say a word or that he did not know anything until the morning he was assigned to arrest my father and deliver him to the German authorities. As a Russian refugee and a Jew, my father was identified as an enemy alien. The policemen, Anna told me, had been very polite; in fact, they had taken my father to a coal depot where he had ordered a supply of coal, so Anna would be able to have some warmth in the house that coming winter. The policemen did all they could for him except letting him escape. For years I carried a grudge against that policeman and the French police for the ways in which they had cooperated with, and sometimes anticipated, the wishes of the Nazis. The Paris police even helped to organize and execute one of the biggest raids against Jews in Paris on July 16, 1942.

It was frustrating to me that I had to suppress my feelings of anger whenever I saw that policeman but had to act as if he were really a valued friend of the family. He did, however, in exchange for some fur pieces for his wife or mistress, make me an identification card on which the word "Jew" was not stamped. He filled it at our house and affixed the proper stamps and then recommended I go to the police station to have the word "Jew" stamped on it so it would be properly registered. I now owned an identification card that was legal, signed under the Vichy laws. It could serve me well if I were caught in a raid in the streets of Paris. I failed, of course, to report to the police station with my new identification card.

On Monday I reported to Versailles, packed my belongings, and informed the principal that given my father's situation, I was obliged to withdraw. To his credit, he felt sorry for me and suggested a few possible solutions, but there was nothing that could be done to help me through the end of the school year. My education was complete. As I left Versailles, I did not think about my future. I just wanted my father to be home. Thus it came to pass that I had to live with Anna, who could not believe that anything bad would ever happen to my father. I was an inconvenience to her, but I was also indispensable. I could serve as an intermediary between her and the French people.

We soon received a postcard from my father, who was interned in Compiègne. The return address was labeled *Kriegsgefangenenlager,* which meant that he was not being detained by the French police as were the other Jews and foreigners in France. It was helpful to believe that he was considered a prisoner of war and would be protected by the Geneva Convention. This belief was reinforced a few months later when Anna and I traveled to Compiègne and caught a glimpse of him through the barbed wire fence. He was wearing a French army uniform as were his companions. The detail was guarded by an SS soldier and his dog.

Later, I would write to the Prefect of the Department of Seine et Oise to ask for his help and for some relief. A social worker came to the house, a young woman sympathetic to our plight. She arranged for us to receive an allowance from the state which was similar to the money given to the families of prisoners of war. The state would also find me a place where I could learn a trade. The irony of that project was that I found myself in an organization of the Petain Youth, wearing the uniform of the ongoing National Revolution. There were few boys in the group, so I was put in a shop by myself and shown how to cut out license plates out of sheet metal. The lunches we were served were adequate for the times. For two weeks, I walked the three kilometers to the train station in Sevran, got off at Blanc-Mesnil, and walked to the youth camp. In the second week, a boxing session was arranged, in which I received more than my share of blows. It convinced me that the youth camp was not the place for me.

Anna and I did not get along. Besides our emotional problems, we could not tolerate each other's cultural differences. Her ways of dealing with the world at-large depended on her

Jewish-Polish roots and had scant currency with the French. She could not or would not understand that certain modes of behavior were not acceptable. She often concluded that the rebuffs she received were due to anti-Semitism or my inadequacies as a translator. It had taken my mother a long time to learn that you do not bargain in grocery stores. Anna was not yet aware of this, nor was she aware that relationships in France were different from those in Lodz. She would order me to go see so-and-so and ask for such and such, but I knew that I would come back empty-handed. I'd go anyway and sadly watch people shake their heads in disbelief at my inappropriate request. This only cemented Anna's belief in my incompetence. I used to hide out at the Manoutsis home and read Jeanette's books until her mother or father, irritated by my prolonged presence, would chase me home. I read a lot that fall, devouring novels by Balzac, Flaubert, Zola, Gautier, Victor Margueritte, Emily Bronte, and many, many schmaltzy stories published in women's magazines. Victor Margueritte's works fascinated me the most, especially the series which started with *La Garçonne*. It was considered a scandalous book but was in fact the prelude of a utopian vision of the world. Even the announcement in the newspapers that Margueritte endorsed a collaboration with Germany did not deter me from avidly embracing his utopian vision. I was taken by his advocacy of the equality of the sexes, his denunciation of bourgeois marriage, and his notion that sexual looseness should be abandoned. Mating was for life, and virginity was necessary until the right one came along. At fifteen, in the midst of a war, one is entitled to dream of new worlds.

During the summer of 1941, I was quite alarmed by the success of the Nazis on the Soviet front. One by one important cities fell; the Panzer divisions kept smashing through Russian resistance. The news from the Eastern front provoked jubilation in the media. It seems that the German Army was invincible. The touted New European Order could become a reality. The Vichy government, in full sympathy with the Nazis, was calling for Volunteers against Bolshevism. When the United States entered the war, we hoped for a quick end to the conflict and that the military power of Germany would at last be broken. Peace would be restored, at the very latest, in six months. We would all be saved, and my father would come home. It was hard to believe in the beginning that Japan was victorious in Asia against the British and the Americans. Such was the power and success of the Axis, that it finally dawned on some of us that the war might not end as quickly as we had hoped. That winter was among the harshest that I had experienced. By 1944, most of the wooden benches in Paris, had been ripped off and used for fuel. The harsh winter did not sustain our spirits.

To escape Anna, I found a job as an apprentice in a fur shop in Paris. I was put to work stretching the skins by wetting the leather side with a stiff brush and pulling on them until they could not be stretched anymore. Finally, the skins were nailed on a wooden board and let to dry until they retained their stretched shape. I wasn't very good at that kind of work; I had no feeling for it even though I had seen my father do it. I don't believe I lasted more than six weeks on the job before quitting or being fired—most probably the latter.

My sixteenth birthday came and went unnoticed. Anna and I traveled to Compiègne and were able to catch another glimpse of my father. A month later, my aunt Raymonde, Anna, and I returned to Compiègne. My aunt Raymonde's husband and brother were also prisoners in that camp. We bribed one of the SS guards with some furs, and we were led into the camp where we had a ten-minute visitation with my father. He looked to be in good health although he had lost weight, and even spoke of a plan he had to escape. Anna reacted with near-hysterical fear upon hearing this plan; she was afraid that if he failed, he would be shot on the spot and that we would be shot in reprisal. He did not try to escape. I'll never know if he could have succeeded and survived the war by hiding somewhere with Anna or whether he would have died sooner than he did. As we kissed him good-bye, Anna cried, and I trembled. My aunt Raymonde slipped some money under his coat collar for her husband and brother. I never saw him again; the Nazis murdered him.

My relationship with Anna continued to deteriorate. I refused to obey her once, so she hit me and kicked me. I knew then that I could not go on living with her. I reasoned that if I had to be miserable, I might as well do it in my mother's house. Anna remained a stranger to me, despite the many months we had lived together under the same roof. I asked my aunt Raymonde to arrange a reunion between my mother and me. A few days later, I left Villepinte. Anna urged me to come back from time to time to visit her. I never slept in my father's house again.

Chapter Seven

In Paris I managed to find another apprentice's position in a shop run by an old friend of my father. His shop was located just a stone's throw from my mother's apartment, which made it convenient for me to go home at lunchtime. David, my new boss, was subcontracting from another furrier and providing fur vests for the German army. By subcontracting the job, David could delude himself into thinking that he was not really working for the Germans. He made good money which helped support a large family. I was paid very little in keeping with my skills, but it allowed me to keep some dignity as I faced my mother. We had agreed on a sum of money I would contribute toward my board and on how much money I could keep for my personal needs.

The money that I contributed hardly covered the cost of my food, but my mother treated me as if I were an adult. She offered to sew me a work smock and even went so far as to discuss its style with me. She proposed to have her uncle make me a suit even though cloth could hardly be found. I understood and accepted that she was trying to make amends for the years in which she had neglected me. I returned her respect, and for the two months that we lived together, not a word of recrimination or criticism passed our lips. We did not become affectionate, but then, neither of us knew how to express our feelings very well. Except for the fact that my father wanted to know why I had left Anna in Villepinte, I was reasonably happy in my mother's home. The emotional storm that had once controlled our lives was over. All was not forgiven and forgotten, but there was a significant truce between us.

On June 1 of that year, a new series of restrictive decrees were promulgated against the Jews in the occupied zone of France. We now had a curfew that went into effect at eight P.M. In June, it is light in Paris until almost eleven P.M. As I recall, Jews had to obey the following restrictions:

Jews had to wear a yellow star with the word "Jew" sewn visibly on their outer garments near their heart. These patches were picked up at the police station in exchange for a textile coupon from our ration card.

Jews had to ride in the last car of the metro and in the rear of busses.

Jews were forbidden to enter the following facilities: movie theaters, theaters, libraries, public latrines, public telephones, swimming pools, public parks, or public benches. The use of bicycles was also forbidden. Radios had to be turned in to the police.

Jews could only shop at certain hours of the day, and they could no longer queue up with the Gentiles. These new hours coincided most often when the shops were closed or when all goods available that day had been sold out. Jews were reduced to buying their food on the black market if they could afford it, or depended on the kindness and courage of the local merchants—something that seemed to be in short supply.

Wearing a yellow star may either humiliate you or bring you great pride. It may also cause you shame and defiance. One thing that is certain is that it will make you feel different forever. That yellow star is imprinted on you for as long as you live. It is the sign of the world's rejection, the symbol of your alienation. In 1942, the glances of my compatriots informed me that I was no longer one of them. I was one of *them*, I was *they*. I had become a boy whose country no longer wished to embrace him, who denied him his very right to live like other people—assuming that he would be allowed to live at all. Yet the more I was denied, the more vigorously I believed and asserted I was French and that I was no different from anyone else. I did not understand what the Jews had done to be singled out in such a manner. My world was being turned upside down; I now lived in a place where the notion of justice was nonexistent. The France of my school days had ceased to be a reality.

On July 15, there was a knock on the door at eight P.M. Nobody Jewish would be calling, not with the curfew in place. My mother and I looked at each other anxiously as she opened the door. A man entered the flat, excused himself, and said he had been sent by the Leizers, my mother's aunt and uncle. He warned us that there was going to be a police raid in the early hours of the morning and that we should hide out. My mother turned to the concierge who was, unbeknownst to us, a police informant as were many concierges at that time. The concierge showed us a place in the cellar where we could hide, so we packed our clothes and some fruit and went down to the cellar. We entered a tiny closet in which we could only stand, and stood there, too afraid to speak or breathe. After several hours, we could not stand our confinement anymore. We went back upstairs, and with stupid fatalism, we went to sleep. Our legs had given out, and fear could not overcome our need to sleep. At five A.M., we were awakened by shouts and heavy steps on the stairs. We did not dare to make a sound or get out of bed. We simply held on to one another. We waited for the fateful knock on the door. That knock never came. Our neighbors, an elderly couple, had been arrested, but we were safe for the moment. Apparently, we had not been on the list of Jews to be arrested that day. Those who had been taken from their homes were mostly of Polish origin.

The next day, the horror of the night before began to unfold as we surveyed the damages. Some of our relatives had been arrested, and with one exception, none would survive. It was quite obvious that we were all liable to be arrested and interned. This time the arrests had not been limited to the men. Women, children, old people, and sick people had been brutally carted away by the French police to the Vélodrome d'Hiver, an arena where six-day bike races used to be held. Rumors spread like wild fire that as many as eighty thousand Jews had been arrested and that there had been many suicides. Even policemen were said to have committed suicide rather than obey their orders to arrest the Jews on their lists. Historians have related that the arrests accounted for about thirteen thousand people, and suicides were not even mentioned.

The massive raid created an atmosphere of panic and despair among Paris's Jewish families. It was high time to organize hiding places or flee to the unoccupied zone. Unfortunately, fleeing to the Free Zone was dangerous. Jews caught on a train, away from their residences, or at the border risked immediate deportation and even death. There were stories of Jews having been shot at the border and of some having crossed the border successfully with the help of a local guide and considerable sums of money. Others paid their guides but were delivered to the Germans. The air was indeed fraught with many a peril.

That afternoon I went out and checked on our nearest relatives. My grandmother was safe, as were a few others. My boss and his family had managed to escape arrest. A few months earlier, his father-in-law and his brother-in law had been able to cross into the Free Zone and were now living in Toulouse. My boss invited me to spend a few days with his family in a house that he had rented in Villepinte. The house was located almost directly behind my father's house. I avoided going to see Anna or anyone I knew in Villepinte. The spirit of living incognito had taken me over. David's family lived with his wife's two younger sisters and his mother-in-law. His mother-in-law and her two daughters had escaped arrest on the night of July 15, but their apartment had been sealed by the police. They were disconsolate because they had no belongings and worst of all were without their favorite dresses.

Because I was French born, spoke without a foreign accent, and looked younger than my sixteen years, I was persuaded by the mother and her two daughters to go back to Paris, break the police seal on the apartment, and stuff as many suitcases as I could carry with the precious cargo. I was entitled to take anything for myself that fit me or that I liked. I was to arrive before eight P.M. to avoid arrest in the streets and sneak into the building through the courtyard to avoid being seen by the concierge. I still had to wear the yellow star that could identify me to the police or the Germans. Avoiding the concierge was the most essential part of our plan, for she surely would stop me or call the police if I were to be seen.

Fools must have guardian angels, whether they believe in them or not; I managed to get from Villepinte into to the Third Arrondissement to their apartment, climbed the four flights of stairs, broke the police seal, and slipped the keys in the two locks as noiselessly as possible. When I entered the apartment I was either all body or I had none left. I did not turn any lights on; I found two suitcases and stuffed them with the items I thought had been requested. I did not look for anything that might fit me. I tried to fall asleep so that I might wake up early enough to leave the building before anyone became aware that the police seals had been broken. Of course these are not circumstances that encourage sleep. I left the apartment at seven A.M.and took the metro to the Gare du Nord. From there I dragged the suitcases the three kilometers from Sevran to Villepinte. I got a hero's welcome that lasted for the rest of that day. The next day, the young women began to cry and whine about not having some of their favorite pieces of clothing, and it seemed to me that they were looking to blame me for their losses.

The raids in Paris soon stopped, so we returned to our homes except the two young women and their mother who now lived with David. Upon returning to my mother's, we both began a discussion of what was to be done about our future. I had no doubts in my mind that we would all be arrested and interned sooner or later. I had no desire to be arrested and even less desire to live my life in an internment camp even though I did not then know that Jews were marked for extermination. Although the propaganda against us was virulent, the repressive measures humiliating, and the mass arrests frightening, we were not yet aware that mass murders of Jews were occurring. It was not until late 1942 that I began to hear stories about Jews being asphyxiated in the wagons of freight trains. Even then it seemed unbelievable, but it did make the fear of death more real. All I knew, as I spoke with my mother, was that I did not want to fall into the hands of the French police or the Nazis. It seemed logical that we leave Paris and head toward the Free Zone where we would be safe from the Germans. But where would we go even if we could manage to leave Paris safely and get across the border? How would we survive there? These questions did not worry me somehow; I was sure that we would survive. My mother, however, was very doubtful about her ability to reestablish herself in an unknown place, especially with her poor French and lack of connections in that part of the country. She was loath to abandon her friends and the few possessions she had accumulated over the years, especially her old sewing machine which was a necessary tool for her trade. Instead she would trust in God, who would watch over her, take care of her, and keep her safe. She had nothing to fear. These discussions repeated themselves many times in the days that followed. My assertions that there was no God or that God helps those who help themselves did not have any impact on her decision to stay where she was. I should have learned then that words are helpless in the face of faith.

Although I was not working, I stopped by my boss's house. I was cajoled into returning once more to his mother-in-law's apartment to fetch the clothing I had not brought back the first time. At that time, there was a woman with two young children who had miraculously escaped from the Vélodrome d'Hiver living in the same building as David's mother-in-law. The plan we devised was very simple. I was to go to that woman's house, and when it was dark, I would cross the courtyard, climb up the four flights of stairs, enter his mother-in-law's apartment, and fill two more suitcases with the precious items I had left behind the first time around. Once my task was done, I would return to that woman's house and stay the night. I managed to execute the plan, returning to my host's apartment well past eleven P.M. with the two suitcases. My host greeted me, breathless, in the entryway. She wore only a full slip as she hugged me and took my hand to her breast to show me how fast her heart was beating. I was a hero, once again. I delivered the suitcases to David next morning, and I was given an address in Toulouse where David's father-in-law was living safe from the Germans, at least temporarily.

My mother never questioned my absences. Our emotions were in such a chaotic state that when I told her that I was going to see my boss or spend time with his family, she just accepted my statement. If she had any worries, she did not share them with me. She responded as if I were an adult and free to act as I pleased. Of course I never told her what I was doing. Our conversations about leaving Paris continued without much success. One day she told me that if I wanted to take my chances and leave for the Free Zone, I should go. I disliked the idea of leaving without her, but in the end I gave in to her offer. She provided me with five thousand francs, which I could use to cross the border and pay a smuggler. I had never seen that much money in my life. I was now responsible for a small fortune and how to spend it.

I left Paris on August 1. That was a good date to leave Paris since most Parisians left for their vacations on August 1. That France was occupied by foreign troops did not seem to have any effect on this holiday schedule. It would be a propitious time to go unnoticed in the crowds at the metro and the train stations. I also hoped that the police would be less vigilant. We spent the day before my departure packing my suitcase with my clothing and a few photographs. We removed the yellow stars from my clothing very carefully; there was not to be the slightest trace of a yellow thread on any of my belongings. My mother told me to be extremely cautious. I was not to speak to strangers, and if I had to do so, I was to be wary about to whom I spoke and about what I said. I was warned that anti-Semites were everywhere and that they would not hesitate to denounce me to the authorities. The moment I stepped out of the house without my yellow star, I was breaking the law and subject to the direst consequences. In order to allay my mother's fears, I confessed to her that I had an identification card on which the word "Jew" was not stamped. Instead of being reassured by this fact, she became quite alarmed and ran to consult the concierge about the advisability of owning such a card. The concierge asserted that the identification card was illegal. It was fortunate that my mother did not consult the concierge about my immediate plans of departure—that was illegal as well. I surrendered the card to my mother, and I left the house with my birth certificate, the decree certifying that I was a French citizen, and my ration card. Our parting was not dramatic. I kissed my mother. She kissed me back. And shortly after eight P.M., I left her house to take the metro to the Gare d'Austerlitz. I bought a one-way ticket to Dax, where I would look around for someone to smuggle me across the border into the Free Zone. I never saw my mother again.

All of the trains leaving Paris were full. No seats were available; even the hallways were crowded with people sitting on their suitcases or smoking at the windows. I sat on the floor next to my suitcase, in a stupor. I was so hot that my shirt was sticking to my back, and I was worn out from my fears. Still I could not sleep. Instead I tried in vain to imagine what would happen in the next few days. I had left Paris before, two years ago, to find my father. This time, there was no one to run to, save an address in Toulouse and someone I did not know. I thought about my father in Compiègne, my mother in Paris, and Anna in Villepinte. What would happen to all of us?

Next to me, seated on the floor, were two young people necking, totally impervious to the world around them. I don't know where I found the nerve to speak to them, but at one point in the evening I asked where they were going on vacation. Mont-de-Marsan, which turned out to be just a few kilometers from the Free Zone. I asked if they knew of someone who could help me across the border. The young man's brother had a truck and even a permit to go back and forth between the zones. The young couple did not ask me why I wanted to cross the border; in those days they knew. It could not have escaped the attention of anyone living in or near Paris that

Jews were being arrested and detained. July 16 had left its mark on everyone.

In the course of our conversation, it turned out that this young couple was living in an illicit situation. The young man had fallen in love with his sister-in-law; both of them were fleeing Paris. Though we were strangers and I was only a kid, he told me their story. I was so engrossed in my own thoughts and feelings that it did not occur to me at that time to judge them or their actions. Instinctively, I had turned to them without much thought as to the wisdom of my own actions, disregarding my mother's recommendation that I be wary of strangers. On that train, everyone was a stranger, and I a stranger among them all. Choosing to speak to the lovers was not the most stupid thing I could have done. In fact, I was well served whenever I called on younger people or couples during my wanderings.

I got off the train at Mont-de-Marsan, instead of Dax. My biggest fear had been that there would be a control on the train or at the train station by the French or German police. My identification was in Paris, and I did not care to explain to a policeman why it was missing, nor did I know what I would say if questioned. I went to a hotel near the station where the young couple had indicated and where I was to wait until I was contacted by the young man's brother. Contrary to established customs and laws, I was not asked for my papers, nor did I fill out a registration form; the police would not be informed of my presence. I was contacted by phone and told where I was to meet the young man's brother in town. It smacked of cloak and dagger, of spy movies I had seen at one time or other. I was full of apprehensions: Was I walking into a trap? Would this man really smuggle me across the border, or would he turn me over to the Germans? I had no choice but to meet him. Returning to Paris meant certain arrest, internment, or worse. I did not give it a second thought. I met the man in that evening at his house. He was a trucker, an ordinary Frenchman, with a wife and children. He did not like the Germans and did not mind making some extra money with his permit and truck. He was risking his life if he were caught. He explained that his fee for taking me across the border was three thousand francs, half to be paid in advance, the other half when he left me in the Free Zone. Most of my fortune would be gone, but I felt reassured by the fact that he had asked for only half the fee in advance. I reported to his house the next day at six A.M. My suitcase was stashed in the back of the truck, and I donned a disguise of oil-stained overalls. My hands and face were smeared with motor oil. We were going to drive to the checkpoint where I was ordered to stay calm and show no emotion. I did not feel very calm.

We drove a few kilometers to the border and stopped at the gate of the checkpoint. A German soldier, a noncommissioned officer, came out. My driver jumped out of the cab in order to put as much distance as possible between me and the German and presented his permit. The German pointed at me, but the driver told him that I was a new worker who had been hired that morning and that there had not been enough time to prepare my papers. Meanwhile, I was needed to fill up the truck with important materials requested by the Germans. The German gave the signal to go on, and the gate was lifted. He started to go back inside his post, but changed his mind and called the driver back. At that moment, I thought that I was undone and began to tremble. Luckily, the German never looked at me. All he wanted from my driver was a light for his cigar. We went through the no man's zone and at the other end, but the French gendarmes did not stop us at their checkpoint. The Germans had let us through, so there was no need for them to be zealous. I was left in a small village. I paid the driver, gave him back his overalls, and I was told where to catch a bus that would take me to a train station and from there to Toulouse.

Chapter Eight

After my trip through no man's land, I thought I was home free. At the very least, I was free from the German occupation forces, though not yet free from the French police. I was still a Jew on the run—a boy without an address or visible means of support. At the bus station, two gendarmes were asking passengers for identification papers before allowing them on the bus. I saw that some people were not permitted to board; they were foreign-looking and mostly Jews. Until then I had not realized that Mont-de-Marsan was a town from which many people chose or hoped to cross the border into the Unoccupied Zone. What the foreign Jews did not know is that the gendarmes would stop them on the other side. I hope that many of these people were let go or were able to bribe their ways out of that village and were not turned over to the Germans, but I fear the worst. I did not know what to do, but I decided to gamble. I showed the gendarmes my birth certificate and the decree of my naturalization, and I was allowed to board the bus.

There were no direct trains to Toulouse, so I had to make several connections along the way. What I remember most about that train ride is the sight of the Pyrénées mountains. I had never seen a mountain before except in photographs. The long delays at my transfer points allowed me to visit Pau and Carcassonne. Pau is a blur in my memory, but the medieval walls of Carcassonne have stuck in my mind for a very long time. I arrived in Toulouse and found the house of David's father-in-law. It was a dingy place in a section of town where there were no connections between the sinks and the sewers. Dirty dishwater ran along the gutters, and foul smells hung in the air.

David's father-in-law was a short, pudgy man with a protruding lower lip and beady dark eyes. His son, in his twenties, sported a thin mustache, and his conversational subjects concerned the seduction of women. He fit my idea of a gigolo. I was well received by these two men, but inevitably the question of my immediate future came up after a couple of days. David's brother-in-law suggested that it would be best if I were to work on a farm, out of reach from the authorities and at the very least, well fed and reasonably housed. He knew a woman in a small village called Fleurance who could help me find a job. I packed again and left for Fleurance, leaving a thousand francs with David's father-in-law. I was welcomed somewhat reluctantly by the woman; her daughter was in bed with pneumonia, and her hands were full. She gave me a room in the back of her house and promised that in a few days she would find a farmer who would take me on.

There were few Jewish refugees in Fleurance. One of these families, Hasidim, lived in a rented house across the street from where I was staying. There was a young boy about my age, whom I befriended. He informed me that there were over six hundred commandments in Judaism. I had always thought that they were ten which I had trouble following to the letter. I was both surprised and incredulous by his announcement, but I was intrigued by his passionate belief in his God. Whenever I had been taken to the synagogue, the worshipers struck me as being ridiculous in the course of the rituals and nothing short of being hypocrites. My grandmother headed the list. Even Dupuy who had tried to convert me to Catholicism was, despite his fervor, a hypocrite in the sense that his faith did not prevent him from being cruel toward those who were not as fortunate as he was. I thought my new friend's fervor was an example of fanaticism and ignorance. My schooling had been nonreligious; I qualified all religions as vestiges of antiquated societies, and religious people as nothing more than superstitious. At any rate, I liked my friend's eloquence, his passion. I have forgotten his name. I hope that he and his family survived.

After my successful border crossing, my arrival in Toulouse, and my trek to Fleurance, I sank into a form of fatigue or depression. For almost a month, I had functioned on nervous energy and adrenaline. I had, so to speak, gritted my teeth until my arrival in Fleurance. One afternoon, feeling lost, disoriented, and unable to handle my feelings, I took a pair of scissors and sheared off my pubic hair.

A job was found for me, at last, on a small farm. The farm consisted of a farmer, his wife, their two small children, and a dozen cows. The first day at five A.M., I was awakened, and after washing my face at the pump in the courtyard, I walked into the kitchen to find that the farmer had filled two glasses with alcohol. That, he said, was to sustain me until we had breakfast later in the morning, after the animals had been taken care of and chores had been done. I was not about to drink any alcohol at that time of the morning, nor at anytime. Monsieur Violle had given us countless lectures on the evils of alcohol and the tragedies that alcoholism had caused in many families. Sure, I had been given wine as a child, but more often than not it had been laced with a generous portion of water. On some festive occasions I had even tasted champagne or hard cider. I was deadly afraid that the glass of alcohol offered by the farmer would transform me into an addict on the spot. I refused the drink as politely as I could but that did not sit well with the farmer. The refusal to drink told him that he was dealing with some sort of misfit—not with some good peasant stock. He was quite right. That morning's scene with the alcohol was repeated each time I started working for a new boss. No one was going to make an alcoholic out of me.

My first job was to clean up the stable. I was given a wheelbarrow, a pitchfork and a shovel and told to gather up the soiled straw. I then had to take it to the dung heap, which stood at some distance from the barn, and which was accessible only if you waded through puddles of mud. Within a half hour, I was exhausted. I had twisted my ankles several times, and I was developing blisters on my hands. Still I had made scant progress cleaning out the barn. The farmer started to yell at me to hurry up and to wonder why it was his misfortune to have hired such an incapable person. I dragged myself through the daily chores for two days, but the farmer had begun to question my background a little more closely. Where did I come from? What was I doing in this part of the country? What about my parents? Finally, he said that in time I might do but that he had to report my presence to the local gendarmes to protect himself. I had no wish for the police to know who or where I was, so I left the farm having acquired two days worth of experience.

I found another job on another farm about nine kilometers from Fleurance. As there was a shortage of men at that time, farm jobs were easy to find. This farm was bigger than the last one and the farmer wealthier and more patient than the first one. It was, however, as far as I understood it, a strange place operated by an unusual family. I stayed there for two months. It was there that I received a letter from one of my mother's neighbors in which she informed me of my mother's arrest, as well as the arrest of my grandmother. I also received a postcard from my father—my last—telling me that he did not need anything and asking me what had happened between Anna and me. I just had sent him a package full of food, but I do not believe he got it. In fact he was already on his way to Auschwitz. All I knew about my family at that point is that the Leizers had escaped Paris and were living in Grenoble, which was occupied by the Italians.

The farmer's family consisted of two generations: the older couple, their daughter, a son-in-law, and an infant. There was another farm boy slightly older than I, and occasionally a woman who came to help out in the field. The family relationships, as reported by my coworker, were complex—worthy of a soap opera. Apparently, the daughter was not the farmer's blood daughter; she had been conceived during World War I while the farmer was fighting for his country. The daughter's husband, born and raised in Italy, had been a hired hand and had become her mother's lover. When the daughter had become pregnant out of wedlock, a quick marriage had been arranged for her with her mother's lover so the child would not be considered illegitimate. The young woman would leave the farm from time to time allegedly to meet her lover, but the son-in-law still shared his mother-in-law's bed. This older woman had a funny habit. She would walk ahead of the men or boys, and from time to time, she would stop, bend over to pull up her stockings, and expose her imposing thighs. We all acted as if nothing was happening, but we snickered behind her back. Otherwise, she was quite friendly and direct. When she learned that I was Jewish, she asked to see my penis. She had never seen a circumcised one. I blushed but did not comply.

My first day at that farm showed me once again that I did not belong. We sat down for breakfast at an oblong table in a large kitchen. A bottle of wine was in front of each place setting, as well as baskets full of walnuts, apples, and bread. Above our heads, from the beams, hung four cured hams. The farmer's wife asked me how many eggs I wanted. I had not seen eggs in the last two years, so I answered timidly that I would like two. A look of surprise came over the woman's face; the farm boy next to me ordered six fried eggs and cut himself a healthy slab of ham. I could not believe the quantity of food that was available and ingested. If I did not eat a lot and drink my bottle of wine, I was told, I would not have enough strength to do the hard work I was supposed to do or last until lunch.

After breakfast, I was taken to a dung heap that had fermented for a few seasons under a straw-covered roof—a sort of acid test for newcomers I was sure. My job was to fill a tumbrel that would be taken to fertilize the fields. I was given a pitchfork, and eager to make a good impression, I dug that pitchfork into the dung heap the whole length of its prongs. To my dismay, I could not budge the pitchfork an inch, much less lift anything into the tumbrel. I struggled stubbornly with it to no avail and noticed shortly that I was being watched by the farmer and his crew. They were laughing heartily at the city slicker who was getting nowhere with his task. I was going about it the wrong way, of course. I was supposed to lift my cargo in layers, the way it had been built. The farmer, good naturedly, corrected my mistake and within a short time, I was enveloped in the heat of fumes emanating from that old dung heap and bathed in sweat. I managed to fill a couple of tumbrels, but by then I was so exhausted and so smelly that I could not imagine how I would make it through the rest of the day. During the next two years I was to experience many such days when all I could do at night was to fall dead onto my bed and rise tired and aching the next day, only to start all over again.

It was during that two month stay, that a painful thought crossed my mind, a thought that was to pursue me and torture me for years. I was in a meadow, guarding the farmer's cows, when I began to think about my parents' fate. I tried to picture them in a prison camp, in a place similar to Compiègne. I imagined them being starved, beaten, and made to do forced labor. How would they come back after the war? Would they have broken bones or be crippled, unable to take care of themselves? What kind of life would they have when they returned? Who would take care of them? If they had to live out the rest of their lives as cripples, maybe it would be better if they did not come back at all. It was a thought so horrible that I ceased immediately to think about it. I was superstitious enough to believe that such thoughts had a magical quality, and I could will them to die. When my parents did not return from the death camps, I recalled the thought I had in the meadow. I knew then, and I know now that my thought did not kill them. The Nazis did. I carried, however, the guilt of that thought for a long time until I forgave myself for their death.

That fall I had my first experience harvesting grapes and drinking the new wine. The first day of harvest, I bit into the bunches of grapes with zest, but on the second day, I hardly looked at the grapes. My back ached from bending over all day. What fun to see the grape juice beginning to bubble in the vat! How sweet it is to drink the new wine! How you run to the toilet the next day! The work was hard, but it was also a festive time. Long tables were set up in the courtyard at noon; food was served in abundance. The wine, jokes, and laughter freely flowed.

As I became more adept at farm work, or as the farmer thought that I was becoming more adept, I was given more responsibility on the field. One day, I was told to take a tumbrel drawn by a team of cows. In all the farms that I worked during the war, cows were used for their milk, flesh, and work;

on only one farm was there a horse and a team of oxen, yet even there, the cows worked. That day, I was in charge of one of the several tumbrels that were in use. At one point going around a corner, one of the wheels of my vehicle fell into a deep rut that I had not been able to avoid and the carriage almost turned over. The tumbrel righted itself, but the center shaft hit one of the cows very hard. She was with calf, and the shock killed it. The farmer did not yell at me, but he dismissed me anyway. After two months as a farm boy, I was not quite yet seasoned.

I was at a loss and did not know where I should go or what I should do next. I did not think that I would find another farm to employ me that late in the year, nor was I encouraged by my past experience to pursue another farm position. I was still a city boy, not yet aware of what I had to accept to make my new life possible or to find some meaning in it other than staying away from the police.

I decided to join the Leizers in Grenoble. I did not know them very well, nor did I like their snobbish ways, but they were family and they had the means to help me. I had not the vaguest idea what kind of help I wanted. Subconsciously, I probably wished to be taken care of. At age sixteen, I was still not ready to take charge of my life. I hoped that something magical would happen to smooth out the rough edges of my existence. I knew that Jews were in a precarious position, but that did not stop me from dreaming of better things to come. As I look back, those dreams were very important. They kept me going, especially when I felt frustrated or on the verge of despair.

On my way to Grenoble, I stopped in Toulouse to collect my last thousand francs from David's father-in-law. David and his family were living there, crowded in dingy quarters. I took the train, without once being asked for my identification papers. I arrived safely in Grenoble where the beauty of the Alps filled my heart with awe.

Chapter Nine

The Leizers did not know what to do with me. There was no room for me in their life. A few of their friends had also settled in Grenoble, but I did not fit in at all. My clothes, my manners, and my outlook on life were all wrong in that circle. One of the Leizers' friends suggested that I report to the Jewish organization in Grenoble which, he said, was set up to take care of people like me—children whose parents had disappeared. I reported to that center, and in a few days, I was on my way back to the region of France that I had just left. I reported to a center in Valence d'Agen where children from all over Europe were sheltered. I was back in boarding school, a place with a religious orientation, prayers in Hebrew, and wishes for a future in Palestine. It's also the first place where I saw young people dance the hora.

I did not stay in that center very long; I was sent to join one that was a few miles away in a large manor. No more than fifteen or twenty boys in addition to a director and one or two staff members were lodged at the center. The manor had been recently rented out, and our sleeping quarters consisted of three or four cots in a room. We ate together in a common room, and we showered together as well. I do not remember there being anything to do. The vast majority of the boys were either born in Germany or had fled their homelands through Germany. All of us were without parents. The main thrust of our conversations was about the plans that were being made to transport us to Switzerland and about the Jews who had succeeded in crossing the Swiss border. Some of the boys spoke French poorly; Yiddish was the language most frequently spoken. Food was scarce even in that part of the world, so we were absolved from kosher food but not from prayer. In the last six years, I had lost the habit of living according to Jewish law and was not disposed to embrace it here.

I developed a foot infection. A doctor was called in to lance the abscess and recommended bed rest for a day. Like the rest of the boys, I did not want to stay in France. I wanted to be somewhere where I would be safe, but waiting for some mysterious person to come and take a group of us to Switzerland did not appeal to me. I was hoping for something more active, where I would be more in control of my life. While in bed, it occurred to me that if I could go to Marseilles or Toulon, I would surely find a recruiting office for the French Foreign Legion. I could enlist for a five-year stint and be sent to Africa. There I would be safe not only from the Germans, but from the French police. I knew that once I was in the Legion, no authority on earth had any power over me. So I asked to see the director of our center and laid out my plans for the future. He did not laugh at me, nor did he treat my project as if it were the most stupid idea he had ever heard. He did not try to talk me out of it either. Instead he deflected the conversation by asking me if I was bored at the center. I replied that I was, and he offered to find me a temporary job near the manor. After that we could continue discussing the pros and cons of my project to enlist in the Foreign Legion. I should think about it for a while before making any decision. Two days later, the Allies landed in Algiers. Unoccupied France ceased to be. My project came to naught.

The director kept his part of the bargain and found me a job with a baker in the village. I started a new career. The bakery was managed by a young man and his widowed father. The old man was rarely in the shop; I saw him only in the afternoons when preparations were made for the next day's baking. I reported each morning at six A.M. The wood was already roaring in the oven, and the flour had been mixed with water in a trough and lay in a lump. I helped move the mixture into the kneading machine. My other tasks consisted of cleaning the machinery, the troughs, the tables and baskets, sweeping the floor, and splitting wood in the afternoons. I could see the customers coming in for their daily ration of bread, and they could see me. But no contacts or conversations occurred. Not even the morning greeting was addressed to me. Bread was, of course, rationed. Some of it was sold at black-market prices or exchanged for other goods. I was not paid; instead, I was served lunch with as much bread as I wanted. My workday ended at five P.M., so I reported to the center for the evening meal. I worked every day.

One late afternoon in November, we were splitting wood in the shed next to a garden where a persimmon tree stood. I had never tasted a persimmon, so the young man handed me one that was not quite ripe. I still remember its acidity and the awful way my tongue felt. That afternoon, the old man began to talk with great conviction about his love of opera. However, he did not understand or approve of the volume of the orchestral music; it prevented him from hearing and understanding the words sung by the performers. Years later I remembered his remarks when I read that Charles Bovary had the same complaint. He also wished to understand what was being sung in an opera.

During the period when I worked at the bakery, we began to hear rumors of Jews being exterminated in Eastern Europe. According to these rumors, Jews were being packed into railroad freight cars or trucks with a thick layer of quicklime spread on the floor. The Jews would die, burned or asphyxiated. It turned out later that this was not an accurate description of mass murder; the realities of extermination were beyond any speculation we could imagine. One evening, a new boy arrived from Paris; he and I bonded almost immediately. We talked all night about how we had ended up at this center, what we had done, and what we hoped to do. He did not want to stay in the center; he was leaving in the morning. He was not waiting for the Germans or for the police to come and get him. Instead he would find a way to London or North Africa and join up with the French Army. Life for him was an adventure that should be lived to the fullest while rejoicing in the beauty and simplicity of nature. The new boy taught me that human beings could transform the world and make it a just, peaceable place. He kept his word and left the next morning.

I did not want to stay in the center either. I did not feel that I was really safe since the whole community knew that the manor was a refuge for Jewish children, and we had to depend on everyone's discretion—including that of the authorities—for our safety. I felt that this was too risky despite the assurances the staff gave us. I had no ambition to become a master baker, and I persisted in asking the director to help me find a way out of France. I was nearing seventeen and thought that an army would surely accept me. The director promised that he would do what he could to help me, but in the meantime suggested that I go work on a farm until a satisfactory solution was found. That is how I found myself back on a farm where I spent the following six months. The center was built high on a hill on the left bank of the Garonne River, and the farm was situated on its right bank at about five kilometers from the manor. I was always out of breath when I reached the center, but I would run down the bank quite fast as I traveled down toward the river.

The farm was located on flat ground and produced wine weak in alcohol. The farmer lived there with his wife and three children. Its size was modest, far more modest than the last farm I had worked on. I was fortunate to get a job in January, the slow season on a farm. There was plenty of wood to split, repairs to make on the barn, and preparations for the spring planting. It was in this farm that I learned to plow a field with a team of cows. A few incidents from that period stick out in my mind.

One Saturday morning, the local butcher showed up with his helper to slaughter a pig that had been properly fattened in the previous months. I had fed that animal and cleaned up his sty; I think he knew who I was, and he could recognize the humans in the farm. When we took him out that morning, he sensed that something horrible was going to happen. Did we all smell of death? Did our behavior give us away? The pig began to yell, roar, and cry out as the sharp knife slit his throat. He cried until his heart stopped. The killing of the pig was quite an event on the farm; not an ounce of edible flesh was wasted, not a drop of his blood, not an inch of his intestines. He was cut up, put up to cure, put up in preserves. He would serve for a whole year. I regret to report that while I witnessed that death with some pity, it did not deter me from taking part in that day's feast.

On another occasion, a fox managed to get into the rabbit-s' hutches, and carnage ensued. The solution for preventing another such episode was to raise the hutches on higher stilts, out of the fox's reach. The farmer's plan was to take a beam and use it as a lever to raise the hutches; when one side was sufficiently raised, I was to slip a pole under the cages, and we would raise the other side. The farmer raised his side, but as I was about to slip the pole under the cage, the beam the farmer was holding gave way and the rabbit cages came down with a crash, tearing my nail from my left thumb. That day I walked with a bandaged hand to the center where I was treated, I think, with sulfa drugs and properly bandaged. The next day, I was back at work. To this day the tip of my thumb is still sensitive, particularly to cold.

One morning the farmer told me that I had to kill a litter of dogs and bury them deep so the mother would not dig them up. I refused to do it. I had seen animals killed since early childhood, but it was always for food. Dogs and cats were not food they were pets, and the idea of killing them was revolting. Why wouldn't he kill them? Well, his children had discovered the puppies and had played with them. He did not want to be directly blamed for getting rid of that litter. I had no emotional ties to the children; it did not matter if I did the deed. He handed me a hatchet and a spade, ordering me in no uncertain terms to dispose of the dogs. That day I became a murderer.

To give us some added protection, the administrators at the center arranged to acquire fake identity cards. Actually, the cards were not forgeries. The blank stamped cards had been obtained from the city of Valence in the Rhône river valley. But names and addresses were fake. We carried these identification cards with us, as was required by law, but I always felt uneasy with mine. One Sunday in June, three men in civilian clothes walked in the common room and addressed us in German. They asked for our papers, first in German and then in French. There were about ten boys in the room, and we handed our fake papers over. While they perused our papers, two boys and I took to our heels through an open bay door. I do not think that I ever ran as fast as I ran that day, down the hill while one of the German shouted at us to stop and calling us *verfluchte Juden.*

I ran all the way to the farm, arriving out of breath and yelling that the Gestapo was after me. I was frightened and had to find a way to leave the country. It was easy to ask the farmer to help me escape. The tide of war had turned, and a mass resistance movement had begun to mobilize. With the Germans suffering major defeats at Stalingrad and El Alamein and the Allies in control of North and Sub-Saharan Africa, it was clear that an invasion of Europe was imminent. Moreover, young Frenchmen were taken to work in Germany, allegedly in exchange for prisoners of war. As the Allies were bombing Germany on a daily basis, French youths were not eager to leave their homes. Instead they joined the underground and fostered a climate of defiance that fed off of Germany's defeats on the battlefields.

The farmer took me immediately to one of his vineyards where he kept a tool shed and told me to stay there until he had an answer to my problem. Food would be brought to me; I was not to worry. I stayed in that shed three nights and three days before the farmer came to fetch me. He led me to another farm in the vicinity, where I was given an address in Toulouse and a password. I could be in London in a week—that was being done on a regular basis, under the very noses of the Germans. The next day, I took my leave from the farmer and his family and took the train once again to Toulouse.

I arrived in Toulouse late that afternoon and found the man whose address I had been given. The man was in his forties, bald and sporting a medium-sized mustache. He was a veteran of World War I with a fiery spirit—the Boches had not gotten to him then, and they would not get to him now. He had, he said, an indomitable nature and had never been defeated. He wanted to be sure that I understood that about him. The man told me I would be in London the following week. Meanwhile, I must eat and go to bed. The next day I was to go to a village at the foot of the Pyrénées mountains and meet my contact at the entrance to a bridge at six P.M. precisely. After an exchange of passwords, I would be hidden until it was time to be taken to London. I hardly slept that night; I was too busy trying to imagine and anticipate the next few days.

The next day I took a train to Pau and from there rode a broken-down bus to the village. I was met on schedule and walked up several paths in the hills for a couple of hours. I arrived at a shack in which a dozen young men were sitting on stones or makeshift furniture. During the course of the evening, I found out that all of them were there to avoid being sent to work in Germany. The conversations encompassed two topics: how soon they might be taken out of France and whether they would wind up in London or North Africa. The desire for either destination depended on the political personality they admired most. Those who favored De Gaulle hoped to go to London and join the French Forces that were being trained for a future invasion; those who favored general Giraud hoped to join him in Algeria. To my surprise, no one had left-wing leanings. I was the only Jew in the camp. I had no preference as to where I went. My only goal was to get out of France. I did not feel any passion for the political figures vying for power after the war. I simply felt that after the war, the conditions that had prevailed in 1939 ought to change and that a world should be built in which wars would be outlawed and justice and brotherhood would triumph. I did not have the vaguest notion of how this could to be brought about.

During the first few days I spent in the shack, we focused on our lack of food. Our supplies consisted of wild lentils boiled in water, and I started feeling hungry again. I was beginning to wonder about our impending departure when a man showed up and declared that all escapes from France were being stopped. Moreover, we would be the first group in the region to start armed resistance. We were not asked if we wanted to participate in armed rebellion: We were told these were our orders, and that we were now soldiers. That night our group was split in two; eight of us assembled and left camp to go deeper into the mountains. We were given two carbines to carry. We marched all night, and in the morning we reached a small valley and were told to build our camp. Though it was early July, it was cold in these mountains. I did not sleep very well that first morning. I shivered from the cold, and probably from fatigue.

In the middle of the day, we started building shelters made of branches. We even made beds out of branches and thick foliage. Other than that, we had nothing to do. We did not know what to do with our carbines, so we hid them under our improvised beds. One afternoon a man showed up and conducted a drill with the carbines. We were told how to fire them, but we were not issued bullets. We were not told to post guards, and it did not occur to any of us that we should. We were camping out in the mountains, quite puzzled as to our role as the future liberators of France. This went on for about a week, when suddenly I woke one morning with a gun pointed at my nose. A platoon of special police, the *Gardes Mobiles*, had surrounded the shelter where all of us were happily sleeping. Armed with submachine guns, they had entered our hiding place and rudely awakened each of us. We did not, could not, offer any resistance, and we were quickly manacled. The shelter was searched and the carbines were found. We were marched out of our little valley carrying the carbines and loaded in police trucks. By noon, we were back in Toulouse and incarcerated.

The prison was overcrowded. There were not enough cells to put us in, so we joined a group of prisoners in the courtyard.

No names were taken, no identification papers were demanded. We sat in the courtyard surrounded by our meager belongings. I thought that I would surely be delivered to the Germans who would not hesitate to have such a dangerous terrorist shot, or at best, deported. The courtyard was very hot during the long July afternoons, but the nights did not bring much relief either. In fact, nighttime was in some respect a difficult time to endure. On my first night there, a prisoner went berserk. He kept talking in gibberish and stamping his feet, but no one did anything to take care of him or make him be quiet. The guards did not intervene, nor did they seem to care. The rest of us were perhaps too frightened to approach him or did not wish to call attention to ourselves. I slept fitfully that night.

I do not remember what we were given to eat or if we were given anything at all. We were not able to wash up; the smell of sweat and bodies mixed with the odors of the courtyard bathroom became pervasive. It's doubtful that I had any desire to eat. My stomach was in knots. That afternoon I was taken into the building for interrogation. I sat at a desk, facing two policemen in civilian clothes. They were in their early thirties, and their demeanor was relaxed—devoid of the brutality that I had seen in the movies. I told myself that I must be alert and not reveal anything that might implicate my host in Toulouse. I realized very quickly that I had not prepared a story to tell them. I had no experience in contriving alibis and became hesitant in my speech. As they became aware that I was beginning to panic, they changed the line of questioning and began to help me fabricate a story that they could type on their report sheet. It became clear to me then that these policemen were annoyed about having to investigate my activities. They wanted to be done with me as soon as possible. What was not clear was what they intended to do with me. Would they keep me in jail or turn me over to the Germans?

After that they avoided asking about the group and concentrated on me. What was I doing in the hills, and why had I gone there in the first place? Was I trying to go into Spain? Or was I trying to find my way to North Africa? Did I intend to use the weapons that were found in the camp and become a terrorist? No, I was not. I had never used a weapon in my life, I replied. I was in the hills because I was a Jew. I had found the group through contacts in the countryside who had sent me to Toulouse, but I did not have their names and addresses. I signed my deposition and was taken back to the courtyard. Toward the end of the evening, some prisoners who were in the available cells came out under guard. I recognized among them my Toulouse host who signaled to me to be quiet. The next day, I was taken again to be interrogated. This time, I felt more at ease. I was asked if I had family that I could rejoin somewhere out of the region. I told the policemen that the Leizers lived in Grenoble, under Italian control. I was given orders to report weekly to the police in Grenoble and a voucher to buy a train ticket. The next morning I was let out of jail and directed to the train station. Apparently, we had been the first group arrested in the region. We did not seem very dangerous, quite the contrary. I do not know what motivated the two policemen to help me, but I owe them my life, and I am grateful to those men. I never knew their names.

For the second time in less than a year, I was on my way to Grenoble. I had never traveled so much in my life.

Chapter Ten

I was not welcomed with open arms in Grenoble, and I was thoroughly scolded after I related the adventures that brought me there. The Leizers and their friends had never seen such a fool. Why would I try to leave France? Didn't I know that I would be safer and well fed on a farm? Alfred Leizer, who was only a couple of years older than I, was the only member of the group who was in any way sympathetic to my misadventures. I made him promise to take me with him when the moment was ripe for armed resistance. He promised but never kept that promise. A year later, he was killed in the Vercors.

In the summer of 1943, there was a feeling that the war would soon end. The armies of the Third Reich were being pushed back on every front, and the Allies had been victorious in Africa. They had even landed in Sicily. Resistance in France was stiffening; it was becoming clearer and clearer that to collaborate with the Nazis was to bet on the losing side. My cousin Alfred had been raised in the same tradition of patriotism as the children of his generation, but he wanted to take part in the demise of his oppressors. We all wanted to slay the monster.

Meanwhile, I reported, as I had been told in Toulouse, to the police station in Grenoble. The policemen read my papers with surprise; they had not received any communication about me, and they made it quite clear that they were not about to call or write their counterparts in Toulouse to inquire about my status. However, they agreed to provide me with an identity card. They also let me know they had no desire to see me and no time to bother with the likes of me. After I obtained my identification card, duly stamped with the word "Jew," I left the station. I never reported there again, and no one was ever disturbed because of it.

I found a job on a farm near Grenoble, but I did not like the farmer. I left after a few days and took a bus in the direction of Voiron. I had no idea where I was going or what kind of job I would find. All I knew was that I wanted to find something before winter. The heels of my shoes were worn flat, and my soles had big holes. After I spent a whole day walking from farm to farm inquiring about a job and being turned down, I was told to go talk to a mason who happened to need helpers. He hired me despite my total lack of experience, and I was taken to a room where there were already two other young men. My bed consisted of a straw mattress on the floor. That night I went to bed hungry.

The next morning, we were awakened at six A.M. and driven to a farm where a barn was being rebuilt. My body ached from sleeping in such an uncomfortable bed, but I did not get much of a chance to recover as I was given the task of digging a ditch that led from the barn to a cistern where the farm animals' urine was collected. Wielding a pick and shovel all day is good exercise, but my muscles and back were quite sore. In fact I don't remember a time when my body did not hurt, yet we labored day in and day out. I worked for that mason for six or seven weeks until I had managed to burn some of the skin off the soles of my feet by mixing lime and sand together. I arrived at a farmhouse the day before the Italians surrendered. They would soon declare war on Germany. One of the consequences of this declaration of war was to make Grenoble and the Alps a more dangerous place for Jews as well as for members of the Resistance.

At my new place of employment, I replaced the farmer's son who had chosen to join the maquis in the Vercors. I got along very well with the farmer's wife, but her husband could not stand me. The woman kept telling me not to pay attention to his temper tantrums and said that he had been as harsh with their only son. I think that he deeply resented my being there in his son's place. There was no way I could have satisfied that man with my work. I became even more disturbed by the whole situation on the day I found lice crawling out of my head. I was soon sent packing. The harvesting of the tobacco had been done, and the ground had been prepared for the following spring. There was no reason to keep me in the winter.

When I was let go from that farm, I felt as if the strength of my body had left me. I began to have serious doubts about my chances of surviving the war. I imagined myself starving or freezing to death in those Alps. I was tired of running; my shoes were falling apart, and the clothes on my back were wearing quite thin. I began to walk from farm to farm, and with each rejection of my services, my depression increased as did my fears. I finally stumbled on a small farm that was operated by a couple of newlyweds named Pierre and Françoise Jaillet. I asked them if they needed a farm boy but also told them who and what I was—they were taking a risk in sheltering me. They took me in without reservation. That day my whole attitude toward farm work began to change. Instead of trying to survive one more day of hard work, I began to take a serious interest in the work itself. I identified with the farmer's concerns, his hopes, and his anxieties. I did all I could to become a good farmhand.

Each night, the three of us would plan the next day's work. Françoise was only nineteen, but she worked in the fields and did as much hard work as we did. The farm was built on a hill, which meant a lot of the work had to be done by hand. Once, a storm flattened a wheat field, and we had to cut the stalks with scythes while Françoise bundled and stacked the wheat. I remember my back aching and the sweat that soaked my whole body, but I also remember the sense of satisfaction that the accomplishments gave me. In those days I felt that I could do anything physically, lift any weight; there was no limit to my power. I stopped thinking about the war, about the Nazis, my family, or my own safety. Working in the fields had become my raison d'être. I learned a lesson that I would never forget, that a commitment to a task, no matter how trivial, enhances one's existence provided that what one does is not evil.

Life was so peaceful in the foothills of the Alps that my fears began to be allayed, and I even dared to go to Grenoble twice by bus. Each time I carried potatoes, flour, butter, and eggs to the Leizers. Once, I brought enough flour to demonstrate what I had learned in the bakery. I baked bread, and my aunt Jeanette baked a chalah and made apple strudel. We were so engrossed in our farm work and stories of young farmers fleeing into the mountains that D-day came as a total surprise. I had hoped all along that the Allies would land in France. The armies of the Third Reich were retreating on all fronts; surely, the war would end soon. Yet when the landings in Normandy were announced on the BBC, I was astonished. The last four years had been filled with tragedy for so many people that I had a hard time imagining that our lives would be different in the future, that the running would stop.

After the Normandy landings came the landings in southern France. For days we heard the roar of German trucks racing north. All I could think about then was that they should keep on racing. It did not occur to us that the American army might be close. We kept working the fields because it was hay-cutting time. One morning Pierre and I were working in a small, enclosed field. Across the field we saw two figures in uniform walking toward us. We could not tell if they were German or American soldiers. We froze as the two tall, well-tanned soldiers approached us. We did not, at first, understand what they were saying to us, but we knew that they were not Germans. The soldiers were definitely American, but we could not figure out what they were doing by themselves in this hay field. We soon found that they were looking for fresh eggs. We took them up to the farmhouse, gave them the eggs, and opened a bottle of wine to toast each other's country. We had just been liberated.

For me the worst was over. I had survived four years of Nazi occupation. But the war was not over; Paris was not yet liberated, and I did not know when I would be able to leave the farm or what I would do when I could return to Paris. I did not expect my parents to return. So many stories of the Germans' atrocity had circulated that I was prepared to accept the worst. Little did I know that the worst scenario I could imagine hardly measured up to the reality of the extermination camps. A few days after I was liberated, I received a telegram from the Leizers saying that their son had been killed. I took the bus to Grenoble to join them for his funeral.

The Leizers were devastated. They had lost their last child. My great-uncle had been arrested by the Gestapo after his son's death and was tortured by beatings and by being burned all over his body with lit cigarettes. He told me how he yelled and cried from the pain and that he would have told them everything he knew if he had anything to tell. He cried again as he related how he had lost all sense of his dignity. He carried on his person the photograph of his son as he had been disinterred; he had to identify him to the French authorities. That photograph stayed with me for years. My cousin was clearly recognizable: his jaw was wide open, as if a last cry of terror and pain were still escaping his lips. His eyes were open because there had been no one to close them when the firing squad had done its work. Months later when there were photographic exhibits of the tortures that young men had suffered in the Vercors at the hands of the Milice, a French paramilitary organization, and the Nazis, I was grateful that Fred and his companions had simply been executed.

Fred was buried in Grenoble with all the fanfare that was possible in 1944. The longest speeches were made about the loss of Jean Prévost. All the young men were praised for their courage, their patriotism, and the sacrifice they had made to preserve freedom for France and for all mankind. The burial was conducted in the military tradition with a salute of gun volleys. No mention was made that Sergeant Alfred Leizer was a Jew. There simply was no cross over his grave. A year later when he was moved to the family plot, a kaddish was said for him.

Two more events stick out in my memory of that trying visit to Grenoble. The surviving Jews went to a synagogue, and I went too. I was not tutored in religious ways, nor did I believe in God or feel that I had to give thanks to what I considered nonexistent. I was, however, immensely moved to be in that community, I felt a sense of kinship with people I didn't know but with whom I had shared a common experience. We were all survivors, and even if many were thanking a silent God for their lives, I was in no mood to mock or challenge them. I understood in that moment that we needed to be together, no matter what our individual beliefs or disbeliefs. Many years would pass before I set foot in a synagogue again, and then only for social reasons.

I also had my first encounter with Zionism and the possibility of illegally emigrating to Palestine. I was riding a city bus in Grenoble when I met a girl whom I had known in Villepinte as a child. Her name was Esther. We had not been friends, but we had gone to the same school, she in the girls' side and I in the boys'. We were positively joyful, and we could not stop hugging and holding hands. Esther struck me as being the most beautiful girl I had ever seen; I think I fell in love with her right then. But being just eighteen, I hardly knew it nor would I have been able to tell her if I had been aware of my feelings. She took me to the home where she was living with other young people, which was run by an adult woman. I was received like a long-lost brother. I was alive; we all were alive. And in the first flush of recognition, we laughed and sang. The sadness would come later. Everyone in the house was full of excitement at the prospect of going to Palestine and of starting a new life. There was no thought of waiting for the war to be over or for legal channels of emigration to be accessible again. Esther and I stayed up practically the whole night talking about Palestine. She told me what I was later to learn was Theodor Herzl's reasoning; that is, Jews can never be safe anywhere because there is no homeland to protect them or for which they can legitimately die. Anti-Semitism was two thousand years old and would never die out; you could not trust the gentiles. In Germany and France, Jews had assimilated—were still assimilating—and had even been granted citizenship. But recent history had proved all that to be precarious. Gentiles and Christians were all basically anti-Semitic, and nothing, absolutely nothing, would ever change that. It was difficult to argue with Esther. I had to agree with her that as French children, we had been betrayed. Many of my younger cousins had been deported despite the fact that they were French by birth. Had not the French authorities and the French police been quite zealous in serving the Third Reich? How useful I could be, how needed I was in Palestine as a farmer. While I agreed with most of what Esther said to me that night, I could not honestly say that all non-Jews were evil. It is true that many of them cooperated with the Germans and were scared or indifferent to the plight of Jews in Europe. To that extent they were complicit with Naziism and mass murder, but many of the same people helped me at various stages and in unexpected ways. I also could not renounce, the way Esther did, all that was French in me and adopt a culture that I knew little about. I was also scared about having to live in an ultra-religious milieu. Moreover, even though I agreed with Esther that anti-Semitism was an age-old problem, I thought that a worldwide revolution would solve all the previous injustices and horrors we had experienced, particularly war. I did not think that nationalism was the answer to the persecutions the Jews had suffered throughout their history. I continued to see Esther in Paris, but since she did not succeed in converting me, she grew increasingly cool toward me. I hope you made a happy life for yourself in Israel, Esther.

Before returning to the farm, I made an attempt to enlist in the French army. The war was not over, and the Beast was still much alive. The recruitment officer refused to even consider my request; new recruits were not needed at that time. At the farm, French soldiers were bivouacking. Senegalese soldiers and noncommissioned officers—all Europeans—were staying in the barn. I found Françoise flirting with one of the sergeants. She blushed but made me promise not to say anything to Pierre. There was a holiday ambiance at the farm except for the fact that I was told not to approach the Senegalese; they were considered very dangerous. There is no end to racism: exit one form, enter another.

Pierre asked me to help him prepare the land before I left the farm for Paris. That was the least that I could do to repay him for having taken the risk of sheltering me for nearly a year. I stayed until the middle of October, 1944. I then joined the

Leizers on the train back to Paris. Almost twenty-seven months of exile had come to an end, or so I thought. I had no idea what the future was going to bring. Where and how was I going to live? What was I going to do in France? I did not realize then that my family had been decimated, and my childhood dreams had been destroyed. I could hope and wish for a better world, but I did not know if there would ever be in it a place for me.

Chapter Eleven

In November, 1944, I returned with the Leizers to their apartment. The trip from Grenoble to Paris had been a long one, almost twelve hours. Trains were slow moving, bridges had been bombed or blown up, and enemy attacks were still feared as we approached the battlefields. Around Nevers the train came to a virtual stop. I could hear my aunt sobbing, and my uncle blow his nose, but I avoided looking at them or saying anything. There was nothing one could say. Where there had once been life, there was only death; I knew of no words to console them. I was too frozen and awkward to touch them, hold them. I would not have known how to do it even if I had wanted to do it. They were close to sixty years of age. How could I speak to them of a future, of hope? On that train ride, I could not even think of a future for myself. I had little hope of seeing my parents ever again, but I could not share that thought with anyone. These were forbidden words. Among us, as long as the evidence was not irrefutable, the language of hope was *de rigueur,* and grieving was not allowed. The Leizers, alas, could grieve.

After they had left Paris to take refuge in Grenoble for the remainder of the German occupation, their apartment, as well as their store, had been taken over by the gentile manager appointed by the Vichy government. That saved their furniture from being shipped to Germany. The manager had emptied the apartment and stored their property in a warehouse, waiting for it to be shipped or sold. A few days after his return to Paris, my uncle was able to recuperate the major part of his belongings, including an antique piano. The first few nights, they managed to sleep on a mattress provided by the concierge. I was sent to a small hotel that no longer exists, where I spent a couple of nights.

The concierge's husband was employed by the famous Lycée Louis-le-Grand, rue Saint-Jacques, in the heart of the Latin quarter. There was a shortage of labor in Paris, so I was hired as part of the cleaning staff. My wages consisted of room and board and a modest stipend to take care of my personal needs. I was given a minimally furnished room under the roof. That did not bother me since less than the bare minimum had been my lot during the last few years, but the loneliness in the evenings did. I enjoyed walking the streets of Paris even though my pockets were empty. I quickly resented the students and their air of self-importance as they went to their classes and ate noisily in the dining rooms while I bussed their dishes. I was terribly envious of them. I endured Louis-le Grand for two weeks before I quit. The Leizers were dismayed by my irresponsibility. Thanks to the concierge's husband's connections, I found a similar position at the Lycée Henri IV. I was assigned to clean the infirmary, which was run by nuns who urged me to put my life in the hands of our Lord Jesus Christ. I quit after a week. The Leizers had no other choice but to reluctantly take me in.

One evening, after my work was done at the Lycée Henri IV, I walked to the Communist Party storefront, not really knowing what I wanted. Fortunately, no one greeted me. I was not asked anything; I just wandered from table to rack and pick up materials to read for my enlightenment. There were a few young people in the store who all talked and laughed among themselves. It was as if I did not exist at all. They were addressing each other as "comrade," and using the familiar *tu*. I stayed a while, read, and left without having dared to speak to anyone. It did not stop me from coming back several times. It is there that I met a young man who was to become my closest friend during the next two years.

How I could earn a lot of money became the leitmotif of the daily admonitions I received at the dinner table. With money I could become a real *mensch*, break the chain of my father's inadequacies, and transcend the errors made in my deplorable upbringing. Through the Leizers' connections, I found a job as a shipping clerk in a wholesale outlet that sold pharmaceutical goods on the rue Réaumur. I had two hours to eat lunch, so I walked home almost every day for lunch. I seldom took the metro; there were too many things to see. The talk at dinner inevitably would revolve around the death of their children. It did not matter who was present; the Leizers had many friends and acquaintances. Conversation might start with current politics, the news from the front, or the retelling of a bawdy story. There could be controversy or laughter, but it would all end up in tears. After a while, I could predict the exact moment the tears would begin to flow. The guests lowered their heads and sighed. Some cried.

In the early months of my stay with the Leizers, I continued to go to the storefront headquarters of the Communist Party. That's how I happened to go to a rally at the Vélodrome d'Hiver to welcome the return of Maurice Thorez to France. The Communist Party and Charles de Gaulle had struck a deal forgiving Thorez his 1939 desertion from the French army and allowing him to return to France under certain conditions. We learned of these conditions at the rally. The Vélodrome d'Hiver was of special significance to me. It was there on the 16th of July, 1942, that the French police had incarcerated some thirteen thousand Jews for several days before sending them to Drancy and from there to Auschwitz. I had never been to the Vélodrome d'Hiver, nor had I ever before attended a political rally. Political life was an abstraction; I had heard speeches on the radio and been impressed by the oratory, but that was all. I thought that the world had to change radically, and that if the people were united, life would be a simple affair. I entered that arena, knowing no one, and climbed the stairs far away from that night's speakers. I looked around intently, trying to imagine how thirteen thousand Jews had managed to live through the several days they spent here. There were no traces of them, just as there were no traces of my parents when I journeyed to Birkenau in 1988.

Shortly after that day, I met a young man on the metro platform at Réaumur-Sebastopol. I had seen him at the Communist Party headquarters, but we had never spoken to each other. He approached me and asked whether I was satisfied with the way communist policy was working out. He caught me at the right time; I had been chewing on a couple of anti-Semitic remarks that a man had uttered one evening at the storefront. I had been left dumbfounded and felt angry with myself for having kept silent. The man had complained that now that the Jews were coming back and claiming their apartments, they were putting out some needy Frenchmen on the street. That remark by an avowed Communist had brought back Esther's assertion in Grenoble that all Frenchmen were anti-Semitic, and none could be trusted. No one had protested the anti-Semitic comment. If I was not considered French by the revolutionaries, what would I be considered if their international goals were realized?

I related all this to the boy I met at the metro station, Raphaël Valensi, on an impulse. I took an instant liking to him, something that was rare for me then. I liked his fine face and was moved that someone would want to know how I felt about such an important topic. He said that he too was Jewish, which surprised me. Valensi was not the sort of Jewish name I was accustomed to hearing, but then I did not know any Sephardic Jews. Raphaël's family came from Tunisia and was aristocratic. Mine came from Eastern Europe and the Balkans and had never shaken off the dust of the ghetto. I was even more astonished when he began to tell me that the Communist Party was not revolutionary and that Stalin had betrayed Marx and Lenin. It turned out that Raphaël was a member of a Trotskyist group, a member of the Fourth International. He had infiltrated the Communist youth with the intention of recruiting more young men to his cause. The Third International, he said, like the Second, had betrayed the working class, and pursued erroneous policies in Germany during the twenties. It had, in effect, facilitated the coming of Hitler to power. The Communist Party had deliberately betrayed the Spanish Republic in 1936; the Stalin-Hitler pact in 1939 was but the logical consequence of these betrayals. The Third International was but an instrument to fulfill Stalin's mad dreams. This was not the history I had learned, and I was overwhelmed. These revelations left me totally dizzy. If all he had told me was true, why was it not obvious to everyone else? We agreed to meet another time and continue our discussion.

In the ensuing weeks I met Raphaël a few times; each time I inquired why we met in this conspiratorial way now that the Gestapo was long gone. He replied that the International Communist Party, as it called itself, was fighting for legal recognition as a legitimate party and fighting to have its newspaper become a legal publication. The Communist Party was blocking the resurgence of a Trotskyist party in France and painted the Trotskyists as allies or agents of Hitler. The French Communist Party, he said, was deathly afraid of the open presence of a true revolutionary party.

When I brought these ideas to Nathan, my friend in the Communist Party, they caused an uproar and almost broke up our friendship. Nathan and I had met in June, 1940, at an evacuation center for children. We had continued to be friends in Paris until I left for the Free Zone in August, 1942. Our friendship resumed upon my return to Paris, but by that time our lives had dramatically changed. Nathan's oldest sister had died of meningitis, and he had been apprenticed to a tailor. He had survived the war along with his mother and his two sisters. Now he was deeply immersed in politics and adhered completely to the doctrines of the Communist Party in France. He could quote speeches, newspapers, and pamphlets with the fervor of one quoting the Old Testament. Stalin had become the god he worshipped. We argued and shouted at each other. In the end, our relationship cooled off considerably, and we saw less of each other. Outside of politics we continued to like each other: We were not hardened intellectuals who would break up a friendship because they suddenly espoused different ideologies.

Nathan was very interested in meeting and seducing young women and tried to get me to join him in his escapades. I was too naive, however, when facing a young woman. I refused to join him in his games. Years later I realized that his sister had made advances to me, but I had not recognized them at all. I excelled best in the realm of fantasies.

Raphaël met me a few more times on subway platforms but decided that my education could be completed by someone else. I was passed on to a young woman who introduced herself as Suzanne. Suzanne was not French; she was a Jewish refugee from Austria, and her name was really Ilona. I did not learn this until a few months later, after we became friends. Ilona's mission was to explain the political positions of the Trotskyists to me and to gain my adhesion to the party. She had a lot of trouble explaining everything to me and was not very convincing. However, I was desperate for friendship, and Ilona, I thought, was beautiful. Most likely I had a crush on her. I kept coming to the fleeting rendezvous on the subway platform of Strasbourg-Saint-Denis. Thus in the early months of 1945, my life was spent in the Leizers' apartment, at work, in disputes with Nathan about politics, and in meetings with Ilona on metro platforms. My meetings with Ilona kept me from sinking into a profound depression. She stoked my hopes of a better world: an end to all wars, famine, and injustice. What my role was going to be in molding this brave new world was not clear at all. It was not even very important that these changes occur in my lifetime. The dream was important. So was listening to Ilona's warm voice and looking at her dark red hair and sensuous mouth. That we were not doing anything to bring about this new world did not bother me at all. Meeting on metro platforms and talking about our dreams, that was what mattered.

I was on my way to work when the Nazis surrendered on May 8, 1945. Paris went wild with joy. I can still see myself standing on the sidewalk, with American jeeps and trucks honking and racing through the streets. Soldiers were shouting, *Vive la France* and waving flags; Parisians were shouting too. I remember riding in one of those army trucks, but I don't know how I got there. It was better than any carnival day. The whole day had a dreamlike quality. My memories of that day are distorted, and no matter how I try, I cannot remember the details of that day. I spent the whole night out, going from party to party. I don't remember eating or drinking. All I remember is the frantic running from place to place.

The end of the nightmare in Europe did not end our collective or personal anguish, for the war's end revealed the horror of the concentration and extermination camps to us all. The first photographs of the living cadavers, the mounds of the actual cadavers, and the lampshades made of human skin appeared in the newspapers and in the movie theaters soon after the Nazis surrendered. Even today, more than sixty years after I first saw these photographs, I cannot find the words to describe what they made me feel. Words such as horror, inhumanity, barbarism, and sadism are miserably inadequate to describe how we all felt. We had been shown before the photos of people tortured by the Gestapo or the French Milice, but the magnitude of these new atrocities was beyond the scope of our imagination. When I saw these pictures, I knew that my parents were no longer alive. I could not believe that they had somehow managed to survive. Still, I bought a newspaper every day and carefully searched through the list of returnees. I read it several times, hoping I had missed a familiar name. Perhaps I hoped I could conjure up their names or the name of the twenty-some members of my family who had been taken away. I spoke of nothing else with my surviving cousins and friends. The Germans were cursed, condemned to eternal damnation.

One day a distant cousin of my mother's showed up at the Leizers. He had been arrested in 1941 and deported to Auschwitz where he spent the next four years of his life until the camp closed down. He went on one of now-infamous death marches. He was liberated by the Americans. He told of seeing his wife and two children arrive at Birkenau; he saw my mother and her mother too. He knew what their fate had been, but refused to speak about it. In fact he did not speak very much. He had been severely beaten he said, his voice choking and the tears running down his cheeks. We did not ask him how he had managed to survive, or what he had been obliged to do. He did not speak, and we either respected his inability to speak, or most likely, we were afraid to hear him describe his unbearable burden. The liberation of the camps revealed in large measure that some prisoners had been made to collaborate in the machinery of murder. We were quick to condemn these men and women; their blood was demanded in the name of justice. We were still operating by a moral code that had no currency in the death camps. We did not, could not, understand the nature of these hells, nor was it within our experience to ask ourselves how we would have behaved under the circumstances. At the end of the war, nothing short of heroism could be tolerated or even talked about. Our cousin occupied a high position on the ladder of sufferings; we did not want to know what price he had paid to survive. Except for that distant cousin, no one in my family came back to France, and my Polish and Romanian relatives were never heard from again. Those of us who were left alive would be bound up in our losses for the rest of our lives.

The exploding of an atomic bomb in Hiroshima filled us all with a kind of euphoria. The world was experiencing the dawn of a new age. The atom had been split, a feat that had once been considered impossible. From then on, wars would be impossible to fight and not a single nation would risk bringing on the apocalypse. There was also jubilation about the potential peaceful applications of this scientific miracle. There were no limits to what the future held. I was at work when the news of Hiroshima broke. I don't recall any demonstrations of joy among my coworkers, nor any celebration in the street. Victory over Japan did not compare to victory over the Nazis. Japan was far away, after all. I do recall a sense of horror when we found that approximately 100 thousand to 150 thousand people had been killed by a single bomb. It was not at all comparable to the mounds of dead we had been shown in the camps. In Hiroshima there were no corpses; the dead had evaporated, and there was no more evidence than there had been in the smoke floating out of the crematory stacks of Birkenau. We were shown the imprint of a human form on a wall where a human being had once been. There was nothing to identify with, no possible empathy. I could not imagine myself as a shadow on a wall. The horror was not comprehensible. I had dreams in which I found myself in the midst of an atomic storm, but I always woke up at some point. I still find it strange that I dreamt more about Hiroshima than I did about Auschwitz. My dreams about Auschwitz always concerned my father or mother. I always saw them as they lay dying, and I reassured them that I was alive. That was all. Years later I was to dream more specific and more dramatic encounters with them.

Shortly after the war had ended, I started working for my father's cousin who had survived the war with his wife and three of his children. Two other daughters were deported to Auschwitz and never came back. How these daughters perished is worth retelling both for the filial devotion it embodies and the irony of fate. In the raids of July 16, 1942, both my father's cousin and his wife were due to be arrested and eventually deported. Their two daughters Hannah and Miriam, respectively twenty-four and seventeen years old, were not scheduled to be arrested. When the policemen came, they told the family that the mother and father were to be taken to perform labor for the Germans. The daughters suggested that they be taken in lieu of their aging parents. The police agreed to the substitution; all that mattered was that two Szykowskis were to be arrested that day. Hannah and Miriam were never heard from again.

In September I went to Villepinte to see some of my old friends and to check up on our property. Anna handed me a telegram from the Red Cross which was an inquiry from my father's oldest brother, now living in California, about the whereabouts of his family. That telegram would later determine my future. I took it to my cousins, and a correspondence was started by my cousin's wife who knew how to write in Yiddish. Soon my uncle asked if I would be willing to emigrate to the United States. It did not take me long to make a decision. The press was full of stories of young people, not all Jewish, either leaving or wanting to leave France. Many youths were going as far as Australia or New Zealand. There was a sense of disillusionment with France and, I dare say, the whole of Europe. Years of war, deprivation, unimagined atrocities, and a feeling that the future held no promise all made for increased desires to go live elsewhere. In my case, with no family to help, no education, and no trade, the future looked bleak. I was beginning to suspect that the Revolution might not come about in my lifetime. I accepted my American uncle's offer.

The American embassy in Paris was a zoo. It had long lines of people seeking visas for the United States. At that time, immigration was regulated by a quota system established in 1924 designed to keep out undesirables. Northern Europeans were favored, but Eastern and Southern Europeans were not. I was fortunate; I had a sponsor, and having been born in France, I did not have to worry about a quota. The French quota was never filled. The French rarely emigrated, and had there not been a war that destroyed my family and my hopes, I would never have thought of leaving France. I had always defined myself more as being French than as a Jew, but the war taught me that I had been wrong. It was not always up to me to define who I was or what I wanted to become.

It took well over six months before I was granted an immigration visa. During that interim period, I had to take many steps to satisfy the American and French authorities. I was required to submit a copy of my criminal record as well as a health certificate by an approved doctor. The French military had to certify that I was free of my obligations. Under normal circumstances, I should have been drafted with the class of 1946. When my class was called up, I panicked: I saw my plans for going to the States disappear. I left the Leizers' residence and took refuge with Ilona. I contemplated running away and going into hiding again. The war was over. I felt no inclination to defend France's honor or her colonial dreams in some distant part of Asia. However, one of Ilona's friends informed me that if I presented myself to the French military with documents certifying my parents' deportation, I would be exempted from military service. I had obtained such documents a few months earlier from a government ministry, specially created to deal with war victims. I was found physically fit, but I was exempted from serving. All of us who had lost their families in the Holocaust had become wards of the nation and were spared further sacrifices. The last act before receiving my visa was to appear before the American Consul or his representative and to take a solemn oath to defend the Constitution of the United States by force of arms if necessary. Little did I realize that this oath was going to land me in the United States Army.

My lot in Paris began to improve with the arrival of care packages from California that included clothing and foodstuffs. In the mail there was also, from time to time, a notification from a bank that a money order was awaiting me. My uncle Leizer criticized the workmanship of the clothing but gladly accepted one of the money orders so a suit could be made for me. I could not be sent to America looking like a pauper as if I had not been properly taken care of by my family, could I? I was kept busy arranging for my transportation and saying goodbye to everyone I knew. I was eager to meet my new family. I was going to be well cared for, and maybe I would be able to go back to school and become the teacher I had always wanted to be. I was going to be spoiled. The war years would in time become part of a distant past. The damage that had been done would be repaired.

On June 1, 1946, my aunt Jeanette and my friend, Raphael, accompanied me to Rouen where I boarded a Liberty ship, the *SS Lawson*, with ten other passengers. We left that evening. I had the same sinking feeling in the pit of my stomach that I had felt four years earlier when I had fled Paris. Back then I had feared that I would never see my parents or Paris again; now I was afraid that I was saying farewell to everything and everyone I had known. I was leaving my childhood, my youth, and my dreams behind and was heading toward a life I could not imagine. My parents had come to France as immigrants, now I was becoming an immigrant, too. I was bitter toward France; it had betrayed me. What was I going to find in the United States?

Chapter Twelve

My first experience with what I had imagined to be the beginning of my American life was a mixture of excitement and disappointment as I stepped, on a rare rainy day in June, onto the ship that was sailing to New York. I had expected to board a passenger ship, crowded with hundreds of immigrants. Instead I boarded a Liberty ship—an essential transport vessel during World War II—but nonetheless, a cargo ship. Instead of hundreds of passengers, there were only twelve men. And instead of an individual or shared cabins, we were lodged in a large cabin on the stern of the deck near the anti-aircraft gun. It might not even have been the quarters of the sailors who manned the gun but their post. The room was bare, furnished with six bunk beds and metal closets. We all dropped our luggage near our beds. I had imagined that we would eat with an officer who would tell us all about our destinations. But we ate in a separate dinning room, sitting on benches surrounding a narrow, oblong table, not with the officers. That evening at dinner, a plate was served up to each of us with two pork chops topped with applesauce. Beside them were mashed potatoes, green beans, and soft white bread with butter. What was I supposed to do? Where to begin? And what was that cup of coffee doing in front of my plate? I was used to having each item served separately: the appetizer, the soup, the meat, the vegetables, the salad, the cheese, or dessert—all in that order and on a dish of its own. Only in dire circumstances had I been given my food all at once on the same plate. But I was hungry, so I quickly overcame my feelings of bewilderment and devoured what I thought was a gargantuan meal. In fact the bread tasted so good to me, and there was such an abundance of it that I forgot all about French *baguettes.*

That first evening on the ship, as we had glided out of port of Rouen on the Seine River, passed Le Havre and taken to the sea, I tried, once again, to envision what my new life would hold for me. My parents and other members of my family had disappeared in the extermination camps the Nazis had built in Eastern Europe, but that evening, I felt exhilarated and free. My uncle in California, according to the affidavits and financial statements I had received, was well off. I would know comfort at last, and beside the California sunshine, I might be able to pursue my childhood dream and become a teacher. Above all I believed that I would live in a real family. I thought that perhaps in America, the world did not need to be changed. I had left home before to save myself from what would have been certain death. I had managed to survive and return to familiar surroundings, a familiar culture, and a familiar language. This time I was leaving my native land with no intention of ever returning. I may have felt apprehensive about learning a new language and adopting a new culture, but my expectations could not be dampened.

No one among the passengers spoke English. We had no choice but to speak to one another in French. I befriended a young man from Geneva, who was going to the States on a lark.

He did not intend to stay; he was a fierce patriot as I had once been. The other men were older, many from Central Europe, and one was Hungarian. The Hungarian claimed to be going to Hollywood to make movies. I hope he made it. It took the ship fifteen days to cross the Atlantic. The weather was beautiful, and the sailing was smooth. We were free to explore all parts of the ship except the bridge. I visited the engine room several times, fascinated by all the machinery and the dials, about which I understood nothing. The merchant seamen tried to talk to me, but not knowing many English words, I was unable to carry on a conversation with them. I could not understand a word they were saying; they spoke too fast. It left me feeling like a total idiot. Even if I had known how many cognates there were between French and English, it would have been of little help to me. In the ensuing years I was to discover that those words which were closest to French gave me the most trouble in English. I struggled for years with words such as *impossibility*; learning to put the stress on the English word gave me fits. What I did understand on the ship, however, were the open faces and the ready smiles. I know that's a cliché about Americans, but it's nonetheless true. We were also delighted when the PX store opened. There, we could buy almost anything from cigarettes to chocolate. For a few days, I went on a chocolate binge, enjoyed the use of my American toothpaste, and smoked Regent cigarettes on deck, looking and feeling like an important gentleman.

We arrived in the New York Harbor on the evening of June 14 and anchored almost at the midpoint between the Statue of Liberty and the Battery. New York's skyline was exactly as I had seen it in the movies and on posters. What was most striking were the patterns of lights created on the highways by cars and trucks. From the deck, it looked as if they were scurrying about like lit toy mice. I had never seen such heavy traffic in my life.

I was to see a lot more. I remember standing on that deck quite late into the night, wondering why we had not docked and why we had stopped in the middle of the harbor. I could not take my eyes from the skyscrapers and stared at the lights in the windows. I was mesmerized by the abundance of concrete. New York, America—what a fantastic place!

The next day we docked at Pier 168 near the Washington Bridge. Custom and immigration officials came aboard. My luggage was thoroughly inspected, and I had to pay duties on some of the perfumes and trinkets I had bought for my California family. One by one the passengers were interrogated, passports were inspected, and destinations were requested. There was no one from my family to meet me at the ship; instead, I was greeted by a representative from the Hebrew Immigration American Society (HIAS), who proposed to take me to a dormitory until I could be put on the train to Los Angeles. I had a letter for my uncle Adolph in New York and also the address of his jewelry store in Manhattan. Adolph was my mother's brother who had immigrated to America in 1934. I had not seen him since then, although I remembered him and knew of his bad reputation within the family. I took a taxi to my uncle's store, but he was not particularly surprised to see me or overjoyed. "Nu, you're here," he greeted me in Yiddish, although he knew French. I stiffened; why was he addressing me in the language of the greenhorns? Yiddish, for me, was the language of those who had recently left the ghettos of Europe. My welcome was curt, and I was not asked any questions. Everyone had seen the newsreels of the death camps, the mounds of corpses, and had, understandably, recoiled in horror. I was to find the same response in California. After a cursory acknowledgment that the past years in Europe must have been difficult, I had to listen to the recitation of restrictions of goods imposed during the war. This was, by far, more disconcerting than the way meals had been served on the ship. When I left Europe, there was no subject more important than the tragedy we had survived and the losses we had endured. It was most probable that my relatives, along with most people, could not confront the unspeakable evil that had befallen their European families. The wounds were too fresh.

On the afternoon of my arrival, Adolph called his wife and closed the store to take me to his home in Queens. My aunt Gisella received me with far more enthusiasm than my uncle. She and my mother had known each other in Romania. In fact they were distant cousins. My mother had acted as a go-between for her and Adolph while he was in the midst of a divorce from his first wife. Their home was modest and was located in an apartment complex. I was impressed by its modernity: elevators, garbage disposals, and showers with hot water day and night. I was even more dazzled during a trip to the neighborhood A&P, where I saw the incredible display of foodstuffs. I had not seen such abundance since the eve of the war. In 1946, France was still a land of shortages. The Nazis were gone, but the wealth had not returned. As I walked around the streets of New York, I was overwhelmed by the availability of goods. If I had had any money, I would have gone on a shopping binge.

My aunt and uncle had a son who was not yet quite eight years old. At home Adolph and I communicated in French. With Gisella, it was Yiddish, which served us. But with Lester who spoke only English, signs and body language sufficed. The evening of my arrival, my uncle disappeared. He disappeared every evening, going for long walks. I accompanied him on one of these walks, and it was one of the only times we talked seriously and amicably to each other. Adolph was a complicated man, a self-made man, often unscrupulous, a bon vivant, an angry man, authoritarian, elegant in dress, charming, arrogant, and vulgar in manner. That particular night we walked together, he criticized the family's failures in response to all he had done for each of its members. He was particularly upset about my father's and mother's inadequacies, and despite the fact that his bitterness echoed my own, I heard myself say that they had done the best they could do. He agreed with me, and it was the first and last time we ever agreed on anything. I had taken the first step toward forgiveness, acceptance. It was a verbal step, and an intellectual one. It would take a few more years of living before I truly accepted that my parents were not to blame for my unhappiness. But that talk with my uncle, I believe, was an important step in the right direction.

That first night in New York, my aunt encouraged her son to take me for a walk around the neighborhood. Lester and I walked alongside the elevated subway until we reached Queens Plaza—quite a walk in ordinary circumstances, but a real adventure for someone just off the boat who was being accompanied by an eight-year-old, with no common language between them. I do not believe that Lester had ever gone that far by himself, let alone with a perfect stranger. When we got home a couple of hours later, his mother was sick with worry. We thought nothing of it; what we had done seemed perfectly normal to me. I saw no danger that could have befallen us. In fact we were quite safe.

After school let out, Lester became my constant companion and my guide. We went all over New York together; we even visited the Empire State Building. In Paris I had never gone up to the top of the Eiffel Tower, but in New York I was a tourist so I did what tourists do. We went to see the Statue of Liberty and visited Coney Island, where we tried the parachute jump—a leftover from the World's Fair. Lester introduced me to hot dogs and chocolate milk shakes. We rode the subway up and down Manhattan and Queens. Lester and I may not have been able to speak to each other, but we had a wonderful time. During these two weeks in Manhattan, I learned the pleasures of having a sibling. I also had a marvelous vacation away from war, persecution, and worry about the future. I was allowing myself to be spoiled and to be totally irresponsible. I was catching up on a lost adolescence.

On my first Sunday in New York, two or three days after my arrival, my uncle took me to Harlem, where he proceeded to knock on tenement doors to collect payment of overdue rents. I did not understand what Adolph was saying to his tenants. I could only judge by the severity of his voice that the situation was unpleasant. I felt embarrassed; money matters always made me feel squeamish. Money was something dirty; it was the root of all evil. I was further embarrassed because my uncle's harsh tones were addressed to poor black people. It was the first of several times that my uncle tried to explain to me that life is a jungle, and the world is a dog-eat-dog world. I disagreed. All my life, my father, his friends, and later on my revolutionary friends had convinced me that a better world was an absolute necessity. Adolph's attitude and his actions were, in my view, reprehensible. Had he learned nothing from the recent events in Europe? In 1946, most people were focusing on the evil nature of the Germans. Naziism, they thought, was a natural outcome of the German national character.

That Sunday, to celebrate my presence in New York, we met my aunt's brother, his wife, and their two daughters at a restaurant on Delancey Street. I was briefly introduced, and we all sat down to eat around several rectangular tables, set together for the occasion. Lester and I sat together at the end of the table, silent while an animated conversation in English proceeded on either side of us. The meal was held in my honor, but it was as if I were not there. No one attempted to speak to me or even ask me a question in Yiddish.

During the war, I had experienced severe hunger, not as severe as it had been in the camps, but still a traumatic experience for an adolescent. I had promised myself that if ever the occasion arose, I would not leave as much as a crumb on my plate. This was to be the occasion, and I felt up to the challenge. The meal was going to cost five dollars per person, which was quite a sum in 1946. A feast would be served. The salad came first followed by the largest sirloin steak I had ever seen on a plate—all this next to mounds of French fried potatoes. I attacked my food with gusto. To my chagrin I failed to finish both the steak and the potatoes. The experiences of that Sunday dinner left me numb and bloated.

At the end of my quasi-magical two weeks in New York, I was put on a train at Pennsylvania Station for Los Angeles, where I expected a life of undiluted joys. It seemed as though the war years had not taught me anything; I was losing all sense of reality and ignoring the need to work and achieve. I was living in a fairy tale. This was a period of euphoria, and nothing could go wrong. I had not felt like this since I had won first prize in grade school. I boarded the train with great excitement, thinking my life was decidedly taking a turn for the better. In four days I would meet my new family. I was convinced that California was a land of perpetual sunshine where all my dreams would come true.

I was greeted by my aunt Eva and my cousin Pearl at Union Station. My uncle was ill and was unable to meet me. In fact he was deathly ill with cancer and would soon succumb to the disease. I was driven to a house in Beverly Hills in a car I thought was enormous. I heard my aunt Eva say that the car needed to be washed. The rest of the way I was glued to the window, searching for palm trees. The street on which I was to live was lined with palm trees and ranch houses. This was precisely what I had expected. I was shown a luxurious room with an adjacent shower. I had landed in paradise. In a short time I had gone from rags to riches. I was far away from the horrors and deprivations of the war.

After two weeks in the U.S., my English skills were still very poor. I was picking up words and bits of phrases, but holding a conversation was impossible. My family had to resort to Yiddish to communicate with me although I insisted they speak English. While in New York, I had visited a family whose oldest members did not speak English despite having spent decades in their new country. I also remembered how poorly my parents had mastered French and the humiliations they had endured because of it. I was determined this would not be my fate. I insisted that English be spoken to me; it did not bother me that in using the little bit of language that I acquired every day I was not always understood and was surely making a fool of myself. Still I was never made fun of. I was corrected but never criticized. My obvious foreignness never caused undue hostility. Unlike the French, Americans do not express their xenophobia by criticizing or mocking the way foreigners pronounce their language. There are just too many accents in America.

My aunt Eva was a pretty woman with white curly hair and large brown eyes. My cousin Pearl resembled her except that her hair was dark, and her face was marked by acne scars. She was married and was waiting for her husband to be discharged from the army. Meanwhile, she lived at home and did her mother's bidding. My aunt was a meticulous woman. Her house was spotless and did not seemed lived in. Except for the fact that her furniture was modern, she and my aunt Jeannette could have been twin sisters. My father used to relate with great delight how she and his brother were married. My uncle Joseph had had a friend in Lodz whom he would visit often. The friend had a sister quite a bit younger than the two boys. My uncle used to bounce the little girl on his knees and tease her that when she grew up, they would get married. As any fairy tale would have it, so it came to pass. My aunt and uncle settled in Patterson, New Jersey, and had three children. They built up a wholesale liquor and tobacco business which they eventually moved to Los Angeles. Theirs was a success story as well as a romantic one. Coming from a broken home, I was quite impressed.

One of the first things that my aunt did was to go through my two pitiful suitcases and discard the clothing that she declared inappropriate for California. The next few days were spent in shopping, visiting the doctor for a physical, and having one of my teeth replaced at the dentist. I was being transformed into a well-groomed, middle-class American. I took all of that for granted, and I was taken by surprise when my aunt asked about my plans for the future. She was aware, through the newsreels, of the effects of the Holocaust, but I was in a new land now where opportunities abounded. I could make anything out of myself that I wanted. The past was best forgotten. My aunt knew a few refugees who had recently arrived from Europe, and who were already busy making money and adjusting wonderfully to their new country. I knew that my vacation could not last forever, but making money was not on my mind. I was very aware that I had no skills, and I could not imagine learning a trade with any enthusiasm. I was back at square one. I timidly suggested that I would like to resume my education. There was a look of consternation on my family's face. Although the second generation would be educated, the first generation of immigrants had another role to play. My aunt proposed to take me to UCLA the next day and investigate the possibilities and requirements to be admitted as a student. The people at the admission office were very helpful in outlining a course of action. I would have to learn English in a high school program, earn a four-year diploma, and then apply. It would take years before I could even consider studying at a university. It would be more sensible, more practical, to find a good job.

I enrolled in night school, where I began to study English in a disciplined manner. Meanwhile, a job was found for me in a record company as a polisher. I polished copper discs on a wheel for one dollar an hour. When I was not going to school, I would go to the movies. I barely followed the plots, but it was great training for my ears. In the years to come, movies became both a source to teach me a new language and a true passion.

My uncle's oldest son, Arthur, owned a liquor store in one of the more impoverished sections of Los Angeles. My aunt was quite worried about his safety. He had been held up several times, but instead of waiting for the police to arrive and eventually letting the insurance company take care of his claims, he had once given chase, on foot, to a robber. My aunt let him know in no uncertain terms that a few dollars were not worth risking his life. Arthur was over six feet tall, quite athletic, and had served in the Navy during the War. He felt confident that he could handle any situation. I dropped by his store a couple of times and noted that most of his business consisted of selling pints of cheap liquor. I quickly learned to recognize the name of the brands being sought, and when the store got crowded, I helped out. I was not excited by the prospect of leading a life like Arthur's, but I liked practicing my English with him whenever I could.

One of the first things that I had to do upon my arrival at my uncle's house was to register with the local draft board. The 1941 Selective Service Act was still in effect, and I was of draftable age. As an immigrant, I was subject to all the laws and regulations applying to citizens, except that I could not vote or work for a government agency. I could serve in the army. My American family lauded the benefits derived from serving in the military. There was a GI Bill. I could go to school, get a loan to buy property or start a business, get free medical treatment at a Veteran's Hospital, and be buried in a military cemetery when I died. After four years of living under Nazi occupation, I was not intrigued by these amenities. I believe that I was very much in the way in my uncle's house. He was dying; my aunt had her hands full. She had raised her three children and was quite worried about one of her sons. I had been brought from Europe, but I was a burden. My departure to the army would be appreciated.

I was ordered to report to Camp Beale, near Sacramento, on September 9, 1946. I was given a physical, an IQ test, and a set of uniforms. Because of my poor vision, I was classified as qualified for limited service, which meant that in time of war I might not be part of a combat unit. Since the war was over, the army could send me wherever it liked. Anyway, I had my first taste of army life that very afternoon, marching in formation, and being shouted at by a noncommissioned officer. Eating in the mess hall proved to be a yet more daunting experience than it had been on the ship. Here I was served on a tray with compartments and felt my stomach going into convulsions when the ice cream began to melt next to the mashed potatoes. I did not know the term yet, but I was experiencing culture shock. I did not quite understand what was being said or shouted, nor what was written on doors or posters. At the end of the day, I climbed on my bunk feeling that I had acquired a new set of left limbs and three heads. The next morning, I became acquainted more vividly with the army's way of communicating. I greeted the soldier next to me with a shy, "Good morning."

He returned my greeting with a, "What's good about it?" followed by a string of obscenities that soon became very familiar since it was practically the exclusive vocabulary of soldiers. My elementary linguistic education was complete by the time I left Camp Beale to report to Camp Polk in Louisiana. I knew all the grammatical variations of the F-word and from which accursed she-dog I had illegitimately been borne.

Camp Polk is situated halfway between Shreveport and Alexandria in the backwaters of Louisiana. Toward the end of September and in the early part of October, the temperature and the humidity are quite high. We were given salt tablets for our long marches. Many soldiers fainted from heat exhaustion. To say that I did not like army life and that I was not disposed to shine as a soldier would be to understate my feelings of discomfort and bewilderment. A couple of inductees acted in such a way that they managed to obtain a discharge. One came back from a Sunday afternoon outing with his hair dyed in violent colors; within a week he was gone. The army had not recognized the first manifestation of a punk hairdo. Instead, it saw it as a form of mental illness. Another soldier started to wet his bed at night. The army tried to shame him into continence. That failed, and he was soon gone to his native Oregon where he claimed to make a living by breaking in wild horses. I would have liked to find a way out, but I was too scared or unimaginative. Besides I felt strong, and I did not believe that I could put on an act of insanity. I was also afraid to appear as a failure in front of my new family. I learned to drag my feet and be as inconspicuous as possible, which is not easy when everyone in the barrack calls you "Frenchy." That nickname remained with me during the remainder of my time in the service.

Basic training was not a bad experience; it was just a bore. The marching and the drills were a relief from the dull lectures on military matters. At Camp Polk we were supposed to be trained to become medics. That might account for the excessive number of films we were shown on venereal diseases—how they were contracted with sexy-looking women. Blindness, paralysis, and madness, flesh peeling off bodies…no fear-producing image was spared us. Alas, nothing could stifle the sexual fantasies or the dirty talk in the barracks. There were other movies shown on the base. I saw *The Jolson Story* five or six times. Of course I could have gone to the PX with some of the recruits and swilled beer. However, I am not very fond of beer and even less of drunkenness, so I tried to learn Jolson's repertoire instead.

On a Sunday midway through our basic training, we were granted a pass. Four of us decided to go to Alexandria, take in a movie, and splurge on a steak dinner. That's when I discovered segregated America. I had not paid too much attention to the ethnic or racial composition of troops at Camp Polk. My unit included mostly Caucasians with a large minority of Asian Americans. I was too busy avoiding trouble to notice that there were no other minority members on the base, not even as civilian workers. But "Colored" were in evidence in Alexandria, as was the presence of Jim Crow laws. When we went to the movie house, the balcony was clearly designated for COLORED ONLY. The water fountains were also segregated, and the bathrooms were, too. I had been excluded in Europe by racist laws, and as I took my seat in the orchestra, I felt ashamed now that I was on the other side. During dinner, I almost caused a scene which could have turned out to be very ugly for me if I had been alone. I asked the waitress for a fork to eat my steak, but the pronunciation of my *r* caused some confusion, and she thought that I was asking for something totally unrelated. She angrily asked: "You want what, soldier?" Fortunately, my companions calmed her down by quickly revealing my foreign origin. When they explained why she had gotten so angry, I envisioned all the images of lynching I had read about in the newspapers. Many years later when I asked a speech therapist for help in correcting this particular linguistic difficulty, he told me that happiness did not reside in an American *r*. He obviously did not understand the troubles I've encountered through the years.

Toward the end my of basic training, I was called to the company headquarters and informed that my uncle in Beverly Hills had died and that I had been granted a ten-day leave to attend his funeral. I had expected his death, and I did not feel as devastated as I should have. I did not know him, and his death left me sad. He was just one more death to be added to the rest of my family who had died and for whom I had not yet grieved or been allowed to grieve A loan for my transportation had to be arranged, after which I was driven to an airport and put on an army transport plane that would take me to Los Angeles. This was my first plane ride, and my anxiety level soared as high as the aircraft. The cabin was not well pressurized, and my ears began to ache. I was given some gum to chew, but that did not seem to help the pain. I did not have a high priority status, so I was bumped off the plane in San Antonio. It was quite late at night when I reached the railroad station where I was able to buy a ticket for a train leaving for Tucson. I boarded the train with my duffel bag and proceeded to find a seat in the coach section where most travelers were already asleep. All of the seats were occupied; I went from one wagon to the next until at last I found a seat. I wondered why the passengers gave me a strange look as I sat down but did not say a word. I was exhausted from the day's travails; I fell asleep as soon as I hit the seat. I don't know how long I was asleep, but I woke up in a daze as the conductor was shaking me by the shoulder.

"You can't stay here, soldier."

"Why not ?"

"You're in the Colored wagon."

"There are no seats anywhere."

"You can't stay in this wagon. It's against the law. Where you from, soldier?"

"Paris."

"Paris, Texas ?"

"No sir, Paris, France."

During this exchange the passengers did not look at us. I spent the rest of the night sitting on my duffel bag, with my head resting against the wall of the platform. I arrived in Tucson with a nice crick in my neck and some unpleasant feelings about the railroad accommodations in Texas. For some reason, I decided to hitchhike to Los Angeles. I reasoned that, at any rate, it was too late to attend my uncle's funeral. I might as well see part of the country. Despite everything that had happened since my leaving Camp Polk, I was still twenty years old and off on a big adventure. Arriving in Los Angeles a day late could not matter that much.

I walked along the highway that leads to Phoenix, thumbing each passing car. In 1946, it was not too difficult to hitch a ride, particularly if you were in the military. Patriotic fervor was high, traffic sparse, and crime was not a major concern. I was picked up by two men who were not going to Los Angeles but were willing to drop me off in Phoenix where I could catch a train. The road from Tucson to Phoenix seemed to be built in a straight line, and the car raced along it at a speed that I found incredible. It took less than two hours, I think, to arrive in Phoenix. I was struck by the beauty of the landscape and was able to see the most extraordinary sunset I have ever seen.

I arrived in Beverly Hills the next morning, much too late for my uncle's funeral. My aunt Eva made it clear that I was not welcome by asking me where I was planning to stay until I was due back at Camp Polk. I found a small hotel near Main Street in Los Angeles and spent the next few days at the movies. I quickly exhausted my funds and started the inverse trek from Los Angeles to Louisiana. I arrived at Camp Polk ten days late. The men I had trained with were gone. I had no duties for the following days, but then the orders came for me to report to

Fort Lawton in Seattle. Christmas of 1946 was fast approaching. I kept writing to my Aunt Eva and to the friends I had left in France and going to the movies. These were my chief occupations and distractions while waiting to be sent overseas. From Fort Lawton, one either went to Korea or to Japan. On New Years Eve, I boarded a ship headed for Yokohama, along with a few hundred soldiers.

I saw my aunt Eva once more after I was discharged from the army. We kept in touch for a few years but gradually lost touch with each other. My hopes of having a family collapsed. Without a doubt, I was a disappointment. I had not embraced the American Dream the way they had wished I would. I expected more from them than they were able or willing to give me. It took me a little while to understand all that. I did not know what was to become of me, whether I would ever find or create a life that would make me happy. At any rate, the responsibility was now mine, and that was no small source of anxiety. I was very far from feeling that I was lucky enough to deserve a life of my own.

Chapter Thirteen

Sailing the Pacific Ocean in January was not as smooth as crossing the Atlantic in June. Compared to the accommodations of the army's transport, those of the *S.S. Lawson* were almost luxurious and afforded me relative privacy. Army life is conspicuous in the absence of both. The bunks are uncomfortable, the living is promiscuous, and the quality of the food depends on the calmness of the sea. During the trip, the Pacific belied its name and turned me off Ritz cheese crackers forever. Still I did not get seasick. The weather did not permit too many outings on deck; instead we stayed mainly in the hole. When I was not writing a letter, I watched the soldiers play games of cards or throw dice. I did not nor do I now understand the game of Craps. The various rituals fascinated me, especially those pertaining to language.

We landed in Yokohama on January 17. It was a cold day. We were lodged in huge tents that were poorly heated by kerosene stoves. I was grateful to the Red Cross for the coffee and donuts. These were available every morning, and I much preferred them to the greenish scrambled eggs and the greasy sausages. Large breakfasts were not yet to my liking, I had huge breakfasts when I was working on farms during the German Occupation, and a hard day's work was required. But the war was over, and I was slowly reverting to the habits prevalent in peace time. Donuts are not like croissants, but then I had not seen a croissant for a long time. The donuts sufficed while I lounged in the tent and huddled around the stove to keep warm. In all the transition camps that I had been in, there was not much to do—no training and no defined duties. Once in a while a noncom would come in and call us out to police the area, but that would only occupy us for an hour. In Camp Beale, I spent an afternoon peeling potatoes. I soon learned that if I did not stay where I was supposed to be, I could avoid most of the chores I might be called to perform and that I could do that with impunity. The camp was disorganized, I could get lost. I made it a rule never to stay in the barracks or tents unless there was a direct order issued.

I wondered for a while whether I might be assigned to Tokyo in some army hospital and be trained as a medic. I did not have to wait too long. The orders came that most of us were being sent to Beppu on Kyushu Island in Southern Japan, where we would join the 19th Infantry Regiment, 24th Division, 8th Army. It was peace time; my limited service status could be ignored. I was going to be a foot soldier. A dreamlike quality had overtaken my life. I was to be taken care of in a benevolent manner, my needs would be attended to with clockwork regularity, and I would join in the normalcy of army companionship by bitching about everything. Paris, New York, Los Angeles—I had never heard of them. While I was in the army, there was only the here and now. All else was irrelevant.

We boarded the train loaded with our GI issues and our K-rations. Our trip was supposed to last two days, but the trains moved slowly in bombed-out Japan. There were no kitchen facilities. K-rations, inedible as they may be, were our fare. We stopped a couple of hours in Hiroshima where we were allowed to get off the train and admire the results of our military power. It's one thing to read about destruction, to see it in pictures or newsreels. But it's quite another thing to see it in its real setting. I remember seeing the pictures of the mounds of corpses, the crematoria, and the walking, staring skeletons after the death camps opened. I had been filled with unbelievable horror and anger, but when my family and I visited these camps forty years later, I could find no words for what I saw. I was struck with a sense of paralysis, trying to understand, to interpret the silence which pervaded Birkenau. The terror the victims had experienced could not be felt. It had left no mark, no trace. A world had vanished. There was only rubble, beautiful trees, and high grass. Hiroshima, save for one lonely building, had been flattened. There was silence, but my overwhelming emotion was of shame. I felt ashamed to be there as a conqueror and refused to embrace the destruction of a city and its population. All the reasons for the bombings of Hiroshima, Nagasaki, and Dresden have not reconciled me to the deaths of innocent children. I was not responsible for what happened in Hiroshima, but I was associated with the nation that had engineered this cataclysmic event. I felt ashamed of the human race.

I did not know enough English to share my feelings with my companions, but I fear that if I had been able to express myself, my opinions would have fallen on deaf ears. Unless the soldiers around me were very adept at hiding their feelings, I never heard them refer to the Japanese people in terms other than derogatory ones, reflecting the dehumanization process popularized by war propaganda. If anyone felt any horror, it came out in a roundabout way; the atomic bomb had saved American lives, and besides all that, everyone was convinced that the Japanese did not value human life as much as the

Americans did. I can't count the times I have heard that lie; that people different from ourselves do not experience pain and sorrow, or if they experience it at all, they do not experience them with the intensity that we do.

In 1947, Beppu was a small fishing town with hot springs of volcanic waters. Parts of the town were off-limits to U.S. personnel, for unexplained reasons. We were warned to avoid eating any of the local foods lest we acquire intestinal diseases whose cure was unknown in the West. Nonfraternization with the Japanese was imposed military law. We did not know Japanese and the citizens of Beppu did not know English, so body language was the universal medium of communication. We were also warned that the Japanese carried the most dreadful venereal infections and that we should keep ourselves pure for the sake of our mothers, sisters, and girlfriends. At the same time, we could not get off or come back to the post without showing our contraceptives or a certificate from the health station in town. The 19th Infantry Regiment was not free of sexually transmitted diseases.

We were allowed to go mainly to the center of town, which had not been bombed. Its buildings were still intact. One of the buildings open to us had been requisitioned by the Red Cross. It was a place to relax, with an old upright piano and a hot sulfuric water spa. Our camp was located several miles out of town. The road in and out of camp was a dirt road, as were most of the streets in Beppu. On the way in to town I was always intrigued by the aromas of the food being stir-fried on porches or on the side of the road. I was also struck by the ritual greetings exchanged between old Japanese women. They would bow to each other interminably, their heads almost touching the ground. They dressed in drab peasant clothing, and I gawked at them. My presence was never acknowledged except in the central market by the merchants peddling souvenirs.

The top sergeant of the company to which I was assigned took a liking to me. He had been a soldier in France during World War I and was awaiting retirement. He liked to recall the towns he had seen in 1917, and wanted to know if I had been there. He reminds me of those people I meet in various parts of the world who want to know if I have met their friends and relatives in the U.S. Like everyone else, he never called me by my name. My name appeared only once for guard duty. Toward the end of my shift, I was called upon to arrest a Japanese man and take him to the guard house. He had been caught on post looking for food. One of his legs was missing, and he walked with the aid of a homemade crutch—a dangerous individual, no doubt. After alerting the corporal of the guard, I walked him to the other side of the camp, with orders to keep my rifle ready and cocked. I felt pretty silly even though the poor man showed no fear. I delivered him to the authorities and was told that he would be let go in a couple of hours after he had been fed. I decided that he had gone through this procedure a number of times and knew that nothing drastic would happen to him. My arrest stopped him from rummaging through the garbage piles. No doubt he and other Japanese civilians would be found on base again illegally. We wasted enough food, which would have fed many people in occupied Japan. That was my sole military venture. It made me feel uneasy, yet I savored its absurdity.

Our lives were thoroughly regulated. I had no worries except escape from some extra detail. During the day, we drilled, learned how to march, turned left, turned right, ran on the double, and went on forced marches in full battle uniforms. At one point, I was given a Browning automatic rifle to carry. I represented the heavy firepower on my squad. I carried that BAR on long marches and bore up quite well. I had developed a strong body with strong muscles while working on farms during the German Occupation. I liked feeling the strength of my body; I had depended on it to survive, and though I might feel tired from lugging the full field equipment, I enjoyed the sweat running on my skin and the feeling that I could do what was asked of me. The army made no sense to me, but I did not care. I would get through; I had survived much worse. So I marched and sang the songs soldiers sing. Meanwhile, I failed to qualify on the first test on the rifle range. I was relieved of my BAR duties. I did not protest.

Most of the boys who served with me came from the South. There were very few of us from either coastal areas. Many were farmhands, and some admitted that their army shoes were the first decent shoes they had ever worn. The vast majority had enlisted in the army and expected to spend twenty or thirty years in its service. They pointed with pride to some of the non-commissioned officers who had received field commissions during the war but had remained in the army rather than going back to a life in the civilian sector. My buddies were full-blown racists. They talked about *Nigras* with unabashed contempt. When I tried to remonstrate with them as my English allowed, I was bluntly told that I did not know what I was talking about and that I did not live with "them people" as they had. My status as a foreigner probably saved me from a beating, and my ideas about equality were a laughing matter to them. I was also in a privileged position as "Frenchy." I was supposed to know all about sex, and I was asked if I was an *artiste.* Only months later was I told what was meant by this expression. This was true for many other sexual expressions and activities—my national origin qualified me as an expert.

Passover was announced, and Jewish soldiers were given the opportunity to travel and spend three days in Kyoto. I had abandoned the practice of Judaism long ago, but I could not pass up the chance to get off post for nearly a week. In Kyoto, we were received lavishly with a grand Seder. Not having to look at army chow was in itself a feast. I spent the next three days visiting the temples and gardens of this ancient city. I was very happy that the war had left it intact. To have bombed such an ancient and beautiful city would have been a cultural disaster.

March in Kyushu was mild with lots of sunshine. The cherry trees were blooming, and the landscape was traditionally Japanese. President Truman had ended the National Selective Act of 1941, which meant that all draftees would soon be discharged. My stint in the Army was about to end. Those of us who were going home were ecstatic. However, we were all called in, one by one, into the commandant's office and pressured to enlist in the regular army. I was asked what my plans were and what I would be doing in civilian life. The benefits of being a soldier for the next thirty years were clearly laid. I declined the opportunity to remain in the military. We were reassembled in Yokohama, and before we were allowed to board the ship, we had to display all of our belongings on the ground. War souvenirs were not allowed to be taken out of the country, nor were weapons that belonged to the army. Bayonets as well as Japanese sabers had to be surrendered, much to the dismay and discontent of those of us eager to import these mementos. Still, some of these articles found their way to the U.S. On the way from Beppu, we stopped once more in Hiroshima. Once more we got off the train, and I found that my distress at the sight of so much destruction had not diminished. After having sailed from Yokohama to Seoul to pick up more soldiers, we arrived in Seattle and awaited discharge at Fort Lawton.

The weather in Seattle at the end of April was in sharp contrast from what it had been at Christmas. I remember clear sunny skies, with Mount Rainier looming on the horizon. Waiting for my discharge papers was a time to lounge around and go through various processes like having to tell to a typist what skills I had acquired in the army. Outside of a better command of the army idiom and some improvement in my English, I was at a loss to describe what benefits I had acquired during my stint with the military. I did not see how my ability to take a M-1 rifle apart and put it back together was going to help me in my new life. I had learned to escape from the noncoms; that too would be of little use. But the eight months in the service did shield me from some of the harsh realities an immigrant has to face in a new culture. I was taken care of while at the same time learning some of the ways American culture and society functioned. I was not about to tell all of that to the typist, however. I muttered that I had experience doing guard duty. Thus, my discharge papers read that I am entitled to a World War II Victory Medal and that I have been recommended for further training.

During that time, I managed to get off the post a few times, and I met a man in his thirties, a Trotskyist. Jesse Simons received me most cordially. A New Yorker by birth, he was college educated and he worked at Boeing. Like many radicals of the time, he was convinced that his place was in the factories, organizing workers to fight for improved working conditions and recruiting them to his cause. The Great Depression of the thirties and the sometimes bloody battles that labor unions had waged against corporations were not that far removed from 1947. As in France, social security, paid vacations, and other employee benefits were recent laws. Jesse had participated in many ideological battles within the factions of the revolutionary groups. Though he led the branch of the Workers Party in Seattle, he was a relative newcomer to that party. Jesse was very tall and lanky, balding, and wore steel-rimmed glasses. He spoke eloquently with his hands. His demeanor was that of an intellectual; he knew it and I think he saw that as a handicap in his mission to persuade workers at Boeing to join the Workers Party. Jesse invited me to come and share his studio apartment after my discharge. Since I had no other plans and no family to return to, I accepted. Seattle was as good a place as any to put down roots.

Jesse took charge of my education by correcting the glaring errors of my English and by introducing me to a body of literature of which I was totally ignorant, namely the writings of psychoanalysis. While expressions such as "unconscious" or "subconscious" were a part of my French vocabulary, I had no idea that these words had a scientific foundation. I considered them part of an individual's nature, a given. I thought that one was born with certain qualities and modes of behavior; that these could be constructs traceable from an individual childhood and culture was astonishing. I was simply the way I was and could not imagine anyone digging into and revealing the springs of my innermost self. Years later, I met French people with similar attitudes; their dreams were no one's business. Of course I had seen books in France that pretended to reveal the secret messages of dreams, but they were always in the occult section along with horoscopes and palmistry. I equated the occult, or spiritualism, with quackery. Jesse's Marxism included psychoanalysis as further illumination of human behavior. He used the word "neurosis" as freely as he breathed. The concept was suspect to me, but I was eager to learn about it and despite my distrust of it, to perhaps find some magical key that would dispel my confusion. Karen Horney's books were linguistically the most accessible to me. I liked the emphasis she placed on the role that society played in fostering neuroses in the individual. It provided me with the naive argument that society was largely responsible for the state of my psyche, so individual therapy would be of little help. Were we not all caught in a vicious circle? Was not the most important task that of changing society? I remember using that reasoning to argue against the proponents of Freudian theories whose key word was "adjustment." Why would I want to adjust to a world that made me ill in the first place? Did adjustment mean that I should accept all the evils of mankind? Moreover, even if I had wanted to avail myself of the benefits of psychoanalysis, I could not afford them. Neither could Jesse. I was smart enough and strong enough to face my problems myself; I did not need anyone to probe my dreams. In fact I did not know much of anything about life or relationships. I had survived a stormy relationship with my mother in my childhood and an adolescence shadowed by death. That hardly prepared me to take charge of my life.

In mid-May, I was discharged from Fort Lawton and came to share Jesse's studio. I shed my army clothing and used part of my severance pay to buy a new outfit. This was the first time I bought something for myself with money I had actually earned. It was a good feeling, and I took it as an omen that change was on its way. To celebrate my discharge, Jesse organized a dinner for me to which he invited his girlfriend and her roommate. Jesse's girlfriend, Helen, was a beautiful young woman—tall, blond, a native of Boise, Idaho. A recent graduate from the Washington University, she had an office job that she did not like very much. She appeared to agree with everything Jesse said during the meal. Her roommate, Ardis, was in her late twenties. She was a statuesque woman with dark red hair who worked in an office and had graduated from Washington University too. We laughed a lot that evening and consumed a couple of bottles of poor wine. Ardis was flirting with me, but I was too inexperienced to realize it. In fact I jumped back when she touched my cheek and commented on the mobility of my face. Toward the end of the evening as Ardis called for a cab, I realized that Helen was going to spend the night with Jesse and share his single bed. There was no wall between his bed and mine. I was caught in a quandary, but I quickly ran after Ardis and asked to go home with her. That's how my first love affair came about. It did not last long. I was enamored of Ardis, but she considered me a fling. I can't say that the end of the affair was a painful one. We stayed friends, which was one of the rare times in my life that a relationship did not end on a sour note. I thought that I could devote my life to Ardis, but when it did not happen, my heart did not break. I was not going to die for love, after all.

I took a brief trip to Los Angeles, picked up my belongings from my aunt's house, and bid her good-bye. I never saw her again though I continued to write to her for a couple of years. Now and then she sent me news of her family or photographs of newborn grandchildren. She remarried; we lost touch. Back in Seattle, I set about finding a job. There was a recession in the country, caused by the retooling of the war economy into a peace time economy. I went to the employment office and was found a job in a bread factory from four P.M. to midnight. My job was to stack the bread on racks as it rolled down from the oven. The bread rolled down rapidly and in considerable quantity. A music system played Emmanuel Chabrier's *Persian Market,* which has a charming light rhythm as I worked. Eight continuous hours of it can, however, become something of a bore. I earned a dollar per hour, which would most certainly provide for my needs. I survived the first night, but not the second. At one point during that second evening, I lost it. I failed to clear the conveyor belt before a second load of bread came down and then the third and the fourth. I had to face a mountain of loaves, some mangled and some on the floor. It was a scene worthy of Chaplin's *Modern Times.* The foreman intervened by stopping the belt and fired me on the spot. This has become one of my most cherished memories of my entry into the American workforce. A week later I was hired as a laborer in a factory that made prefabricated showers. Laborers' duties are never easy; on the bottom of the ladder there is neither autonomy nor dignity, and certainly no future. The worst aspect of this job was working in the paint room, where the shower walls were spray painted and then baked. The combination of fumes and heat were at times unbearable. None of the workers wore any protective clothing. During the time that I worked at Colotyle, Jesse and I almost had a falling out. Jesse had agreed to pick me up every day after work on his way back from Boeing because public transportation was not convenient or frequent in our section of Seattle. Jesse had a car, a beat-up car that got him to and from work. One day he did not show up. I waited for two hours before I was able to board a bus. By the time I arrived at the studio, I was furious. And before he could offer an explanation, I exploded self-righteously on the subject of responsibility. Poor Jesse, even his apologies did not calm me down. He allowed my anger to pour out. I guess he understood more than I did that my anger was not just about having been kept waiting. When I was a child my father had failed to pick me up at school for a weekend visit and my mother, taking advantage of my absence, had gone out with her friends. I had been left stranded. Ever since that happened, waiting for anyone has been difficult for me.

Shortly after our argument, Jesse and Helen left for New York. I could not keep the studio, but I was able to rent a room with a couple I had met at an organized picnic. This lasted a couple of months until I was a laid off at Colotyle. I was not very successful in my efforts to make a life for myself in Seattle. I enjoyed meeting people there, especially some old anarchists and dock workers who had wonderful tales about their struggles. That was also the time when I became acquainted with Daniel Guérin, a historian and an anarchist who was touring the United States to promote his book on the French Revolution in radical circles. Its title, *La Lutte des Classes sous la Première*

République (Class Struggles Under the First Republic), did not at first impress me since I had been taught that Revolution came about as a result of class conflicts. It was part of the radical canon that Robespierre and his cohorts were the left wing of that Revolution. Guérin's book contradicted that thesis and proposed that within the bourgeois Revolution of 1789, there was a budding proletarian movement much to the left of Robespierre. It was during that visit that Daniel Guérin took me out to dinner, and while talking about France and my experiences, he affectionately put his hand on my shoulder. I recoiled as if a hot iron had touched me. It had been years since an adult had touched me. When I met Guérin again in New York, his coolness made me regret my reaction to his gesture.

In Seattle, I felt that life was passing me by, a feeling that I would have for many years. I was a spectator and did not know how to get on the stage. So I decided to leave Seattle. I wrote to my uncle Adolph and asked if I could stay with him and his family for a while. A week later, toward the end of October, I took a Greyhound bus to New York. This time I was not expecting a vacation, nor was I expecting to find a family. Instead, I wanted to start my real life. What that was supposed to be was still quite vague. I did not have many choices given my lack of education, skills, and competence in personal and social relationships.

Chapter Fourteen

The eagerness I felt to start my new life did not prevent me from stopping along the way and visiting cities. I got lucky gambling at the bus station in Butte, Montana. I played the slot machine and won enough money to pay for my trip and then some. I boarded the bus with my pockets full of silver dollars. Traveling by bus across the U.S. is an awe-inspiring experience. I was lucky enough to secure a window seat all the way from Seattle to New York City. I remember being glued to it whether the bus was crossing the Badlands of the Dakotas or approaching a major city. It was as if I were trying to imprint the landscape upon my memory. It was an experience I did not want to forget. Years later when I visited Minneapolis or Chicago, I discovered that my memories of these places were hazy. In fact these cities appeared to be totally different from the places I had visited in 1947. While it's true that American cities change very rapidly, I have also been disoriented in the neighborhoods of Paris which I used to know very well. Memory plays funny tricks on people. I was not an avid tourist; I did not explore the cultural wealth of these cities. I was content to walk through the downtown sections and occasionally take in a movie.

I returned to my uncle Adolph's home in Sunnyside. I had no intentions of staying there very long. He was not very pleased to see me. He had worked hard since his childhood in Romania and felt that everyone around him had to have a project, a job, or a definite plan. If you did not conform to his ideals, you were a bum. My aunt Gisella, on the other hand, was delighted to see me and have me in her home. I reminded her of my mother, and she liked the company. I listened to my aunt and did not criticize her. Above all, I did not yell. Lester was happy to see me, too. He, of course, was in school most of the day. But because of our previous encounter, he saw an ally in me. Adolph's tyranny had to be countered. I was enough of a rebel to challenge his opinions and support Lester's objections. During these confrontations, Gisella never said a word. I've been told that later in life she rebelled against Adolph and that he accepted it. Perhaps that is all he needed all along, someone to challenge his bullying ways. It was not my privilege to witness her transformation.

I set about finding a career for myself. I had been told that the Veteran's Administration offered vocational tests and guidance, so I took advantage of that service despite my uncle's sneers. The tests revealed what I already knew: teaching was the profession for me. I could not see how I could receive a teaching degree with an eighth-grade education and a mediocre command of the native idiom. I was entitled to educational benefits under the GI Bill, but that was for college, not high school. My uncle was not about to finance my education. To him, a teacher was not the kind of professional who commanded either money or respect. Instead, he thought that I should get a job as a salesman. With smarts and determination, I could make something out of myself. I wanted a better life, but to him the world was a jungle where only the strong survived. I disagreed. He told me to move out, hoping I'd learn my lesson. My last order was that I show up for dinner from time to time. We saw each other very seldom after that encounter. It was obvious I did not measure up to his expectations. In truth, I didn't care what he thought of me.

I found a job as a printing apprentice in a nonunion shop on Twenty-third Street, where I was paid seventy-five cents per hour. I rented a furnished room on Thirty-third Street across from the central post office. I paid seven dollars a week for that dark, musty room. With the rest of the money, I managed to buy my food, do my laundry, and see a movie every day. The movies were my language laboratory for English and American culture. I saw all and any genres of movies, from westerns to horror films. I joined a book club in the hope that I would not only enrich my vocabulary, but become conversant with the literature on the best sellers list. I settled into a routine of walking to work while giving myself enough time to gawk at the shops and buildings on my route. Walking to work was a habit I had acquired in Paris, but walking to work in New York was a totally different experience. Manhattan has often been described as a forest of concrete and steel from which nature has been eradicated with broad treeless avenues. The tall buildings made me feel minuscule; this was not a town built on a human scale. I did not feel the excitement of the city, in fact I was rather lonely. If I were not going to the movies, I looked forward to going to work. Three other people worked in the printing shop—two partners and a linotype operator. It was a one-room shop with a cubicle for an office. The partners were of Irish and Italian descent. The linotype operator was a German Jew in his late twenties who had come to the States before the war. He still spoke English with an accent. Together we represented a substantial ethnic proportion of the New York population. The ambiance in the shop was friendly; there was plenty of laughter, and no one seemed to mind the clanging of the machinery or the fumes emanating from the linotype. We all smoked and did not notice that breathing was difficult. It was not easy to breathe in the streets either. My memory of fresh air had been erased.

I did the work an apprentice was expected to do. In addition to sweeping the shop, I distributed type, made proofs, fed bars of metal into the linotype, helped with the proofreading, did errands, and in time was working on a hand-fed press that printed small lots of postcards or envelopes. It was not hard work. I was barely making ends meet, but my basic needs were satisfied. I was neither happy nor unhappy and had nothing to worry about. If it had not been for some recurrent nightmares, I would have begun to forget about the war. In my present circumstances there was no one to talk to about it. My earlier attempts to talk about my experiences had not been successful, so I thought that silence was the only possibility. However, the blurring of one's memory is not the road to heal one's wounds. What is thrown out the door has a habit of coming back in through the window.

Out of loneliness, I turned again toward the radical political movements I found in the city. The headquarters of the Socialist Workers Party (SWP) were around the corner from Union Square, and those of the Workers Party (WP) were on West Fourteenth Street. The world still needed changing, and I thought we were on the brink of World War III. The French were mired in Indochina, the Jews were fighting the British in Palestine, India was struggling for independence, and the Cold War was heating up. Some thinkers were advocating a preventive war against the Soviet Union. The U.S. was the sole possessor of the atomic bomb; it was better to strike now before the enemy had the necessary technology to destroy the planet.

There was a side of me that continued to hope for a better world and another side which feared the coming of the apocalypse. After having seen the aftermath of the concentration camps and Hiroshima and listening to the speeches of politicians, heads of state, and former left-wing intellectuals, my fears were not entirely irrational. Moreover, I was lonely and needed a friend.

I decided to attend the meetings of the WP and its youth organization, the Socialist Youth League (SYL). The WP had separated itself from the myths fostered by the supporters of the Soviet Union in that it did not consider the Soviet Union a socialist state, and it rejected the notion that state ownership of the means of production, in and of itself, constituted a sufficient basis for socialism. Socialism without democracy was not valid. The WP was anti-Stalinist and believed that it was the authentic heir to the thoughts of Marx, Lenin, and Trotsky. The ambiance of these meetings was friendly, though it was always intellectually intense. Political positions were fiercely defended, and I found out later that these disagreements could lead to enmity. I remember having had a discussion with one of the youth leaders at a time when I was questioning an article of faith and being told that people like me, after the Revolution, would be put up against the wall and shot. I do not think he was joking. What I was discussing with him was the necessity of individuals to transform themselves and become emotionally healthy in order to preserve the integrity of the new world that would be brought about by revolutionaries. Thinking of the self was the incarnation of "bourgeois idealism." "What the Revolution needs is discipline, selflessness, and loyalty to the ideology of Marxism," he said. Totalitarian tendencies are not easily discarded. Utopian movements, and Reform movements, like religions, are prescriptive. At the time, so was I, but it is always a matter of degree whether prescriptiveness becomes evil and whether one has the power to impose it. In a futuristic society, my new friend had the potential of becoming an unfeeling bureaucrat.

The youth group I joined was composed of college students who attended either City College or Brooklyn College. Macy was the exception. He attended Columbia University. In the course of time, we became close friends, and while I lived in New York City, he was my best friend. Soon I moved out of my furnished room to share an apartment in a tenement house on the Lower East Side with a member of the group. His name was Richardson, but I am not at all sure that Richardson was his real name. Many party members had aliases, even some of the younger ones. I knew the names of some of the young people around me as well as the names of the public figures of the WP, such as Schachtman and Irving Howe. I knew most people by their first name or their assumed names. This was part of the old revolutionary tradition; the fear that the FBI was spying on the radical groups or watching them very carefully. That fear was not entirely unjustified. When the Attorney General published a list of subversive organizations, the Workers Party was on it, along with the Communist Party and the Ku Klux Klan. It took years of negotiations before the WP got itself off that list. Today, the WP does not exist. I hope that list of subversive organizations is also history. The Cold War had begun. Dissent was being repressed, loyalty oaths were instituted and the terrain for McCarthyism was being prepared. Harry Truman is now touted as one of our great presidents, but he and Attorney General Tom Clark responded to totalitarian Stalinism by curtailing civil liberties.

An "apartment" in a tenement house on the Lower East Side in 1948 was a misnomer for the kind of cold-water flats that were common in the area. Richardson's flat was on the second floor, in the back of the building. There were no windows on that side the street. It was dark, and the lights were on day and night. The apartment consisted of two rooms and a kitchen, set side by side. The front door opened into the kitchen, which included a sink and a bathtub with a steel-enameled cover. The toilet was in the hall, and we shared it with the other tenants. The location and state of the toilet's cleanliness often gave rise to arguments among the renters. The flat was very modestly furnished. There was a gas stove and even a refrigerator. Yet there were still deliveries of ice blocks and coal by men who drove horse-drawn carriages. In 1948, New York City was not yet ultramodern. We had gas heaters to warm our rooms in the winter. But rent control was in full swing. Our flat cost twelve dollars a month, but there were some that were as cheap as nine dollars per month. My share of the rent was less than I had paid for a week in my furnished room. I was delighted to have a place of my own with cooking facilities. Life was definitely looking up. My roommate was charming, quiet, and rarely home. He wanted to be a writer, a novelist, and a poet. He gave me some of his short stories to read. They were all about the rapes and murders of young black girls by white males or about lynching. I had read *Native Son* by Richard Wright, a novel in which a black youth was condemned to death for raping and killing a white girl. In Richardson's stories, white men raped and murdered black girls with impunity.

During the late forties, the Lower East Side was already in a period of transition. Its ethnic composition was changing. Monroe Street was situated a couple of blocks away from the *Jewish Daily Forward* and within walking distance of Chinatown. The street was no longer exclusively a neighborhood of Jewish immigrants from Eastern Europe. The Jews I saw in the streets were mainly older people; their children had moved on to more affluent quarters. The corner store was now owned by an Italian family. I used to get a monstrous ham and provolone sandwich on Italian bread there when I was too tired or too lazy to cook a meal. I was rarely able to finish eating that sandwich despite my healthy appetite. My neighbors across the hall were of Asian descent. The man was of Japanese descent and his wife Chinese. They lived with three small children in a small apartment. The man was a graduate student at the New School for Social Research. He studied philosophy and allegedly smoked marijuana. I never understood any of the philosophical concepts he talked about, but I was dazzled by the intricate language he used. His wife raised the children, and she often bore the marks of having been beaten. They lived on the money provided by the GI Bill of Rights. They were not members of the Beat Generation, but they were close to it. In those days, I did not even like to think that I was living a traditional *Vie de Bohème*. True I was poor and rootless, but I was very far from thinking that life was gay and fancy free. I had no defined goals, nor did I aspire to be a starving artist in my garret, or even an artist at all. There were no girls knocking at my door, and I did not believe that any ever would. My world revolved around work, movies, and meetings. I was surviving, dreaming of a better world where peace would reign and we would all be equal partners in the building of a rational society.

One girl, Helen, did knock at my door. I met her at a SYL party. Girls were always scarce in radical circles, especially in the late forties. I don't remember how I approached her. The standard operating procedure at the time was to ask whomever you were interested in what she thought of a political position. Asking someone what she thought about the Soviet Union was almost a form of flirtation. I learned later that among religious youth, the big question was about God. The dance of seduction may change with the times, but the goals are always the same. Helen was a new arrival from Philadelphia, and as a newcomer, she drew quite a bit of attention from the love-starved boys in the group. Competition was always fierce. At the party's end, I offered to accompany her home on the subway. She accepted, and we got off near the Brooklyn Museum of Art. It was a balmy spring night, so we walked to the museum and sat down on the surrounding wall. Our conversation became more intimate, and Helen promised to have dinner with me the following week. I went home dancing on air.

Helen and I had a very brief affair. She had just left a long-standing relationship in Philadelphia. I was just an experiment in her search for recovery. I accompanied her to the train station; she was on her way to Philadelphia to say good-bye to her boyfriend. When she returned, she made it clear there was nothing between us. She had not given me enough time to fall in love with her. I was left feeling neither pain nor regret, just anxiety about whether I would ever find anyone to love. As far as my experiences in the realm of love went, I had been a lark for Ardis and an experiment for Helen.

While I was living at the tenement on Monroe Street, a few members of the SYL moved into a nearby apartment. They were the nucleus of a diverse group of rebels, musicians, and painters. The first one to appear was Jack Tatarsky, who in many ways became the catalyst for our small community. Jack had graduated with a degree in accounting from City College, but had no intention of exercising that profession. The offspring of a Jewish father and a Catholic mother, he was raised as a Catholic but was now a fierce atheist. He was short, and a childhood accident with a firecracker had taken away the thumb and index finger from his right hand, which he aggressively thrust at anyone he greeted. That was his way of putting the person he faced at a disadvantage; he had no scruples in exploiting the discomfort that his missing fingers could create. That hand of his was a test thrown in your face; you could not ignore it, pretend it did not exist, or that it did not matter. I was always conscious of it. Jack would not allow anyone to forget it.

Jack could have been cited as a classic example of an unresolved Oedipal complex. He could not abide, he said, his father's rigid adherence to the American Dream. According to him, his father had no life in him—a sort of authoritarian, mechanical robot. He felt both pity—to the extent that Jack could feel pity for anyone—and hate for his father and vehemently rejected his values. His mother, he claimed, was full of life and struggled valiantly against her husband's passive acceptance of his lot in life. Jack's rebelliousness had led him to the SYL and to leave home upon graduation. When I met him, he was busy setting up his flat, furnishing it with odds and ends he found discarded on the street or by attending auction houses where boxes and barrels full of treasures were sold for as little as a dollar.

Jack kept insisting that I come over for breakfast some day. I was not sure that I wanted to be involved with him; I had enough skeletons in my closet to haunt me without taking on his. I knew enough about myself then to know that I would try to counsel him. Being an only child, with a history of conflicts and having faced tragedies as well, I felt that it was my responsibility to dispense wisdom. Against my better judgment, I knocked on Jack's door one Sunday morning. He was about to prepare bacon and eggs. In fact the bacon was already sizzling, and the greasy fumes were overwhelming. His frying pan had a half an inch of bacon grease in it, and he was getting ready to fry the eggs in it. I stopped him, horrified by what he was about to do. Deep fried eggs had never been a culinary delight for me. Jack had a habit of opening his blue eyes wide and smiling crookedly whenever he wanted to seduce you or make you feel like an idiot. He began to explain. "Frying pans, especially a cast-iron pan like this one, should never be washed. It makes them better."

"But Jack, grease gets stale, how does that improve the taste of your food?"

"You'll see, Mathis. I've done it this way before, and the eggs taste great!"

The two eggs he served could have been used to sole my shoes. To his dismay, both the eggs and the grease found their way into the garbage can. The frying pan was wiped with a paper towel, and new eggs were cooked in butter.

Jack was an avid reader like the rest of us, but his search was wider than ours. Most of us were looking for a better world; Jack was ahead of his time in looking for alternative lifestyles. He was not content to reject bourgeois values, and he did not want to postpone his life for some distant and nebulous future. He was seeking solutions that could sustain him while struggling against the capitalist system or by taking advantage of certain aspects of it. His book collection always had a number of new titles from the New York Public Library. Any so-called innovation would command his attention and send him into a frenzy of research. For a few months, for instance, we were bombarded by Jack's fascination with hydroponics. With it we could sustain a whole community with vegetables grown in a greenhouse and have no need for expensive land. We could even turn it into a profitable enterprise. Of course we never got to the stage where a greenhouse was to be built, or to where and with what resources the nutrients for the plants would be bought. We never even discussed whether the enormous tomatoes produced would be safe enough to consume. The main thing is that Jack could create excitement among us. He was more apt to say yes to an experiment than we were, even if the experiment should prove disastrous.

In his search for a more rational world, Jack was more focused and more amoral than the rest of us. He believed, like the philosophers of the eighteenth century, that the world could be understood, and that there were laws that governed the universe. All you had to do was to discover the philosophical system that would provide the key to understanding these laws and adapt human relationships to them. Marxism was for him that system: dialectical materialism could not only explain the broad movements of history, it could open the doors to true science. I liked the idea that there was a system, a road to truth, even though I did not understand the intricacies of dialectical materialism. I was more rooted in historical events than I was in theories. The fact that big business in Germany had embraced Hitler and his regime, albeit reluctantly, and that most of Europe had been predisposed to accept and sustain fascist regimes, made it easier to believe that Fascism was a logical outgrowth of capitalism. I could not then, and could not now, tell you what laws of economics made it necessary for Krupp or I.G. Farben to support Hitler in order to save their enterprises. In retrospect, even if they were motivated by the fear of bolshevism, their endorsement of Hitler does not make sense. The fact remains that they and others supported the Nazis, profited from slave labor, and embraced the "Concentrationary Universe." That was more than sufficient for me to condemn the whole system. After all, I had seen first hand the results of the Holocaust and Hiroshima.

Jack had no scruples about being dishonest. He would shoplift in a commercial bookstore but never in a public library, sneak out of a cafeteria without paying his check, and refuse to leave a tip to a waiter or waitress. He claimed that they should organize and demand a decent wage. He would give a wino money if the wino was honest about his plans for the money. Still he decried charity on the grounds that it was only given to assuage the guilt of the giver. Jack thought the state should be responsible for the care of derelicts. He would borrow money from his friends and never pay it back. We were there to share everything with him.

One of the ideas Jack brought to our group grew out of his reading Wilhem Reich's *The Sexual Revolution*. Jack thought that as young revolutionaries, we should direct our energies toward high school students and inform them of their sexual rights. The main thrust of Reich's argument was that sexual repression was the means by which capitalism kept people in bondage. Jack reasoned that sexual liberation would lead inevitably to revolutionary activity. Some two decades later, Herbert Marcuse's *Eros and Civilization* would contradict this theory, claiming that sexual freedom was a way to distract people from political realities. *The Sexual Revolution* quickly became the most circulated book in our crowd. We talked about creating an information sheet and distributing it to high school students. Nothing ever came of it. Jack did, however, manage to find a high school dropout and convince her to move in with him.

Once we had started reading Reich's works, there was no stopping. We were attracted to Reich's assertion that he had completed Freud's work by establishing psychoanalysis on a sound biological basis. All of our emotional problems were anchored in the muscular structure of our body. If you could free the body, you could free the person. If you could get rid of irrational behavior, you could be healthy. If we could have health and socialism, the Garden of Eden would be ours again. *Character Analysis* and *The Function of the Orgasm* combined with dialectical materialism, replaced the Holy Scriptures.

At the end of 1948, other people of our group began moving to Jefferson Street, and a little community began to evolve. Donna and Fred moved in on the fifth floor. Fred was raised in Saint Louis, and Donna had grown up in Chicago. Fred was the political activist of the couple. When we spent time together, Donna would knit with a faint smile on her face. She rarely spoke, and we never knew what she was thinking. I found out later on that some people in the group did not like her. I had no such feelings toward her; in fact, I liked her.

During the spring of 1948, I spent most of my time going to work, improving my English at the movies, attending political meetings, and getting into intense and lengthy discussion with the group who lived on Jefferson street. We talked endlessly about the take over of Czechoslovakia by the Stalinists, the unfolding cold war, and whether there was an alternative to the Washington/Moscow confrontation. A third world war seemed imminent and eminently apocalyptic. However, the questions about our individual lives, of who and what we were or what kind of lives we would have, were far more daunting than the state of the world. We were after all, in our early twenties, and our dramas far exceeded the reality of our banal lives. Naturally, we proclaimed that we were ready and able to change the world.

Having decided that Revolution should come through the sexual revolution of adolescents, Jack managed to talk a high school dropout named Gerry, into living with him. Gerry was only seventeen. Her face was still covered with pimples. Jack set about educating her. Gerry came from Queens; her background was Irish Catholic, and was rebelling against it. From the beginning of their relationship, Gerry was in awe of everything Jack said or did. She became his parrot save for the mystical tones she adopted when speaking about Schumann or Mozart. WQXR or WNYC, the local classical music stations, were on all the time. Gerry's face was soft with a wide-eyed innocence. Jack's was hard and had a mocking glint, along with a perpetual cigarette dangling from his mouth. We were friends, but I much preferred the company of Fred and Donna.

On the fourth of July weekend, Jack convinced me that we should spend three days at Montauk Point at the very end of Long Island. It was not the first time Jack and I had gone away together. We had gone camping and hiking a couple of times in the Catskills. I had enjoyed being outdoors despite the cold of the early spring mornings. Once we had gotten lost on a trail; finding our way back made a very good story that we liked to tell over and over again. Jack and Gerry were going to the beach that weekend and suggested that I invite a young woman who lived in the same building to come along. Ida was in her thirties and earned a living as an artist's model. I hardly knew her, but I had seen her once or twice in Jack's flat so I was surprised when she agreed to come along with us. We went by train and took over a deserted beach. There we went skinny dipping and were burned by the sun, only we did not feel it until we returned to the city. On that trip, I almost got caught in the undertow. Jack took me by the hand and guided me back to shore, which was a good thing since I did not know how to swim. On Tuesday morning after returning to the city, I could not move. I was burning with fever. Ida later told me that she had taken a bath upon her return to the city and that she had become quite ill. I could not go to work, and when I showed up a couple of days later, I was fired. My boss did not accept my excuses or my protestations of good faith.

A week later I found a job at Greer Hydraulics in Brooklyn as an assistant to the shipping clerk. I had to join the union, the United Automobile workers, I believe. I was now a bona fide member of the proletariat. The work was not hard, and despite the monotony, the hours passed quickly. The union contract dictated that we have a ten-minute coffee break in the morning and another in the afternoon. This was the time when people talked about subjects outside of the workplace, pretty much like it happens in most workplaces. I heard a lot about baseball scores, batting averages, and car performance. It was all incomprehensible to me; I was not able to participate or contribute to the often passionate expression of opinions. Where was the class consciousness the radicals were talking about? There was no talk of politics on the job, no hostility toward the management.

As the 1948 presidential election campaign progressed, comments about President Truman or Governor Dewey were occasionally made. I was surprised to hear so many favorable remarks about Dewey; this was contrary to what I had expected. I had been led to believe that union members were always in the vanguard of progress and that the Republican Party exclusively defended the interests of Big Business. The Cold War was on; left-wing politics were regarded with suspicion. Under these circumstances, it was understandable that there was no mention of Henry Wallace and the Labor Party. Nor was there any mention of the Dixiecrats.

There were no black people working at Greer Hydraulics; that may have been the reason I heard no racist remarks. I did my job and was totally bored. This job was far less interesting than the job I had at the print shop, but it provided for my daily needs. For some reason, I was assigned to the machine shop where in addition to sweeping floors and taking away barrels of shredded metal, I was to help the machinists. In time I thought that I might learn how to operate one of the machines and become accepted by my fellow workers and as a worthy member of the union. First, I would have to learn about baseball and digest its vocabulary. Do not think that baseball lore is the exclusive property of the working class; getting excited about a Yankee-Red Sox series is a necessary part of American culture. There was no way I could become an American without becoming conversant about baseball. Some of my radical friends proclaimed that football was more intellectual than baseball, and some preferred the game of chess. But to me, baseball was king—the national passion.

It was during that period that Fred and Donna broke up, and Gerry became pregnant. Macy had moved in with me after Richardson had left. We became the best of friends. One weekend evening while we were dining, Donna and Helen came knocking at our door. None of us had a phone in those days; when we wanted to see someone, we just took a chance and showed up, hoping that we were not intruding. For me this was not strange at all. None of my friends in France, and very few of my relatives, had a phone save for business purposes. So Helen and Donna's visit did not cause any surprise. What did surprise me, however, was that Helen started flirting with Macy that evening, and Donna followed suit with me. I had no idea that Donna had any romantic inclinations toward me. I had always seen her as part of a couple. Since she was usually very quiet, the discussions I had in her presence took place between Fred and myself. It must be said that, with only a few exceptions, the boys did most of the talking. Girls were a minority in numbers and in decibels.

Despite our commitment to emancipation, our loud rejection of bourgeois values, and our affirmation that we were radically different from our conventional contemporaries, my friends and I were basically romantics. I had yearned for a companion, a lover, and a family ever since my return to Paris after its liberation. It was a yearning I did not know how to translate into reality. I was now twenty-two years old. In the four years that preceded Donna's advances, I had tried to imagine what would become of me. Yet, it did not occur to me that I was not ready or capable of sustaining a serious relationship or that I did not have any goals that might define my life's work. I had ideas about changing the world, but I was at a total loss when it came to changing anything in my own personal life. In short, I had nothing to offer except my naiveté, as well as the heavy baggage I carried from my European experience. When Donna started flirting and dancing with me, I forgot about all of that. I was dancing with a beautiful young woman. All I could feel was the trembling of my body, the excitement in the pit of my stomach. Ready or not, I was ready to fall in love with this woman. There was no reason or logic behind it; it was just youth asserting itself. In 1948, we did not have the sophistication or casualness that the present generation has toward love. We were looking to have partners for life, regardless of our vow of fealty to freedom.

Within a few weeks, I moved in with Donna at 59 Jefferson Street. Richardson moved to Harlem, and the flat was passed on to two young comrades. Macy and Helen had a very brief affair. A new chapter of my life started. I was going to begin to learn the ways of a shared life.

Chapter Fifteen

Donna and I started our life together without knowing much about each other. In retrospect that seems to have been something I did a lot. I am not naturally trusting although I am often gullible. But when it comes to love, I throw all caution to the winds. Despite my failures, I have been steadfast in believing that life must go on, no matter what difficulties it brings. Once, after a difficult divorce, one of my friends announced that he was giving up on relationships because of his fear of suffering. I replied that if he were to suffer, he would know he was alive. We both laughed at this, but we recognized that the avoidance of joy and pain was tantamount to a form of death. I was not thinking of any future pain when I moved in with Donna. The excitement of new love was more than sufficient to blur any thought of the future. In love, the present is paramount. The future will take care of itself. It seldom does.

I went to work every day, but at the end of each day, I came home to a very complex woman. Donna did not have a job, and it did not occur to me to ask why she was not gainfully employed. I did not know whether she had ever been in the workforce, nor did I inquire. Like most of the men in my generation, I assumed that I was supposed to hold down a job that would provide for my family. This was a very strong ethos, even in Europe. My mother had always worked; my father did not and could not. That was the major cause of conflict between my parents. It never dawned on me that I could have a life that was not defined by work and the ability to support a family. Working as a laborer at Greer Hydraulics for a meager hourly wage did not provide enough money for a decent life. Though I was part of the working class, I was neither proud nor satisfied with my job. I was hoping for a higher status in life, but I saw no way to reach it. So, we lived from hand to mouth. While I did not worry about the lack of money in front of Donna, I don't think that she felt the way I did about life or money. Money was not important to her, but she wanted to feel secure and be able to afford some niceties from time to time. I was not the first man with whom she had lived, and that accounted for an enormous difference in expectations of each other.

When I came home at night, she was often in a melancholy mood. *What was wrong? Had I done something wrong? Had I failed to do something she expected me to do?* My anxiety level rose every day. I became solicitous, as is my wont, which caused exasperation. Donna had too much time on her hands. She could reflect and mull over her life, especially her childhood. For some reason that she never clarified, she and her brother had been put in a foster home in the early thirties. Though she and her brother were Jewish, her foster parents indoctrinated them in the Christian faith. For Donna, this was both a source of conflict and fascination. I was totally taken aback when she told me that she often dreamt of Christ in Technicolor. I had never been struck by any color scheme in my dreams, nor had I heard anyone else refer to the color of dreams. But the woman I lived with and with whom I hoped to spend the rest of my life was fixated on Christ. That was a most serious problem for the militant atheist I had become. Donna was not religious and did not wear any exterior sign like a cross or a star of David. *What was the dark meaning of her Technicolor dreams? What was she doing about it?* She was seeing a counselor whom she trusted to help her sort out her life. I should consult him too, she said, because in her opinion I had serious problems to solve.

At first, I resisted the suggestion. *Where would I find the means to pay this counselor? How was she paying him?* She replied that he had a few patients he did not charge, and he also had no fixed rates. He charged people according to their ability to pay. If he liked me, he might not charge me, or he might charge me a nominal fee that I could pay when I had the money. This was a socially conscious counselor. *But then, why would I want a counselor?* I was young, strong, and smart. I could solve my own problems. I could not go to a total stranger to discuss my recurrent dreams. In reality, I used to have several persistent dreams that would last for nearly twenty years until my life and self-esteem improved dramatically.

Two of these dreams transported me to Auschwitz where alternatively I witnessed my father's or mother's death. They were both lying on bunk beds just like the ones I had seen in pictures. They were emaciated, almost unrecognizable. As they were dying, I sobbed although in real life, I never was able to cry. I told each of them that I was safe and alive, but neither of them looked at me or uttered a word. In my dreams as in life, we had not said our goodbyes. I was left with my unspoken grief. My third dream took place in Villepinte after my father had returned from Auschwitz. He was with Anna, whom I had evicted from his house. I ran toward my father, but he turned a cold, angry face to me and would not speak. I cried. I sobbed. I pleaded with him. It was all to no avail. I was rejected, exiled from my father's love, and engulfed by his hatred. I would wake from this dream, still dry-eyed. My fourth dream involved me flying to Paris and arriving at my friend Nathan on the rue Rochechouart. No one there was particularly surprised to see me, but I was always at a loss to tell them why I had come back to Paris or what my life was like in the U.S. It is hardly necessary to wonder at the meaning of these dreams. They speak for themselves.

Furthermore, I could not envision that an American would be capable of feeling empathy for someone who had survived persecution and was now lucky enough to be living in God's country. So my defenses were well drawn. I was strong enough not to need help, and even if I were to seek it, there was no one who could help me. Donna insisted that I consult this man, and since I loved her and valued our relationship, I agreed to see him.

Dr. Bradley was in his fifties and had been a Protestant minister before he became a therapist. His age and mane of white hair did not bother me; the culture in which I grew up did not make a fetish of youth. The popular songs of the day celebrated the joy of being twenty years old, but beyond that magical number we were all supposed to settle down and assume our responsibilities. His ministerial background did not instill me with any confidence that he could understand my rejection of faith and any tenet that suggested mysticism. I entered his office with reservations; I was not going to be manipulated by a mere ecclesiastic. Dr Bradley's mannerisms were those of a kind man. He asked me a few questions, and I quickly realized that Donna was the person who most interested him. I decided to play his game, and if he were to take a liking to me, I thought he would become an ally and praise my good qualities to Donna. There are three sessions that stick out in my mind because parts of them border on the absurd. At least, I thought so at the time.

Dr Bradley was what you would call a hands-on therapist. There was no couch in his office, and he did not analyze dreams. We did not speak of the past or even of my childhood. He was, in his own way, a forerunner of Gestalt therapy in the U.S. Dr. Bradley did not question what I was doing now or how I felt about it. Rather he set about changing my beliefs and values. At one session, he started by declaring that he thought Abraham Lincoln was a greater man than Lenin. That was a game I could enjoy. I had very few heroes at that time; all statesmen or historical figures were found wanting in my eyes. I revered the names of Einstein, Curie, Hugo, Zola, and Balzac. My history teachers had failed to instill in me a recognition of "great leaders." The events of World War II had further disillusioned me as it had many of my generation, in the capacity of political leaders to come to the rescue of the masses. Too many of these leaders were either abetting the slaughter, collaborating with the criminals, or simply indifferent to the situation. Lenin was not my hero, but neither was Lincoln. I could amuse myself with Dr. Bradley by pointing out that the Emancipation Proclamation was not what it seemed—drafted in the hope that it would incite the slaves to revolt in the South, helping the war effort. I thought then that slavery had been but a pretext for the Civil War; no one, on either side, cared about the slaves being freed and becoming full-fledged citizens. Didn't the Jim Crow laws still prevail in the South? Was the North free of ghettos? This whole discussion wasted an hour during which my problems were neatly avoided. I realized much later that by engaging in this particular "game," I had lost an opportunity to discharge myself of the history of grief I had been carrying for years. I needed then to begin to harness my energies and find a focus for my life. Comparing Lincoln and Lenin without any serious intentions but the sole purpose of arguing with Dr. Bradley was an arrogant deflection of my very real problems.

In another session, I was astonished that Dr. Bradley started the session by asserting that my nose was a substitute, or a symbol, for my penis. By now I had read enough books about psychoanalysis and spent enough hours with my friends discussing the subject to be aware of symbols and terms such as projection and transference. Still, I was surprised by this turn of events. My nose had never been mentioned in any previous sessions, nor was I in the habit of rubbing, scratching, or playing with it. This struck me as absurd. I did not laugh at this suggestion, as I perhaps should have. Instead, what his question evoked was the memory of Nazi propaganda. As a Jew I could allegedly, be recognized by the length and shape of my hooked nose, which was considered a sign of the satanic character of the tribe of Israel. The Nazis had also painted Jews as being sexually perverse and well endowed. I remember contradicting him by telling him that my nose was my nose and my penis was my penis, all the while suppressing my anger. There was no way he could have understood the source of that anger. He most probably would have concluded that his insight had hit a nerve. My conclusion was that he was a charlatan, but that I'd best say nothing of this incident to Donna.

Dr. Bradley also suggested that I go to college, and that the college I should attend was Oberlin. He had ties to that institution, which welcomed unusual types of individuals. He would be happy to write me a letter of recommendation. I thought this suggestion was totally unrealistic. I had never heard of the place, and I was not about to leave New York City for the Midwest. Besides, why would a college accept anyone who had only an eighth-grade education? I had all sorts of arguments in my arsenal against his idea. One of the most potent being that it was too late to undertake such a project. I was not aware of the openness of the American system of education. I thought that after a certain age, many doors were closed.

When I finally left Dr. Bradley, he emptied his clothes closet. I inherited a package of shirts and a seersucker suit which I never wore. He also forgave me the debt I owed for my therapy sessions. My problems were still with me, but I was working and had settled in a routine sort of life. My relationship with Donna was stagnating. The glow of our first few months together was gone, and I did not know how to revive it. Donna suggested that our relationship would improve if we were to get married and have children. She argued that many couples often had a child, hoping that the baby would cement the relationship. In reality, the results of such attempts tend to deepen the rifts and prolong the agony of a failing relationship. I did not know all of that then, and even if I had, it would not have changed anything. Losing anybody was unbearable. I would have borne any burden to avoid being alone once again. I agreed that we should get married. That's when Jack and Macy arranged to see me by myself to talk me out of the marriage. It's also when I discovered that they had an intense dislike of Donna. They talked about her body language, her pursed lips, and her manipulative character. But it was all in vain. I would not change my mind and was very angry with my friends for interfering in my life when I had not sought out their advice.

Donna and I were married by Dr. Bradley in Newark, New Jersey at Jesse and Helen's home. That modest celebration was to be the last time Donna and I were happy together. Our relationship deteriorated rapidly. We did not have fights or arguments, but there was a deadly silence between us, exacerbated by abstinence. I was quite aware of our intolerable situation, but I did not know how to change it, nor did I have the faintest idea how to resolve our difficulties. Our love had been so wonderful when it began; it was almost magical. I could not understand how it had become moribund, especially with no apparent conflicts. All I could feel was despair and guilt. My marriage was failing, along with my hopes to have a family. Within a couple of months, Donna left me for another young man. I was crushed but could not find neither the tears nor the anger that would have helped me surmount my torpor and depression. I quit my job. I did not bother to show up or notify anyone, and I did not collect my last paycheck. I left my flat and moved in with Macy across the hall. That was the only time in my life I deliberately set out to be without a job and to live on welfare. Summer was coming; the twenty dollars I would receive weekly from my GI Bill benefits would suffice to take care of my basic needs. I could bask in my depression.

During the time I lived with Donna, Truman was elected president of the United States in an unexpected victory over Dewey. At the time, I had not cared about the outcome the election. I did not care which of the candidates would best serve the interests of the capitalists. Besides, I was so involved with Donna that I did not care about anything or anyone, except her. Elections were as interesting to me then as the World Series. I did not understand their importance in American life.

In the spring of 1949. I applied to Columbia University's School of General Studies. The dream of continuing my education had not entirely left me. All I had at that time, beyond my eight-grade French education, was a New York State High School Equivalency Diploma that I had obtained on a whim. I took the entrance exam and to my surprise, was admitted. The GI Bill would provide for my tuition as well as for a small allowance. I could hardly believe my eyes when I read that letter of admission, and neither could anyone else around me. When Donna left me, attending school lost its meaning. What good was school? My fate was sealed.

Another important event occurred at 59 Jefferson street that spring. Gerry gave birth to a baby girl she named Erika. It was an event that fascinated us and also solidified our opposition to conventional medicine, more specifically what we considered the unnatural methods of modern obstetrics. As soon as Gerry became pregnant, Jack, as was his habit, explored the holdings of the New York Public Library and found a book titled *Birth Without Pain*. We all read it avidly. The book put forth the idea that labor pains were not necessary; they were part of the biblical myth designed to perpetuate sexual repressiveness and subjugate women. This was one more way for us to put Western civilization on trial. We decried the use of anesthetics during labor as being harmful to the child. The episiotomy was another evil invention of the medical establishment. Circumcision was no longer accepted as a hygienic measure, nor was it considered a traditional renewal of Abraham's covenant with God. It was a blatant act of symbolic castration. As Jack's parrot, Gerry had no other choice than to have the baby at home, with the help of a midwife. I don't know whether Jack and Gerry discussed the possible consequences of having a baby delivered in a tenement under questionable sanitary conditions or if they were ready to be parents. I am not even sure if they had made a commitment to share their lives with each other.

We all had talked about the subject of abortion and thought that a couple should be able to decide whether or not to have one. Abortion, however, was still illegal and was very expensive. None of us had any money; an unplanned pregnancy meant that a child would be born, kept, or put up for adoption. I must add that Gerry's pregnancy surprised us in another respect. We all knew about Margaret Sanger's work and had heard about a doctor who would fit an unmarried girl with a diaphragm for a very modest sum. At that time, birth control devices, except for condoms, were not readily available. Still we wondered why Gerry and Jack had allowed this pregnancy. They had acted irresponsibly.

We all assumed that Jack and Gerry would keep their baby and start a family. That was part of the honor code of behavior of men and women in 1949. Only a heel would abandon a pregnant woman or desert a woman and his child. When Jack announced that Erika would be given up for adoption, I was shocked although I did not protest what I thought was a disgraceful action on his part. I say his part because I was convinced that Gerry had accepted this solution after listening to Jack's cold way of rationalizing the decision.

Erika was adopted by a couple desperate to have a baby. That was best for the child. Gerry, however, went through a period of insanity, which was induced by the loss of her child and her abandonment by Jack. It is doubtful that Jack had ever loved Gerry. She was part of his ideological package. He was not about to be caught in the web of bourgeois responsibility, and he was totally unaware that he was acting with the same callousness that the sons of well-to-do families had shown in nineteenth-century Europe. It is ironic that this self-proclaimed revolutionary behaved in a manner that was decried by Marx in an earlier century. Jack left Gerry to be with another girl; Gerry dealt with her pain by becoming promiscuous and bragging about each of her new lovers. Each one of them had a better technique of lovemaking than the last. Jack was now relegated to the dustbin reserved for ineffectual lovers. He had been her first, but now he was the lowest of the low. We kept in touch with Gerry for a couple of years, but she disappeared quietly from our lives. Jack and his new girlfriend, Charlotte, moved back to Jefferson Street in the fall.

That summer Macy, in an effort to help me out of my depression, invited me to spend a couple of weeks with his family in Rochester. I arranged for my unemployment checks to be transferred temporarily to Rochester. That could be done back then if the unemployment office was told that I was looking for a job elsewhere. All I had to do was to report once a week at the unemployment office in Rochester. I was not required to show proof that I had sought employment. I was taking advantage of the system without a second thought. The opportunity to get away from New York City and my loneliness were more important than telling the federal government a lie.

Macy and I hitchhiked to Rochester because neither of us had the money for a bus ticket. This was the second time I had hitchhiked in the United States. I can categorically affirm I did not encounter the fabulous adventures Jack Kerouac describes in *On the Road.* Not being able to control when and where I am going at any given time brings about an unpleasant state of anxiety in me. To be passed on the road by motorists always brought on feelings of discouragement and rejection. I have repressed all memories concerning the vehicles or the people who picked us up. I have forgotten where we stopped, where and what we ate, and how long it took us to travel from New York to Rochester. I do remember that I found the landscape of New York State to be magnificent. What a relief from the heat, noise, dirt, and humidity of the city!

I felt immediately at home with Macy's family. It was a real home with a spacious kitchen. It felt lived in. It had an ambiance I had long wished could be an integral part of my life. Most probably I idealized his home. I liked Macy's mother at first sight. She was welcoming, affectionate with her children, and laughed easily. Macy's three brothers and his father also lived in that house. The first morning that I spent there, I was awakened by the sound of prayer. Macy's family practiced Orthodox Judaism. Before going to work or eating breakfast, the males of that family would put on their phylacteries and proceed to do their morning prayers. When I heard these prayers in the fog of my half-awake state, I thought I was back in my grandmother's house. She used to get up and pray after her morning ablutions. Macy's older brother, Yale, was the most devoted and the most rigorous practitioner in the family.

He was not unfriendly, but he never looked at the person to whom he was speaking. He had other idiosyncratic traits, such as always wearing white socks. Macy's father worked as a tailor at Bond's and was active in his union. He struck me as a silent man. Macy's younger brothers, Sheldon and Alan, were typical teenagers. Macy did not practice Judaism or believe in God; he was the rebel of the clan. I was also impressed by the fact that all the boys participated in household chores from cooking to vacuum cleaning. What was even more impressive was that they loved and accepted Macy even though he had broken with family tradition. I had not grown up in a family where tolerance and acceptance was the norm. Moreover, I had never encountered orthodox people of any religious or political creed who would not brand nonbelievers as their enemies. I could not understand why there was no hostility between Macy and his family. In the two weeks that I spent in Rochester, I never heard a word from the family about Macy's atheism. Perhaps that was worse for him to bear than open criticism.

In Rochester I met one of Macy's childhood friends who was to have an extraordinary impact on my life. Marvin was an honor student in English literature at the University of Rochester. He had embraced Marx and Freud. He was attending school on the GI Bill, as was Macy. He had served in Italy and had been, he told us, the heavyweight boxing champion of his regiment. He was a bulky man, full of energy. When you met Marvin you were assaulted by a myriad of ideas and suggestions. In the coming years, I got used to hearing Marvin presenting some fabulous idea or tale as he was crossing the threshold of my door. Some people found him to be offensive and even obnoxious. I was often baffled by his outlandishness, but I was never bored. You could depend on Marvin to keep a conversation going. He had and still has, beyond his bounding energy, a generosity of spirit.

I met Marvin in his apartment near the Rochester campus and was given all the honors papers he had written that year to read. I was supposed to read them right there and then and offer a critique; it is understandable that I might have been initially put off or overwhelmed by his actions. He could also be hurt if you said something unkind to him. After that you might have to spend some time discussing the motivation for the unkindness. Marvin's saving grace, if he needed one, was that he laughed easily at the absurdity of the world and even more easily at himself.

When I met him, Marvin was separated from his wife. He delighted in relating how he had organized his wedding and how he had spent his wedding night. For Marvin the marriage ceremony was a grotesque, bourgeois, and even commercial ritual. This was a normal reaction in our little group of rebels. If we married, it would be quietly, before a judge or minister, without any fanfare. At best there might have been a party of friends to mark the event. This was not Marvin's way. If the ceremony of marriage had a commercial component to it, he was going to take advantage of it and make a profit. His bride wanted a big wedding. It is a custom at Jewish weddings to bring gifts and money to the young couple. Each gift, traditionally, is announced loudly during the feast that follows the wedding ceremony. Marvin calculated very methodically what each guest was worth and how large the check would be. On the strength of his expectations, Marvin and Ruth invested in new furniture for their apartment and negotiated with a caterer. Marvin is a great optimist, and his research is always impeccable. What he buys is always the best and at the most reasonable price. After the wedding, he wanted to know if indeed his expectations had been met. He spent his wedding night adding up checks and cash while his wife was on the phone with her mother lamenting her fate. This was not a marriage made in heaven. Marvin also acknowledged with peals of laughter that the wedding expenses exceeded the revenues. So much for his foray into capitalist venture.

I enjoyed my two weeks in Rochester. We went canoeing on the Genesee river and swimming in Lake Ontario. Macy stayed in Rochester while I hitchhiked back to New York. Our flat at Jefferson Street was almost bare. I slept on an army cot. I did not like it; I did not like the poverty in which I lived. For some of my friends living on the Lower East Side, poverty was a new adventure. They had been raised in middle-class families and were busy rejecting their parents' "materialism." The Great Depression had soured their vision of the American Dream. They wanted, as I did, to change the world. But unlike me, they had resources. They had families to which they could turn in case of emergencies. Many were still in college and had not entered the workforce. I remember going to one of my friend's summer home in upstate New York. His parents were old time radicals, union members with money.

I was not poor by choice. Sleeping on a cot, not owning a decent suit or a good pair of shoes, and not being able to walk into a store and buy what I wanted bothered me. Why would I want a Spartan life? I decided I had to change my way of life. How to proceed and where to begin was the problem. It was obvious that if I did not like my bed, I needed to acquire a new one. That bit of logic was not too difficult to grasp; all I needed was the money for a purchase. I also felt that I was emotionally ill and that I needed help.

My friends and I had read the works of Wilhem Reich, spending countless hours in intensely idle conversations about what it meant to be healthy. The axis of sick-healthy was at the core of our preoccupations. It pervaded our personal lives as well as our social and political concerns. All events, actions, and feelings were weighed and judged on the scale of health and sickness. It's a good thing we were not in power for we surely would have revived the Inquisition. To be judged unhealthy was very perilous for the one being judged. I was strongly reminded of that years later when I was studying the literature of the Holocaust. The Nazis had declared the Jews to be a cancer on the body of Germany and of Western Civilization. We know what happened to that cancer.

I may have talked about my emotional health, but I did not know how to find a therapist or how I would pay for one. Among the groups of young people, there is always a functioning grapevine about all sorts of things. I discovered that Reich directed an Orgone Institute near Union Square. I went to his office, and a secretary gave me the name of one of the therapists who might take me on for a small fee. I telephoned Dr. Gold, whose office was located on Twenty-third Street. After we talked briefly on the phone—which increased my anxiety because I thought him to be brusque and unfriendly—I made an appointment to see him.

Dr. Gold was about five foot six with curly gray hair, a round face, and a round body. I could not read his face; his expression was neutral. His office contained a chair and a couch which was covered by a sheet. The walls were bare. He wrote down a brief version of my life history on a yellow legal pad. He asked no questions and made no comments. He told me to take off my clothes, all of them, and lie down on the couch. Intellectually, I knew what was supposed to happen. The theory and practice of Reichian therapy was based on the notion that the body was a vessel that contained our emotional traumas. Through our musculature and breathing, we controlled our emotions, our irrationalities, and prevented ourselves from living healthily and orgastically potent lives. By liberating our breathing through manipulation, the therapist could help the patient to achieve health. After locating in which part of the body a patient had repressed anger, guilt, or shame, a therapist could help the patient release these emotions. Reich claimed that his methods brought about faster catharses as well as financially less expensive cures. Like Marxism which proposed a scientific theory to unravel the mechanics of history and society, Reichianism put forth a biological paradigm that defined healthy psyches and their relationship to society. A healthy being could not easily be marched off to war an idea that predated the slogan *Make Love Not War*—and could not be caught up in the mystical adoration of flags, military parades, or national leaders. I had read all that, but I was not prepared for the actual experience. The deep breathing and the pressure and pinching applied to the muscles of my body made me feel like I was being assaulted. Both my arms became paralyzed, and I could not move them. I screamed my head off; Dr Gold's examination was relentless. When he finally let me off the couch, I was shaking with tremors from head to toe. If Reich was right about body armor, I was indeed a very sick boy. Dr. Gold agreed to take me on as a patient at the rate of $5.00 per session. That was almost a charity rate. I was to see him once a week.

I walked out of his office, reeling with pain, confused about where I should go. I did not want to go back to my tenement flat; I was afraid I would sink into a state of depression. I felt like I had taken quite a beating in that preliminary session, and I thought that being around people would take my mind off my aching body. I dragged myself to Fourteenth Street where the WP and SYL used to meet, hoping there might be a meeting. Shortly thereafter, two girls walked in; one of them was unknown to me. She introduced herself as Aline and said she had just come from Buffalo to pursue her interests as a dancer and actress. I remember being quite rude to her, and I realized that I was not fit to be in anyone's company. I went home. It had been one of those hot, humid New York City days. I undressed and threw myself on my cot.

That was not to be the end of my adventures that day. At midnight I heard someone banging furiously on my door. When I opened it, Gerry flew in stark naked and crying, threw herself at my feet, and begged me to make love to her. Her despair was overwhelming, but I was in no condition to oblige her. I had never been attracted to Gerry, nor she to me. We did not even like each other. We simply tolerated one another for the sake of our relationship with Jack. I had quickly understood that when Jack left her, she had taken lovers not only to dull her grief, but to improve her self-image. She was also taking revenge against Jack who most likely didn't give a damn about her or what she was doing. Despite my aches, I was able to keep my cool. Since the war, this has been a pattern of mine: I always appear calm when facing a dangerous situation. I may not feel that way, but that is the way I usually react. In any case, I firmly declined Gerry's offer, but I continued to talk to her. After she had dried her tears, I asked her if she had eaten. She had not eaten all day. My cupboard was empty, so I proposed that we go to the cafeteria on the corner of East Broadway, near the *Jewish Daily Forward.* In New York City, food could be obtained at practically all hours of the day or night. Some cafeterias stayed opened twenty-four hours. I had not eaten that evening, either. It was not too difficult to convince Gerry to get dressed and come out with me to get a bowl of soup. We talked until three A.M. I think that Gerry was relieved that I had not taken her up on her offer, and so was I.

Summer was coming to an end. Macy was coming back from Rochester to graduate from Columbia. He was also bringing a childhood friend with him, Seymour Geldin, who was enrolled in Piscator's theater acting classes. The apartment was still bare of furniture, unfit for three people. Jack had discovered an auction house on University Place where household goods could be had very cheaply. For twenty-eight dollars, I bought three beds, a kitchen table with four chairs, a refrigerator, a very large bookcase, a couple of stuffed chairs, lamps, and several barrels of dishes, silverware, pots, and pans. I rented a pushcart and took it all home. It was the highlight of my summer. I began to forget Donna. I was twenty-three years old. I was on my way to health. I would resume my education. Things were looking up.

My problems were not yet solved, but I was beginning to emerge from torpor and depression. Two more events occurred that summer that were to have an influence on my future. The rent was so low on the Lower East Side, apartments became occupied by young people who had broken away from their families to build a life that was not middle class or bourgeois. In addition to radical students like Macy, there were musicians, painters, and dancers—all aspiring artists. I went once to one of their parties where, because of my naiveté, I had to be told some were smoking marijuana. It was called tea back then, and I was told I should not mention this to anyone. In those days, I looked with horror upon anyone who consumed drugs. In my opinion, a drug addict was a dangerous person flirting with madness and death.

Once again it was Jack who became acquainted with a Columbia student, Bob McDonald, who turned out to be, like Macy, majoring in anthropology. Bob had totally transformed his apartment. He had a real gift as a carpenter, a cabinet maker, and an interior decorator. The landlords of these tenements did not care about what the tenants did to these apartments. They made no repairs, no improvements. Their properties, being rent controlled, brought them no profits. Bob's apartment, in our eyes, had become a jewel. Bob was also an impeccable dresser and very formal in his deportment. Years later we realized that he was probably gay. At the time, it never entered our minds. We did not recognize homosexuality unless it was pointed out to us or acknowledged. If you do not see difference, it does not exist. If it does not exist, it does not have to be addressed. As one who had been singled out for being a Jew, it suited me to have all differences blurred. It never dawned on me that I was adopting Anglo-Saxon culture. On the contrary, I rejoiced that I could dislike catsup and not fear for my life. Through Bob, Macy and I were able to get part-time work in the fall at the Institute of International Education. The job would enable me to buy my books and pay for my therapy while I was attending school.

Gerry left Jefferson Street and Jack returned to his apartment. He was having an affair with a girl named Charlotte, also known as Chaindi. Chaindi's roommate was Aline, the girl to whom I had been rude the day of my consultation with Dr. Gold. One evening Jack knocked at my door and invited me to go with him to his girlfriend's house and meet her roommate. I followed him. I was not really in the mood to be sociable. The weekly therapeutic sessions I was attending made me aware of the stiffness and soreness of my body. At the same time, my moods were growing more somber. I was not working and was getting tired of the lack of structure in my life. School had not started yet. I was going to the movies every day, getting to bed late, and not rising until well past noon. I went with him, reasoning that it was a better thing to do than stew at home.

After an evening of exchanged pleasantries, Jack and Chaindi retired to her room. Aline and I were left alone, looking shyly at each other, unable to say either hello or goodbye. Somehow we managed to start a conversation. Conversation is, perhaps, the wrong word. I asked Aline about herself, her life, and her plans. I learned a lot about her that night. Aline was the daughter of a Sicilian father and a Polish mother and was the middle child of three girls. She was raised a Catholic but had broken with her faith. Her sisters had done the same. Her older sister who, she claimed, was her father's favorite child, had married a Jew. He had been welcomed into the family with open arms. This was fairly unusual in the forties. A marriage between Catholics of different ethnic backgrounds was hardly accepted by the respective families, and interfaith marriages were rare. Although Aline complained about the dictatorial nature of her father, there must have been some form of commitment on his part to America as a melting pot or an attachment to his children that was strong enough to withstand such unusual behavior. The father's behavior was made most evident in the ensuing months. Aline hated dinner time for it was a time of strife in her family. She ate very fast and silently in order to avoid conversation. The grievances of the day or of the past were inevitably served with the meals. If silence at the table occurred, that was a boon for her. I judged it to be a total denial of her life. I think her father had been a barber and had become involved in either Democratic or Republican politics and eventually had become a sheriff's deputy in Buffalo. Aline never talked much about her mother or the Polish side of her family. Her mother may have been submissive to her domineering husband, but she did not lack common sense. I remember Aline writing her a letter in which she tried to convey some of her emotional difficulties. Her mother had replied that she should take care to eat three meals a day and when troubled, to get down on her hands and knees and scrub the floor. That way her anguish would be absorbed by her fatigue. Good habits make for good health, she reasoned. Aline was hurt by this response. Her mother did not understand her and was an ignorant woman.

I learned that night that she had dropped out of college after a brief love affair with one of the leaders of the Socialist Youth League in Buffalo. She had followed him to New York hoping to renew her relationship with him. It had not happened. She told me she was still in love with him. At the time I thought Aline was a strange-looking girl who acted strangely, too. She was tall, with a small head and large eyes. She had inherited her eyes and mouth from the Italian side of her family. The rest of her face had Slavic features: high cheekbones and very fair skin. She had a way of holding herself that resembled a bird folding its wings and head upon itself. Her head would bend down and her shoulders would hunch forward as her chest seemed to have collapsed inward. She appeared to have the typical posture of someone who is self-effacing, or who is terrified of being approached. Her voice was often whiny, child-like. I did not think it was cute. However, it was also obvious when I probed a little longer, that I was facing a young woman with an interesting mind—a mind which could become vigorous if only she would allow herself to trust it.

As part of our group activities, we used to go camping at the foot of the Catskill Mountains. Because we had very little money, our camping expeditions and equipment were very modest. We could not afford a tent. Instead we carried a back-pack, a sleeping bag, and some cooking implements. The sleeping bags were most likely borrowed. I do not think I could have afforded to buy one myself. Shortly after meeting Aline, I invited her to go camping with me. That first night under a star-studded sky, inside two sleeping bags zipped together, we became lovers. However, I was not ready or willing to make any sort of commitment to Aline. I was still licking my wounds and quite confused about the future. I was in therapy and quite content to see what might happen. Who knows, health and happiness might descend upon me in a miraculous way. Meanwhile I'd slide along. I went to see Aline and laid out all the reasons why we should not pursue our relationship any further. I did not ask her what she wanted. I felt guilty about the whole affair, but I wanted out, and I thought that was what I got.

In the fall of 1949, I started going to Columbia University under the GI Bill. I had a part-time job at the Institute of International Education where I operated a mimeograph machine. I saw Dr. Gold once a week. I quickly mastered the mimeograph machine and the Pitney-Bowes stamping machine. But I almost lost that job because my manners were found wanting, first to my immediate supervisor and then to the secretaries who came up to our part of the office to deposit mimeographing orders and pick up office supplies. I was totally unaware that my manners were offensive. It was my habit to answer a question to the point, perhaps too pointedly, but I did not intend to hurt anyone's feelings. My manners had been perfectly acceptable in France, but they were not here. I had never known how to put on the charm. In fact, I was philosophically opposed to charm; I thought it to be mere hypocrisy, worthy of a bourgeois society where everything is bought and sold, and nothing is for real. Smiling too much or acting flirtatious were the masks people put on to hide their real selves. But what or who was my real self? I was deathly afraid to find out, and yet I wanted to know.

I found that two serious obstacles still stood in the path of my studies. By 1949, I could read English with good comprehension. But I lacked training in writing—both in handling grammar and stylistic devices. My English compositions came back with dismal grades. If there was help available, I was not aware of it. It was not part of my French education to seek help from a professor. I fared passably in the courses that required no term papers. At the end of the first term, I failed to complete an assignment in American History, a course I had thoroughly enjoyed. I might have persevered had it not been for my therapist's attitude. He disapproved of my going to school. The mind, he said, expends a minimal amount of energy. It wouldn't help me breathe deeply and would most certainly stand in the way of my getting healthy. Getting healthy was paramount in my mind. I could not jeopardize that all-important goal while dwelling in life-negative academia. I quit school without a pang of regret. My health came first. Jack and Macy had also become patients of Dr. Gold. Macy did graduate in 1950 from Columbia College. To be sure, Dr. Gold may have had a purpose in discouraging me from going to school. I trust that it was a purpose that was alien to the anti-intellectual climate that was beginning to dominate American culture. It was surely part of the Reichian revolutionary tenet that the body held the key to a more rational society—a peaceful, loving society, committed to cooperation. Fie on the greedy competitive ethos that led to wars and repression! True, my intellect might have been an obstacle to my emotional life and an ally in the damming up of my energies. However, the contempt I developed or adopted toward the life of the mind was not justified. In the almost four years I spent with Dr. Gold, a balance between mind and body was never struck. That work was left for me to finish. The irony of denying any role to the intellect is that the intellect is one of the means used to deny itself.

Meanwhile, life at Jefferson Street continued with a sort of community of young people, most of whom attended college. Macy had come back that fall, and Seymour, the aspiring actor, had arrived shortly thereafter. Jack and Chaindi, lived downstairs. Val and Victor, another young couple, had moved into the flat that Donna and I had once rented. Young people were always dropping in. We had to develop a hands-off policy in regards to our refrigerator. It had been raided too often, leaving us without the necessary supplies. For some people in the group, that was not much of a problem. For me it was not only a breach in etiquette, but a major cause of anxiety. The fact that I had experienced hunger a scant decade earlier had left its scar. To this day, I cannot tolerate an empty refrigerator. The only difference is that I now can laugh at myself for still hanging on to such an irrational fear. Hunger resembles torture and provokes a loss of trust in the world.

Among the people who knocked at our door was Aline. She came every weekend and stayed overnight. Though we had declined a commitment, we were lonely and young. Seymour, who had not broken with family traditions, found our bohemian way of life unacceptable. He once qualified our place as an emotional bordello. From its lack of order and the intensity of our emotional discourse, that is surely what it was. Yet, these friends took the place of our families as we were blundering our way toward adulthood.

Early in 1950, Macy found a studio apartment on the corner of West Fifty-seventh Street and Ninth Avenue. We decided to rent it together. It was, I thought, a charming little place, well-heated, with hot water and parquet floors. The old woman who had been renting it was retiring and was eager to sell us her modest furniture for a modest price. The studio was still rent controlled at $37.50 per month. I was now working full time at the Institute of International Education, so I could afford it as well as the cost of my therapy twice weekly. Seymour moved out of Jefferson Street. We gave our flat to Aline along with all the furniture we had acquired at auction. Moving uptown was painless and full of promise.

Chapter Sixteen

For Macy, Jack, and I, participating in Reichian therapy signaled the end of our connection with the Socialist Youth League. As non-Freudians, we were not accepted and could not in turn belong to an organization that did not embrace our principles. We had become convinced that revolutions would inevitably fail if the revolutionaries paid no attention to their emotional health. In time, power without health would transform the revolutionaries into bureaucrats. Freedom would become nonexistent, and repression the norm. Our first task in changing the world was to change ourselves, to become healthy and free. We had no idea how all consuming that could be.

This new direction affected our social lives. We had to convert some of our friends or find people who were similarly engaged. Reich and his theory of the orgone became, for a while, household words and even attracted the attention of the media as one of the new fads which they denounced. If the conventional press was hostile to Reich and his methods, we reasoned that Reich was on to something that threatened the medical establishment, and beyond that, the fabric of society. We must surely be on the right track; truth was on our side.

Aline was among the first to join our little group and find a therapist for herself. Marvin had come to New York to earn a Masters at Columbia University. He also adopted Reichianism, but did not abandon his socialist ideals. To this day, he has remained faithful to democratic socialist ideals. He was proud to report that his therapist was not a pincher. Once again he had acquired the very best, opining that pinchers were basically incompetent in breaking down the body armor. Chaindi followed in Jack's footsteps. Pretty soon we became acquainted with a number of people who were undergoing treatment. They seemed to be coming out of the woodwork.

Creative work and the orgasm were the hallmarks of a healthy life. Dr. Gold was not very understanding about my lack of means. He was almost peremptory in telling me to make money: "You need money! Go out and make money!" Imagine! He had no philosophical position on money, no theories either. You need money in this world in order to survive. Well, you earn what you need, it's as simple as that. Your sex life is a bit more complicated; it involves your body armor.

Around the time my job description at the Institute of International Education changed, my relationship with my immediate supervisor also improved. Mrs. Stovall's initial hostility had disappeared; either she got used to me, or I was watching my mannerisms. I made up for what I lacked in finesse by my hard work. I was impressed with Macy's ease at work. I don't know how he did it, but the people in the office took an instant liking to him and never wavered in their feelings. I've always had to work hard to win people over. Unlike Macy, I was not a quiet person. I often felt awkward and did not know how to hide it. I imagine that I impressed people as being somewhat strange. The personnel officer at the Institute had called me in to propose that I work as a maintenance troubleshooter. I was scared to death. Tinkering and fixing things, whether they were electrical or mechanical, was not one of my strong suits. When he explained I would not have to do any repairs that entailed professional experience, I was relieved. My new duties were in fact easy to discharge; they required more brawn than brains. For the rest of my tenure at the Institute, I replaced light bulbs, moved desks, and adjusted the height or backs of office chairs. It was a good experience for me. I came to know everyone at the Institute and learned that a smile, as well as the quiet acceptance of absurd or frivolous requests, went a long way toward maintaining friendly relationships. It began to teach me that there are levels of seriousness in the workplace. The trivial and the inconsequential must be treated seriously, without the slightest comment about their nature. Although I was doing something menial, it raised my self-esteem that I could do it. I had always considered my hands and eyes as a handicap, but they were now helping me to gain a certain measure of self-respect. The fact that I had taken on and completed tasks that initially had frightened me and was holding on to my job and my therapist meant I was making progress. I was not earning the kind of money that Dr. Gold insisted I should earn, but I was paying my rent, my therapist, and buying my groceries. I felt lucky to be able to do that much. Dr. Gold's insistence that making money was easy and simply a matter of will baffled me. When I tried to resolve that problem a few years later, it cost me dearly.

My love life was not very stable. Aline and I kept breaking up and getting back together. But neither our separations or reconciliations were filled with drama. It could be said that our relationship was permanently unstable. At that point in our lives, it would have been impossible for either one of us to say we loved each other or that we loved or even liked ourselves.

There were too many times when I was unapproachable, which caused Aline to cling to me and whine. I felt guilty about my cruel behavior and feared I might become violent. I never did. I do not recall having any angry arguments or even disagreements with Aline. In my eyes, she was too fragile to tolerate open confrontations. According to her therapist, Aline was schizoid. I was inclined to believe that she was, though I doubted her therapist had told her any such thing. Beyond feeling unhappy, lost, and depressed, I could not have put a clinical label on my problems. There were moments when Aline and I managed to have some good conversations on a wide range of subjects. She was the first person whom I told with some details about the war and how I had survived it. I listened to her stories about her battles with her family. It was good to discover I was not alone, and that somebody else had been raised in a dysfunctional family. It was also good to discover that, in her childhood, Aline had been a fighter. I realized that by leaving home and coming to New York City where she knew no one, she had shown spunk. Had she battled with me, I don't think our relationship would have been as muddled as it was.

I came home one afternoon and found Macy all excited. He had just bought a table radio-phonograph, but we didn't have a table to set it on. We put it on the floor, in the corner of our dining/living room and alcove kitchenette. That was the first new object to appear in our new studio. This acquisition was as a kind of revelation for me. I discovered long-playing records and the Sam Goody's store in New York City. We all owned radios at Jefferson Street and listened to the classical music played on WQXR and WNYC. Sunday nights were reserved for Jack Benny and Fred Allen. The Sunday *New York Times* was a must. Listening to your own record and holding it in your hands was almost a magical experience, reminding me of the first book I won as a prize in first grade. For many years, I rummaged through the secondhand bookstores on Fourth Avenue and Broadway. I could get lost looking at books. I began to have the same experience going through the stacks of records at Sam Goody's. Once in a while I could afford to buy a paperback, but records were a luxury. Macy had bought two records with the phonograph, Mahler's *Songs of a Wayfarer* and Copland's *The Plow that Broke the Plains.* I listened to them endlessly. I decided that if I ever had enough money, I would be happy to live in a room full of books and records. That seemed to me the ultimate in luxury, a never-never land of my own.

Macy and I began to meet people who were also undergoing therapy. It seems logical to me that Macy, who was more socially adept, discovered them and began to build a network. In today's terminology, they would be called a support group. We began to hold meetings to study Reich's works. Our therapists would most certainly have disapproved of this kind of activity. Dr. Gold was emphatic about his dislike of gossip and intellectual discussion of therapy. Reich had labeled many of these activities an "emotional plague" that underscored "life-negative attitudes." As I reflected upon this statement later in life, I should have been aware of the manipulative nature of that language. I had experienced the devastating effects of Nazi propaganda; Marxists as well as other brands of radicals were experts at creating lexicons designed to arouse indignation. Freud and his followers invented a vocabulary that quickly pervaded intellectual and artistic circles. At parties or other social gatherings, the use of that vocabulary could be devastating. One could be swiftly dispatched to the dung heap of some unacceptable neurosis or accused of harboring a bourgeois trait by an "emancipated" individual. I should have been wary of this new language, but I was only too eager to adopt it. Like many young people of my generation, I needed something to believe in. Today we call this spiritual needs. We can do that now, for we are not afraid that the world is about to explode in our faces. In 1950, the future still looked bleak. The world needed healing. Me, too.

Our group met the first time and perhaps the last, in an apartment in the Bronx. I thought it was very posh, very bourgeois, and far more formal than my uncle's house in California. The stuffed chairs in the salon were elegant, not made for the likes of me to sit in. I thought that the people at this gathering were as apprehensive as I was about the conversation and where it would lead us. I was afraid of not being intellectually sophisticated enough to participate in the discussion. It soon became obvious that most members of the group were more interested in gossiping about their individual treatments—which they were not supposed to do—and passing judgment on each other than discussing theory. It was disappointing. Once again the original purpose of a group I was joining had been foiled. However, it was almost reassuring to meet people who, at first sight, appeared attractive and were serious about healing themselves. Despite our differences, we were equally screwed up. Within our group, we were free from social disapproval. In 1950, it was very risky to tell anyone in the "real" world that you were emotionally or mentally ill. Even in the late sixties, one of my colleagues at Oberlin College whispered into my ear that someone on our staff was unstable and seeing a therapist. There was a great deal of shame attached to a person's inability to solve psychological problems by oneself.

One of the consequences of joining a new group is that new relationships occur. One of the women in the gathering took an instant liking to Macy. Evelyn was in her early thirties, divorced, and had an eight-year-old daughter who was being raised by her ex-husband and his new wife. She was a waitress in mid-Manhattan but let it be understood that it was only a temporary job. Shortly after our first meeting, Evelyn and Macy became involved. This relationship would lead Macy into a very strange financial adventure.

Before I relate that story, however, I am going to write about one of Evelyn's more impressive habits. When Evelyn came home from work, she used to strip off her clothing and walk around her apartment in the nude. It was her way, she claimed, of being natural, of rejecting society's repressive constraints. She had no qualms about opening her front door in the buff or disrobing whenever I was present or even alone with her. However, her nudity was to be entirely respected. It was not to be interpreted as a sexual signal. Any sexual gesture while she was in that condition was considered a symptom of sickness. She could, at the same time, publicly celebrate her natural body and demand you pretend that it was not there. Your own body, of course, had no relevance. After witnessing this exhibition a couple of times, her naked body left me indifferent. Instead I was outraged by her attitude. I felt violated, denied as a person. It had the effect of making me feel hostile toward the cult and practice of nudism, particularly if its ultimate goal was to desexualize individuals in the name of nature.

I saw less and less of Macy. He was, for all intents and purposes, living with Evelyn. I became more involved with Aline. In the fall of 1950, she moved in with me. But, she kept the flat on Jefferson Street; we had broken up and gotten back together all too often. I was often impatient with her and intolerant of her mannerisms, especially her theatricality and her little-girl act. When she was not functioning in these modes, a bright, incisive woman would emerge. If I were open to her, we could spend some marvelous times together. Perhaps we could have forged a lifelong relationship. I was not ready or willing to commit myself to her. I do not believe that she was ready to make a commitment either.

While Macy and Evelyn were living together, Evelyn's ex-husband, Joe, moved to New York from California. He was an electronics engineer and a self-proclaimed genius. He occupied part of Evelyn's apartment with his wife, his daughter, and a friend named Orin. Joe had a scheme that would make them all rich. All they needed was some capital to start this great venture. The scheme that Joe had devised was ingenious, and as I understand it, not without merit. It consisted in charting the patterns and results of betting at the races. Joe had it all worked out on paper. He thought there was a relationship between the way people bet and the outcome of the races. Betting and winning correlated in cycles. At its high point, the cycle showed horses that were favorites winning. At a lesser point, the favorites came in second or third. At the nadir, they lost. If one could chart the insights of the bettors, one could make a fortune. I am told that following the races would bear out Joe's theory. They all pooled their resources. Macy even cashed his war bonds. They began to savor their future wealth. Macy never apprised me of his future plans; the whole affair was hush-hush.

There is always an unforeseen problem with any get-rich-quick scheme. The plan does not account for the fact that, in reality, most people are not disciplined enough to adhere to the plan. In the excitement of betting, Joe began to forget the plan he had devised and started betting irrationally. Between the joyous living and the wild betting, the investment capital melted away at warp speed. Macy was devastated and penniless. He came to the studio one Sunday, broke into tears, and threw himself on the bed. That's when I learned about his misadventure, and that he had lost all his savings. I was to learn much later that Joe had a history of starting projects that somehow never succeeded. I believe that Macy's relationship with Evelyn began to cool after that, partly as a result of having allowed himself to be seduced by the lure of instant wealth. We were very good friends, but there were boundaries that we never crossed. We never mentioned any details about our therapy, nor did we ever discuss any other intimate subjects. The only time that Macy ever intruded into my life occurred when I was about to marry Donna, and that was most likely at Jack's behest.

Meanwhile, in the fall of 1950, I was trying to establish some order in my life amidst the tribulations of my relationship with Aline and the anguish my visits to Dr. Gold incited. My earlier difficulties at the Institute of International Education had disappeared. I was almost proud that I had not only overcome some of the problems my attitude had created, but that it was possible, in this milieu of college graduates, to be liked and even respected. Macy had moved out and was living with Evelyn. We saw each other on a regular basis, so our friendship did not wane. As I reflected upon it in my latter years, I realized that our affection rested upon our struggles to accommodate our lifestyles, to make compromises, in short, to grow up. True, we had shared the same ideologies when it came to changing the world: either Trotskyism or Reichianism. There is no doubt in my mind now that these "isms" were far more a means to change ourselves than to change the nature of the cosmos. The world was surely a mess, given that the Cold War, McCarthyism, and the Chinese Revolution were in full swing, but my own life was nothing to crow about. My beliefs were clearly some sort of screen to hide the discomforts of my existence. Despite the fact that I doggedly traveled to Dr. Gold's office every week and returned home with a body aching from the pinching and poking of my muscular armoring, I felt no miraculous transformation. I had learned to gag in order to liberate my diaphragm, but I was still vainly waiting for my chest to heave long and deep. I didn't dare complain to my therapist or my friends, lest I be accused of having embraced the all-encompassing emotional plague. One had to pretend that one was making progress. Never mind the pain, the depression, the sadness, the loneliness, or the feelings of unworthiness. The body armor was being broken down, was it not? We were in the avant-garde of a new Revolution. It would have been tantamount to blasphemy to deviate and dissent.

Aline had resumed her studies at Brooklyn College, intending to obtain her BA in English. She had a fine sense of the artistic, although at times, she struggled mightily with language. Finding the precise expression for her perceptions seemed to mirror the extent of her confusion with her realities. That was perhaps also at the center of her creative aspirations. She had trained as a dancer, desired to become an actress, and later in life a writer. I saw her on stage several times in the ensuing years. I always saw her, not her performance. Her favorite role at one time was that of Blanche in *A Streetcar Named Desire*. Discussions about literature and life filled many of our evenings. We were very serious, but we laughed too. Aline had a tendency for flubbing language: her most charming and significant malaprop was her writing idolatry when she meant adultery. It was most likely the same in her mind. She did get angry at me once when I sold my political library. I was turning away from Revolution, and that was not yet acceptable. I was also resentful of her inability to participate in the routines of life. It was up to me to cook and do the shopping. Most of all, I could not tolerate her withdrawals, her dark moods. I had troubles of my own and told myself wrongly or rightly, that I could not afford to wait for someone else. That spring saw our final break up, but we remained friends.

My legal situation with Donna was also solved that spring. Donna sued me for divorce on grounds of adultery. At the time, those were the only grounds permitted for divorce in New York State. The courts granted divorces if there was circumstantial evidence that adultery had been committed. An old law even prescribed a fine and jail sentence for adultery. If an adulterous couple was shown in a compromising situation, that satisfied the courts. Of course lawyers and their clients were adept at fabricating circumstantial evidence and avoiding perjury. Judges were also reluctant to jail people under an antiquated law. I had also read in the newspapers, of a case about a man who had been denied his American citizenship because he had been convicted of adultery. Though I was not yet a citizen and in no particular hurry to become one, I was in no way willing to risk jeopardizing its eventual possibility. That year was not a good year for liberal policies. McCarthyism was in full swing. Once again the mood in the United States, fueled by the fear of Communist conspiracies, was turning toward a reaffirmation of traditional moral values. These were the years when togetherness was touted everywhere. *Ah! The wonderful years of Levittowns and Organization Man! Where have you gone?*

The other way to end a marriage legally was to take up a brief residence in the State of Nevada or to seek an annulment. I had no other choice but to seek an annulment. Donna agreed to that procedure, and Jesse recommended one of his lawyer friends to take my case. It would cost two hundred dollars, which at the time represented a fortune. I appealed to my aunt in California. She flatly refused: If my wife wanted a divorce, she could damn well bear the financial burden. Our telephone conversation was the last communication we had. At various times in my life I've looked for her name in the telephone book and even made some phone calls, to no avail. I have lost track of that side of my American family.

My lawyer was very careful to explain that what I had to prove in court to obtain an annulment was that Donna had intended to not keep any of the promises she had made when we got married. I had to prove that the marriage ceremony had been conducted under fraudulent conditions and was therefore invalid. I could not, for instance, go into court, claim that Donna had promised to have children and now refused. That was not fraud. A person is entitled to change her mind. A promise had to be made with the express intent of not being fulfilled. And the accused would have had to admit before a witness that her intent had been fraudulent. Macy agreed to be such a witness. Before we went to court, we were told that the judge, Peter Schmuck, had a reputation for irritability. The lawyer warned us not to react to what the judge might say to us. The annulment would be granted in due course. An appearance in court, before an official, is always an unpleasant experience for me. Sitting in the witness stand, telling a story that was untrue made me tremble. At one point, the judge asked where I came from and where my wife came from. He then added under his breath, "They all bring their dirt here." The annulment decree was granted. I paid the lawyer in installments. I believe that the divorce laws of New York State have changed. If divorces are still painful, I hope that the proceedings are perhaps less farcical.

After graduation Macy started to work as a counselor at the Wiltwyck School for Boys in Esopus, New York. The school, a residential facility, operated under the directorship of Dr. Papanek, a prewar refugee from Vienna. Dr. Papanek's reputation rested on the work he had done in Vienna with homeless boys after W.W.I. His project paralleled the work that A.S. Neil had undertaken in England during the same time. It operated on the philosophical premises that democracy and self-government by the children was the road to their rehabilitation and the way to restore them to health and prepare them for a productive life. Their writings reflected the successes of their methods. Summerhill is a name that resonated in the sixties and seventies among the educated classes of America. Floyd Patterson and Claude Brown were celebrities that came out of Esopus.

The boys at the Wiltwyck School ranged from six to fourteen years of age. They were assigned there by the courts of New York City. They ran the gamut of abused or abandoned children, as well as those who had been convicted of thievery and arson. This was a school without walls, gates, or guards. Children who ran away, mostly to rejoin a missed parent, were brought back either by their counselors or the state police. No punishment or reprimand was ever administered. When I worked there later on, I heard complaints from some of the counselors that the runaways were given ice cream upon their return, thus creating an incentive for further escapades. In my opinion, the ice cream signaled that the child was wanted. Of course, the institution's policy did not necessarily square with the longings of the child.

When Aline and I separated in May of 1951, I moved to a friend's apartment in the Bronx. Miki Bernardik was about forty-two years old. To most of us, anyone forty and over was considered old. We had met Miki through the Reichian discussion group and continued to see him occasionally. He was married, had children, and had a good job as a fund raiser at the Jewish Federation. Why was he in need of therapy, we wondered? Our tolerance and understanding for anyone in that age bracket were almost nil. We certainly hoped and asserted that by the age of forty our emotional health would be in fine shape. There was another man, age forty-three, who had appeared in our midst with severe alcohol problems. He discoursed about health continuously, looking exclusively at Aline. After he left our flat, Aline and I would have performed rituals of exorcism, if we had known how to do them. Miki was entirely personable, with kind eyes and an open face. His marriage was not a happy one, and he had conflicts with his father. He did not know how to resolve his dilemmas. Neither did we. For a few weeks, I had the use of his home while he and his family went on an extended vacation.

Through Macy, I began to meet some of the people from the Wiltwyck school. One of them was Herbert Nixon, who called himself Nick. He was a big man with a booming voice and a very expressive face. Nick was in his forties and worked as a counselor at Wiltwyck. He was full of life, and everyone liked him. He was not college educated, but he seemed very wise to me. The details of his life, I would bet, were incredible; I would have loved to hear him relate them, but beyond his mask of friendliness and laughter, he was impenetrable. I wanted to leave the Institute of International Education because there was no future for me there as a handyman or troubleshooter. It was time to find a direction, a focus to my life. I was twenty-five years old. I had bungled a marriage, taken part in a failed relationship, and spent almost two years in Reichian therapy. Was it not time to find a job where I could both be useful and earn a decent living? In this mood, I approached Macy and Nick to ask if there was a possibility of me working at Wiltwyck.

My experience with inner-city kids was nil, and my academic credentials were nonexistent. All I had going for me was my idealism. It was discovered that my experience as a camper might be useful. The school was planning to have a camping program that summer. Nick would be in charge of it, and I could be his assistant. On Nick's recommendation, I was hired for three months. I was only one of two white counselors; the rest of the staff was black as were most of the children. Once again, as I had been in France, I was a minority with the most important difference that I was minority within a minority. Nonetheless, despite my lack of experience and knowledge, I felt confident that my idealism, shored up by my Reichianism, would prove to be most useful in the supervision and guidance of troubled children. Macy, who had worked at Wiltwyck, was spare in the details of daily life at the school.

I expected to spend the whole summer in the woods, but the administration at Wiltwyck was remiss in implementing its summer plans. Instead I found myself in charge of a dozen kids. There was supposed to be two counselors per group, but the way the schedule was arranged meant that I took charge of the group three and a half days per week and was off the rest of the time. Our day started early and ended late. Sometimes, we had night duty as well. When I was free, I could travel back to New York City to unwind. Because of my lack of experience and lack of direction, I found the job to be quite stressful. Despite my good intentions and my theories about freedom and self-governance, I was not up to the task of guiding the children in the most elemental ways. At times I would lose my patience, yell, and become quite angry. The kids were testing me, and I was not, in my own eyes, making the grade. The staff did not feel that way. Despite the overt philosophy of Dr. Papanek, counselors would punish and even hit the children. I could sense that I might be equally tempted, and I did not like it.

One could be tested in the least expected ways. One evening, as I was going through the dormitory, a boy threw off his blanket and began to frantically masturbate. I understood immediately that he was trying to provoke a scene, so I did not respond. When I reported the incident to the Assistant Director, hoping to get some advice for the future, she told me angrily, or perhaps just forcibly, that I should have sat down with the boy and asked why he was doing what he was doing. I thought that her advice was the stupidest I had ever heard. I was probably more concerned with my needs and my self-image than I was with those of this boy or any one of the boys.

That summer we did manage to have at least one week of camping. It was there under the tent that I learned about a game they called the Dirty Dozen. It began when one of the boys started talking about another boy's mother, followed by the boy's reciprocation. Soon the meanness of the game would escalate. The object was to see which boy would loose his cool, therefore losing the game, and resort to tears and violence to end it all. Nick allowed the game to go on until he judged the violence had reached its acceptable limits. Most of these children had either been abandoned, abused, or neglected by their mothers, yet in public they clung desperately to the idealistic fantasy. These tough kids believed, or made believe, that they were loved. Nick thought that by letting them fight he was helping them deal with the anger they felt. A bloody nose was the least of their problems.

At the end of the summer, I was asked to stay on as a permanent counselor. I was afraid I would not be able to survive without losing my commitment to nonviolence, so I refused. Besides, a new love and renewed hope was waiting for me in New York.

Chapter Seventeen

I met Gloria at Wiltwyck that summer. She had come with a friend from New York on a Saturday to attend a party. Her friend, Frances, knew Nick and had encouraged her to come and meet men. It was a Saturday night at the end of June. Once in a while, the counselors and staff members would have a party and invite their friends. Before I had taken the job at Wiltwyck, I had given myself a lecture about not getting involved with anyone, especially not with any woman from a different race. I had enough problems to solve, and the last thing I needed was to take on an interracial relationship. I believe that I must have discussed this with Macy, unaware of the inherent racism of my thinking. It seemed totally rational to me at the time. The last thing I wanted was to have to face society's hostility. I had paid a heavy price during the Nazi occupation, and I felt I was entitled to a life free of racist hatred, wasn't I? True, I believed in equality and that mixing the races would end racism, but that did not have to begin with me. After all there had to be some peace in my life, some time to relax and have fun.

However, the mind often works in one way while the emotions work in another. I had forgotten the ancient Pascalian dictum that the heart has reasons of which reason itself is ignorant. My resolve not to get involved with anyone came quickly to an end when Gloria and I met. Flirtation has never been my strong point; I have been accused of being aloof or abrupt when I was simply timid and anxious. To be more precise, I foresaw my defeats before I was in any sense engaged, and I was afraid to take the first step until it was absolutely necessary. The evening was practically over before I asked Gloria to go for a walk with me. Gloria was a striking woman. At twenty-five, she was tall, with large facial features, copper-colored skin, a radiant smile, and a wonderful melodic voice. I had never seen an Indian woman outside of a Hollywood movie. Besides, most of the actresses who portrayed Indians were white. I did not find out about Gloria's origins that night; I had to pass some tests first. She had to make sure I liked her as she was, not for some exotic reason. Gloria was looking for someone who did not carry the prejudices of American culture. She liked foreign men, but among the Americans she favored young, Jewish intellectuals. Much later in our common life we used to joke that Gloria hated everyone regardless of race, creed, or national origin—but some of her best friends were people. The supreme test I had to pass would prove I was in no way attracted to her older sister, Elizabeth. I understood this very quickly. Gloria told me that most men preferred Elizabeth. Elizabeth was prettier, lighter colored—almost white—with thick curly hair that the straight-haired Gloria envied. She was the darling of the family, but she was selfish and unscrupulous. Elizabeth was smarter; she moved with ease in the white world and cared only for Elizabeth. If I wanted to stay in Gloria's good graces—and I did—I had to make it clear that I was not and never would be attracted to Elizabeth. Despite the competition, they were very attached to one another.

The first night that we spent together I had to pass an altogether different kind of test. One of the ways Gloria used to earn money was to pose as an artist's model. She did it for art schools, as well as for individual painters. One of the things that offended her deeply when she disrobed, were the oohs and aahs and the allusions to Gauguin. She understood or sensed that these reactions were not quite innocent. She recounted how she used to divorce herself from her body as she stood naked before an audience. She did not relish being a form and hated being the object of some exotic fantasy. Fortunately for me, I made no comment about her body that first night. I only asked why she was hiding behind a closet door as she undressed.

The ultimate test was meeting her family. At this stage of my life, becoming involved with my lover's family was the last thing I wanted to do. Experience with my own family had taught me that it was best to keep one's distance. To me, families were nothing but organisms of repression. I could easily identify with André Gide's cry of *"Familles, je vous hais!"* (Families, I hate you!). Of course I wanted a family of my own, but I thought that it would be a new kind of family where the children would be raised without the hypocritical shackles of conventional morality. My children would be authentic people. Gloria, too, wanted her children to be part of a new world, but unlike me, she had a family she loved. Her family was complex, and her relationship with her sister was just the tip of the iceberg.

Gloria's father was born in the San Blas Islands between Panama and Colombia. He was a Kuna Indian. He became a merchant seaman, was adopted by a White captain, and was known to some people as Jim Foster. I knew him as Antonio Miguel, which was not his real name either. He had entered the U.S. by jumping ship, which was not unusual in the first quarter of the twentieth century. The borders of the U.S. were open; stiffer immigration laws would not be imposed until

1924. By that time, Tony had married and had a child on the way. We learned later that Tony had gotten married in San Blas and had abandoned his wife and son. Besides his three legally recorded children, we do not really know how many children he sired in his lifetime. There are a number of stories of children showing up at his door, looking for their father. Some are even said to have attended his funeral. His wife denied these children access to their father. If this bothered Tony, we never knew. It did not seem to bother his three children. They recognized that a girl from the neighborhood looked very much as they did and was most likely a sister of theirs. Still, they took no interest in her. Neither they nor their mother carried any grudge on account of Tony's infidelities. His wife always glowed as she spoke of her husband's good looks. She had more serious problems to deal with besides his philandering; mainly his alcoholism and its devastating consequences on the family.

Gloria's mother's family history are more complex. She was baptized Elmira but was always called Ella. She was the youngest of eight children, three of whom died as the result of a croup epidemic. I've never been able to unravel the ethnic origins of Ella's mother. She was part Rapahaneck Indian, a tribe that had its roots in Virginia. I was told that she was part white and was very fair in color. She married John Spencer, a black man, who was allegedly related to Frederick Douglass. The truth of that assertion is doubtful. It is useful, however, to the family mythology. John Spencer was an educated black man from Baltimore. When Elizabeth Ashton, an Indian woman from the back country of Virginia married him, she was marrying up. In Virginia, she hardly had a legal status. When my daughter Monique researched the family history, she found documentation for her great-great-grandmother Ashton, but none at all on her great-grandmother Ashton—which suggested that she was illegitimate. It is likely then that her father was white, given she was described as pale. Elizabeth's children always referred to themselves as Indians. That made life somewhat easier in New York. How this marriage came about at the end of the nineteenth century remains a mystery. Nor do I know how this interracial couple fared in Brooklyn or whether they were considered interracial in the first place. They were simply people of color. Gloria reported that her neighborhood was mainly populated by Italians, and that beyond the occasional war whoop, they were tolerated and even protected from severe harassment. Still, being whooped at leaves children with scars.

From all accounts, Elizabeth Spencer was a domineering woman, a religious woman, and was very protective of her children. Her three oldest children, George, Frank, and Ida, never married. The family suspected that Frank was gay. He always had young men hanging around the house and collected the lamps he retrieved on his sanitation route. Hardly a word was said about his sexual orientation, but his collection was a target of merriment. Very often he greeted us with: "Come and take a look at this, it will knock your eye out." He proudly lit all his treasures and regaled us with the saga of his discoveries. After his death, the family discovered that these "garish" lamps were indeed valuable and that his current protégé had made off with a substantial number of them.

Gloria remembered her grandparents quite well. She was struck by her grandmother's habit of hiding behind a curtain whenever a stranger entered her home. It does not take a genius to figure out that this woman was living in fear of the world outside her home. That fear may have been irrational but was entirely understandable. In the Virginia of her youth, Indians had a lower status than blacks and many of them, especially the half-bred, chose to be black. Blacks were allowed to own land, the Rapahanecks were not. That fear was passed on to her children. Today we recognize this phenomenon as internalized racism.

Her two youngest children did manage to marry, most likely against her wishes. Ella and her sister Elizabeth, or Lizzie, married Kuna men from the San Blas Islands whom they sometimes referred to as savages. They often excluded their husbands from family matters. Ella, Lizzie, and their husbands lived together in the beginning in their parent's house and later on in the same apartment. The two sisters lived out their lives together. Ella was very fond of telling people that when she lived in her mother's house, she would prepare a huge meal for her husband, who would visit his mother-in-law on the lower floor and put away another huge meal. Tony could never say no to food or drink. Lizzie's husband was given the name of Joe Henry. Thanks to his hard work, both the sisters and the children had food. Tony was a hard worker, but he often came home empty handed, having spent his entire paycheck on drinks.

Reluctantly, I agreed to meet Gloria's family. I was a bit scared too. By that time we were living together, and I did not know how I would be received. In 1951, living together without the sanction of the state or a religious institution was still a rare practice, except in radical or bohemian groups. Fifty years later, the imagery of that evening is still vivid. I can see a little lady coiffed with a chef's hat, opening the door with a wide smile on her face and giggling as she greeted us. That was Aunt Lizzie—sweet, unknowingly funny Aunt Lizzie. Then, I met the rest of the family. There was Ella, probably as nervous as I felt, smiling, flirtatious. Joe came next, extending a limp hand, and then Tony, who greeted me with a hmm. I am sure that my jaw was agape and that I must have been staring at everyone all evening. I found myself in the midst of a family where warmth and laughter were evident. The unpleasantness would come later on. For the moment, I was surprised. There was no hostility or opposition regarding our way of life.

Gloria had reluctantly moved in with me that fall. She had left her parent's home the previous spring and was living by herself in a flat on the lower West Side of Manhattan. She enjoyed her independence. The prospect of giving up her first apartment made her anxious. What would happen if things did not work out? Besides, I was upsetting some aspects of her life.

"Gloria, instant coffee is not acceptable. Spaghetti sauce has to be made from scratch. Salad dressing does not come out of a bottle. Steak will taste better when it is not fried until it feels like shoe leather. Vegetables are not to be boiled to death. A meal is better for you when it's balanced."

My cultural background had instilled a sense of order and decorum in me. Beyond nourishment, eating was a ritual, a celebration, and the ultimate proof that humans were not animals. No doubt my European upbringing was a decided good. I insisted on it.

Gloria should have thrown the jar of instant coffee at my head. Instead she set about incorporating my dos and don'ts into our daily life. I was to be reminded often of this as proof of many sacrifices she made for me.

One aspect of Gloria's character I never understood and made no effort to understand was her need for romance and heroes. That need is best illustrated by this story: as a child growing up in a religious Methodist family, she had pinned a picture of Jesus above her bed. The family would also participate in revival meetings from time to time. That was for Tony's benefit who according to Ella was a fine man, if only he would stop drinking. In her teens, Gloria had a crush on Nelson Eddy. Down came the picture of Jesus, up went the picture of Nelson Eddy. When Frank Sinatra became the teeny boppers favored idol, Gloria played hooky from school, stood in line at the Paramount in Manhattan, and screamed along with the rest of the enthusiastically demented teenagers. It was the first time she and her sister Elizabeth had ventured out of Brooklyn alone or had been on the subway by themselves. Frank Sinatra's picture replaced Nelson Eddy's picture just as the latter had replaced Jesus. Not only did I not understand the worshipping of matinee idols, I openly sneered at the practice. Romantic behavior, flirtations, coyness, the whole gamut of seductive ploys, revolted me. I thought that a person ought to know his or her own mind and avoid playing hypocritical games. It did not occur to me that my total rejection of bourgeois romanticism was in itself a form of romanticism. I thought that the expectation of total, uncompromising honesty was the hallmark of liberation and equality. Gloria believed that too, but she also wanted to be wooed as a woman, not treated as a comrade. I inflicted many emotional wounds in the name of ideology. I did not buy flowers, candy, or open doors for Gloria. The time was not yet ripe for opening a door for a woman to be considered a macho act. When it became de rigueur in the seventies I delighted in the irony. By then I had learned the importance of opening doors for everyone. However, some of the damage to my relationship with Gloria had been done. It's easier to talk about equality than to really practice it.

Gloria had a beautiful mezzo-soprano voice; she was much praised for it and asked to sing on many occasions. Unfortunately for her, she did not have many opportunities to study with a professional. Nor did she have a family with the knowledge or the financial means to help her develop her talent. Gloria did get a voice coach, but even that could not be sustained. She was taught songs and arias. In the late fifties, she enrolled at the Henry Street Music School where she continued to train her voice and learned to read music. Since childhood, however, academic subjects had been an obstacle for her. Written words and abstractions confused her and made her feel inadequate. Her family simply accepted the fact that Gloria was not ever going to be as successful as her sister Elizabeth. According to her mother, Gloria was Gloria: "She'll be all right. She'll take the rag off the bush." We never knew what that expression meant. Of course frustrated and angry, Gloria responded with tantrums and earned the nickname, "battle axe." It was not until later that we guessed she had probably been left-handed and was forced to become right-handed. This affected her ability to drive: She always confused right and left. Gloria tried hard to learn to read music but did not quite succeed. It was yet another example of her inadequacies. Gloria could argue for hours with consummate skill that she was ugly and stupid. One dared not laugh or agree with her; she frustrated any effort to contradict her. Although I appreciated the irony of the situation, I was struck with utter disbelief.

I think that of all my friends from that period, Gloria really bonded with Macy and Maren. The rest of my friends she either tolerated or despised. We have all of us experienced a similar phenomenon.

Many of Gloria's friends had an enormous influence upon our life together. Because they came from such different backgrounds and had such different ideologies and life experiences, I learned from far more than I could appreciate at the time. There was Sidney, Gloria's first lover, who had been a student at Union Theological Seminary in New York. In the late forties and early fifties, that school had a reputation for being progressive and radical. They had met at a Lisle Fellowship meeting after he had become disenchanted with religious asceticism. Through psychological therapy, Sidney discovered that he liked sex better than God. When I first met him, he was trying to sell log cabins. He was looking for an alternative life style where his needs would be satisfied and his schedule would remain flexible. I have already mentioned that Jack Tatarsky had similar goals, but Jack was a scalawag and was totally unscrupulous.

Sidney was honest and sincere in his quest for a different kind of life that he hoped to share with a perfect woman and perfect children. Gloria was perhaps lucky that she did not fit the bill because she had her own dreams of perfection. They did not coincide with his.

I also met Ralph who had been another one of Gloria's lovers. Gloria's complaint about him, as I recall, is that she could not start a fight with him. Ralph was a radical pacifist. He came from West Virginia, had trained to be an opera singer, and refused to serve in any capacity during World War II. As a result he served time in a federal penitentiary, participated in hunger strikes, and was often beaten. He and others like him were deprived of their citizens' rights. In a personal relationship, however, radical pacifism may result in the refusal to confront the issues that inevitably arise. Passive resistance is not only a way to frustrate, it may also be a way to leave a messy situation intact. When Ralph joined the chorus of a budding opera company on Bleeker Street, we went to hear him. After all, Gloria was a singer too. But we never became friends.

Gloria had also met Bayard Rustin. He had come to her church and had related his ordeals in the South as he tried to break the Colored Only rules and wound up in jail. In a recent article in the New Yorker, I learned that Bayard Rustin had once been a communist. When I met him in 1953, he was involved in the War Resisters League, along with his friend Igal Roodenko, who, like Ralph, had spent time in a federal penitentiary for refusing to aid the war effort. Because my family had been destroyed by the Nazis and because I had seen, if only in photographs the consequences of that war, I could admire their idealism, their courage, and their determination, but I could not embrace their refusal to oppose radical evil, by force if necessary. To this day, I do not believe that Hitler could have been stopped by passive resistance. Neither Gandhi nor King were dealing with a social order like the one Hitler engendered. I was eventually told that both Bayard and Igal were gay. I had known gay people before, and my response had always been one of indifference. It was not my business, and it made no difference to me. In the same way, I proclaimed that a person's color made no difference to me either. Still I refused to acknowledge the differences around me. To strive for a world in which equality is the norm means that differences must be overlooked. I was a person of my time.

In the brief time that Gloria lived by herself, she became acquainted with her neighbor, Sally Sullivan, who was to become a dear friend. Sally's life was one that I could hardly imagine. Born and bred in Iowa and educated at Grinnell College, she had chosen to teach in a Japanese relocation center during World War II rather than enroll at Columbia's School of Journalism where she had been awarded a scholarship. In retrospect, I am convinced that her choice was as much due to serendipity as it was to her idealism. Or perhaps I could say that the idealism makes the serendipity probable. At any rate, the time that Sally spent in the relocation center had a profound effect on her. Gloria told me that Sally had joined the Congress of Racial Equality, or CORE, and picketed Palisades Park in New Jersey to protest its discriminatory practices. The picketing had turned ugly, and Sally had wound up in jail. In those days, I took it for granted that the most peaceful demonstrators would suffer violence. But in the late forties and early fifties, racism and civil rights had not yet permeated the nation's consciousness.

Sally and CORE were influenced by the examples of Ghandi and the pacifists. CORE was mainly a white-dominated organization. The number of blacks at CORE parties was sparse. When I met Sally in 1951, her marriage was coming to an end, and she was raising a little girl. She had married a much older man, who had leftist ideas but was societally and economically dysfunctional. At that time, most of my friends were driven by ideology rather than by the urge to fulfill personal potentials. Macy had majored in anthropology at Columbia where he had been more involved in Socialist politics than thinking of what he might do in the future. Marvin was working on a MA in English but went first to work at Wright Aviation before he tried his hand at teaching. We were all preoccupied with the transformation of society. Even as we entered into therapy, the oft stated goal was to be in a better position to create a better world. Sally, her husband, all of us, were not involved in the American Dream. We were likely to condemn bourgeois values, which for us meant any type of conventional behavior. It is important to remember that we were in our mid-twenties, and were the heirs of two bloody world wars, totalitarian societies, and genocide. The fact that the Truman administration had instituted subversive lists, McCarthyism was rising, and the flag of the red scare was being furiously waved made it even more imperative than ever to transform society. Fundamentally, we were politically impotent. By the time that the struggle for Civil Rights had blossomed and that the Sexual Revolution was in full swing, many of us had gone in a different path.

For me the question of earning a living was always a daunting one. Unlike my friends, I lacked a formal education. Moreover, my Reichian therapy had fostered in me a sneering attitude towards academic endeavors. My therapist had stated in no uncertain terms that intellectual pursuits did not produce a sufficient amount of healthy energy. I wanted desperately to be healthy, so much so that reading a book provoked guilt. The state of my body "armor" was to be the only barometer of my existence. At the time, I did not make the connection between my therapist's attitudes and the perennial distrust of American culture towards "eggheads." Nor did it occur to me that certain forms of McCarthyism might have invaded the mental health community. Reichians who decried the ill effects of nationalist and religious mysticism cleaved to a mystique of their own—the body and the ultimate sexual orgasm. Needless to say, I bought into that. I was going to be healthy no matter what.

Regardless of what I thought or felt, it was necessary that I bring home a paycheck. Gloria and I had started our life in common, so work had to be found. I tried to find a job through the newspaper ads as well the local employment agencies. For a week or so, I tried to sell vacuum cleaners door to door. I quickly understood that that was a job for which I was totally unfit. I had tried that once in Paris; I could not stick my foot in any door. Besides, any form of rejection deepened my sense of unworthiness. Eventually, I found a job as a laborer in a sweater factory in New Jersey. I had to travel an hour each way just to move boxes around all day. I left after a couple of weeks. The people at the employment agency asked me whether I would like to learn to operate a small offset press. I thought that this would be my opportunity to learn a trade. I was sent out to Witty Brothers, a quality clothing firm. The firm had bought a multilith with the intention of reducing the advertising costs, but needed someone to run it. A three-day training period ensued. I was back in the printing business that I had entered in 1947, but this time I was no longer an errand boy. I had a machine to conquer. Witty Brothers was a an old-fashioned business and very paternalistic. It was not just a place to work; it was a family. Most of the company's employees had worked there for a long time. There were actually three brothers running the firm. The oldest one, Ephraim, Effie, was the company president and had a fondness for gadgets. He would often come down to the basement where I worked and discuss the possibilities of the press. He eventually bought a hand press, with which I did all the display advertising for the store windows. I was paid a dollar an hour. That was normal for someone in an entry level, semiskilled job. As Marvin was to tell me a few years later: "If anyone of us ever earned five thousand dollars a year, we'd be living on easy street." In 1951, any man earning that kind of money would have been considered a good catch. Not having enough money to buy a decent suit or pair of shoes bothered me. For me, these would have been the hallmarks of comfort. I could not afford these things, so after three months at Witty Brothers, I asked for a raise. It was denied. So, as a good self-respecting rebel with solid principles, I resigned. My therapist had encouraged me to be assertive and take control of my own life. I was not going to be pushed around by an oppressive, greedy organization. I was called in to talk to the firm's vice-president, who proceeded to lecture me on work ethics, salary policies, and my future. I was, after all a twenty-five-year-old immigrant with very few prospects. It was in my best interest, and that of the firm, to reconsider my decision to resign. He would like, he said, for me to become "a member of the Witty family." I was astonished. This was not the sort of behavior I expected from an American boss, and a Capitalist, at that. I stayed. I had learned a lot from my experiences on French farms, at the Institute of International Education, and at Wiltwyck. Most of my work relationships at that point had a human face. My ideas about the owner of a big enterprise were abstract, stereotypical, and wrong. My uncle Adolph's conviction that society was a jungle, "a dog-eat-dog world," was inaccurate. A better image to describe the world is that of a zoo.

Gloria did not have a steady job although she would occasionally substitute at a day care center. These centers did not require the teachers to have any kind of certifications, that would come later. She also continued to model whenever she was asked by the Arts Students League or an individual artist. She decided to enroll in the School of General Studies at

Brooklyn College and earn a much-desired college degree. At that time, matriculation in any of the city-run colleges meant free tuition for high school graduates who had passed the New York State Regents exam. If a student had failed the Regents, he or she, for a modest sum, could enroll in evening courses. If the student earned a certain number of credits and maintained a B average, he could apply for regular status and free tuition. Many people in New York City took advantage of this program. Gloria had difficulties with language. She was articulate, but when it came to the written word and assimilation of grammar rules, she became inexplicably confused. Today, this would be recognized as a learning disability and help would be provided. For Gloria, it was a curse. It made her feel unworthy and incompetent. Without adequate reading and writing skills, college was a harrowing experience for her. I did not understand the complexities of Gloria's situation. If she could just overcome her emotional blocks, she would succeed. Emotional blocks, neuroses, sick attitudes—those were the catch phrases I tossed around to describe her difficulties.

Beyond the problems of work and learning, we were very busy nesting, being in love, going to parties, and taking modern ballet classes. We also had to confront our fear of racism. Interracial couples were rare in 1951. WNYC's motto that New York City was a place where eight million people lived in peace and harmony was not entirely accurate. There were the hostile stares and glances everywhere: on the subway, the bus, and the street. I thought that we should ignore them, but it was really impossible. Gloria had lived with that hostility her whole life. At best, some people perceived us as being exotic—that is strange, abnormal, the other. Other people spat at and on us in the streets. Once we were almost physically attacked by a gang of roughnecks in Greenwich Village. Our landlord threatened to evict us; the neighbors did not like Gloria's presence. I was subjected to a long interview with him until he finally realized that, as a lawyer, he was on the board of his local NAACP.

Our first year of living together was without a doubt the wildest, most carefree period of our existence. We met a lot of people and went to a lot of parties. It almost seemed to me that I was forgetting the traumas of the past. I began to see that I could be happy. I was in love. I was loved, what else could anyone want? If the world would leave us alone, we could build a wonderful life. In fact, something happened in 1952 that proved it was possible to negotiate with society.

Gloria was hired for the summer as a camp counselor in Rangeley, Maine. Rangeley was not a just another beautiful summer place where vacationers from New York City took refuge from the heat and humidity. Rangeley was also the residence of Wilhem Reich. Emil and Penny Caccavo, the people who ran that camp, had been associated with Reich. Emil was a teacher and he and his wife had established the summer camp on principles of self-regulation put forth by Reich and A.S. Neill. According to Reich and Neill, children raised on these principles would grow up free of neuroses and be creative. Given the opportunity, children would create a democratic, peaceful world. It was up to the adults to understand and accept the fact that children innately know what is good for them. Adult rules were simply a microcosm of societal oppression. Many of us, especially the ones with no children, knew all about child rearing. All parents, in our opinion were by definition oppressors and castrators.

For some reason, relations between Reich and the Caccavos had become venomous. Reich had declared that Emil had become infected with "emotional plague" and had become a *persona non grata* in Reichian circles. Neither Gloria nor I were aware of this at the time. Gloria's only problem with the job was that we would be separated for the summer. I did not want to leave my job at Witty Brothers. The Korean War had provoked a mild recession, and jobs were not easy to find. Besides, I liked my job. I was eligible for a paid vacation, but that would not give me much time away. I requested leave without pay, and to my surprise, it was granted. I would spend a month with Gloria in Maine, but what would I do there?

Gloria arranged a meeting with Donny Simms and Renée Davis who where both camp counselors to discuss my qualifications and expertise. It turned out that I could do the cooking in exchange for room and board. Renée had an MA in early childhood education, a profession she would practice until she was swept up in the Day Care Movement of the sixties. She and Gloria became very good friends. Renée, who was in her early 20s, was unhappy about her weight. She was the first vegetarian I ever met, and an addict to failed diets and Weight Watchers. Soybean hamburgers may have been healthy fare, but I found them unpalatable. I found Renée's kitchen paraphernalia fascinating. It was cuisine art long before cuisine art became popular. Renée was seeing an analyst, but her favorite topic of conversation outside of teaching was men and how few of them she could attract. She was at times outrageous in her comments, which was not an uncommon trait among all of us. There are two particular incidents that shed some light on her character. The first occurred on a Sunday afternoon in Greenwich Village when we were almost physically attacked by a band of roughnecks. Renée stood in front of us and very calmly said: "Okay, if you want to beat up somebody, you can start with me." She believed gang members had a code about not beating up women. I am not convinced that she was absolutely right. Still, we admired her courage. Another time, after we had moved to East Twelfth Street, Renée spent the evening at our apartment, and we talked late into the night. She lived on the West Side of the village, and her only means to get home was either to take a taxi or walk. Renée always walked. She could not be persuaded to take a taxi.

"Renée, that's a long walk. The streets of New York are full of desperate and dangerous people."

"I'll be perfectly safe. Who would attack me anyway? I have no money."

"There are rapists out there. You read about rapes every day in the newspapers."

"Well, if a man tries to rape me, I'll tell him to wait a minute so I can go home and get my diaphragm." Then she laughed.

One of the theories that was prevalent at the time, and still hasn't died out completely, is that rape victims have something about them that invites rape. It was currency that there was an emotional link between the rapist and his victim. I think that it was Sartre who had proposed that there was perhaps a complicity between the torturer and the tortured. At that time, the Marquis de Sade's writings were in fashion among French intellectuals. The psychopathology of rape and torture might have been a fit subject to study in the wake of World War II. Yet rape and torture are totally unacceptable in human behavior.

Donny was an elusive personality. He was born in the Midwest and was once a theology student. When I met him, he had become involved in Reichianism, the messianic movement of educating children to be totally free of the negative strictures of bourgeois society. At the moment, he was associate director of the camp at Rangeley and Renée's sometime lover. I never knew to which Donny I was talking, the committed educator, or the taciturn, brooding man he often turned into. He once burst in on me while I was showering and said: "Mathis, you scare me. I am afraid of you," and ran away when I asked him what it was in me that provoked that outburst. I never did get an answer. Over the years whenever we met, a distance remained between us. We never became friends. In 1952, I felt weird enough.

Donny's outburst added to my feeling that I really did not belong anywhere and that I was not doing anything that really mattered, outside of living with Gloria. I lost sight of Donny when he left New York and became a television cameraman.

When I arrived in Rangeley that July, I found Gloria very upset. She hated Emil Caccavo's manner of directing, and therefore, she hated Emil as well. Emil was, by profession, a high school teacher. He was energetic, self-assured, and loud. He most likely reminded Gloria of the men in her Italian neighborhood. Emil wanted things done fast, without questions from anyone. This rubbed Gloria the wrong way. She was responsible for his son Steve and a few other three-year-olds. Gloria could not function without some sense of order or planning. She had fought all her life against the disorder of her family. Spontaneity and creativity had to have a context. This did not quite fit in the philosophy of the camp and the fact that Steve was the only child of the directors and was to be treated in a very special way. Gloria did not complain about the situation, but Emil acted atrociously toward her. Emil was kind of gruff and could get on people's nerves.

I had no problems with Emil despite the fact that I wound up painting the front of the house even though I had been hired to cook. I had looked forward to cooking at the camp for a month, but it turned out that Penny did not trust anyone in the kitchen. Anyway, when I realized that lunch consisted most often of peanut butter and jelly sandwiches, I was happy not to be in charge. Personally, I feel that peanut butter and jelly spread on Wonder bread is an abomination. It may have some doubtful nutritional values; but the taste and texture are atrocious. I did some cooking when Penny and Emil left for a week, but my main job was to scrape and paint their house. Of course I was too slow a worker for Emil, and too inexperienced as well. I was too meticulous with my scraping, and I laid on too much paint—all probably true. Emil and I had a conversation that I never forgot and that I often used to advise my students, in latter years.

"Mathis, you're a smart guy. Why don't you get back to school and learn a profession? Is there not a job you really would like to do?"

"I have always dreamed of being a teacher, but I am past twenty-five and I only have a high school equivalency diploma. It would take me years of night school to earn a degree. I'd be too old."

I did not lack for excuses.

"Time will pass by anyway. You'll get older whether you like it or not. Why not pursue your dream? You won't be any worse off than you are now, and most likely things will be much better."

I did not listen to his advice, but I never forgot it. I passed it on whenever the occasion arose, even if I knew the person I was talking to wouldn't listen. I had to hit rock bottom before I was ready to hear that kind of advice. I may have had a dream, but I had no right to it. Not me. It was incredible enough that a woman loved me. I did not really believe that it could last. Something would happen to spoil it. I knew.

I had a happy time at Rangeley. There was a lot of laughter in between the anguishes of life. I remember two young boys, brothers, the oldest not quite ten years old, who prefaced all his objections with, "I've read the Constitution, and I know my rights!" There were the walks I took at night with Gloria. Once or twice, we observed the Aurora Borealis. You could see the huge white flames dancing in the not-quite-darkened skies. I had to leave camp at the end of July and go back to Witty Brothers. While waiting for Gloria to return, I tried to take acting classes with a man who taught the Stanislavsky method of acting. I did not pursue the classes beyond that August. Instead

I remained a fervent advocate and admirer of method acting. In retrospect it is evident that I was striving to find a key or a method to unlock a life which was without direction.

Chapter Eighteen

As in most relationships, our first year together was one of discoveries, surprises, and emerging conflicts. New people and friendships came into our lives. Gloria enjoyed folk dancing with the Hermans. I went with her a few times and took an immense dislike to Mary's strident voice. I was in my third year of Reichian therapy and was all too quick to judge people by physical traits that denoted a less-than-perfect emotional health. I thought that Mary's voice was an unimpeachable sign of her hysteria and authoritarian character. Her voice amounted to a direct attack on my principles. I gave up on folk dancing, thinking it too rigid for my taste. Gloria gave up folk dancing, too. Folk dancing, she claimed, was a good way to meet people, especially men. Folk dancers were different from ordinary people. Their political attitudes were liberal and left-leaning. It was in that milieu that Gloria discovered that foreigners and Jews did not have common racial prejudices. Her relationships with Indian males had always been poor. She was too dark-skinned for their taste, she claimed. Her black heritage was not accepted in her family. In New York City, it was better to be Indian than black. It was clear that her friends and lovers would originate among liberal Europeans or rebels.

Naturally, we had to adjust to each other's friends. Given our expectations that friends ought to be mirror images of ourselves, this was not easily accomplished. We mistook our censorious judgments for analytical acumen. Gloria accepted Maren and Macy instantly. That friendship has lasted for more than fifty years, through both good and bad times. We were privileged to know Maren's family, whose history reflected the major events of the first half of the twentieth century. Maren's family was the first non-Jewish German family that I ever met who had an anti-Nazi history and a commitment to the arts. They were a revelation. In 1951, the wounds of war were still fresh. I regarded anything or anybody German with a deep suspicion that at times bordered on open hostility. Unlike many Jews in the U. S., the question of whether I would buy a Volkswagen never arose. Day-to-day living was difficult enough. Buying a car was a purely academic question. Back then I believed that the whole world was collectively guilty for the Holocaust and World War II. Naziism had risen in Germany, but the rest of the world was complicitous. I could point to historical events that had fostered the rise of totalitarism and to the many failures to counteract it. Hitler and Mussolini could have been stopped early in their careers. They had not been taken seriously and were considered clowns. The threat of bolshevism and of world revolution was far more serious. It might have made good sense to support these clowns, who had shown us how to deal with Bolsheviks and the other undesirable elements in society. The radical left with its egalitarian programs was far more threatening than the rantings of a racist corporal or the posturing of a reformed socialist. Law and order would guarantee the status quo. So, Hitler and Mussolini were not seen as a threat. That perception cost millions of people their lives.

Maren's parents were early members of the German Communist Party. They had been swept up in the waves of Revolutions that followed World War I. For many intellectuals and artists, either from the Right or Left, war was seen as the ultimate demise of the values that had dominated Western civilization since the Renaissance. The cult of the individual had led to the sanguinary destruction of the whole. Depending on your outlook, you either leaned toward an edenic world of social equality governed by consensus, or you yearned for a world where the strong would lead the weak and impose strict moral values through a strong leader. For both Heinz and Lisa Muller, the Russian Revolution represented a crucial historic moment in the liberation of humanity from hunger and wars. They had been cultural pioneers, in ridding themselves of bourgeois values, especially Heinz who was brought up in a bourgeois family and earned his living as the director of a toy factory. By contrast, Lisa came from a very poor background. The spirit of revolt had permeated their childhood. Their marriage, at a very young age, defied traditional conventions. Lisa joined Mary Wigman's dance classes and after her exile from Germany opened a dance school in Amsterdam. By the time the family settled in Amsterdam, their circumstances had changed dramatically. Lisa and Heinz were divorced, Heinz had remarried, and Lisa was living with a Dutch Jew, Job, who was later deported and killed. Heinz and Lisa had three children: Ruth, Jan, and Maren. After Hitler came to power, Heinz was arrested and sent to prison. Thanks to a police officer who had similar political views, Heinz was set free and went immediately into exile. He left for Paris. Lisa and the children went to Switzerland, then to Paris, and Holland. Toward the end of the war, Maren and Lisa were returned to Germany and were "liberated" by the Soviet army. Lisa often retold the story of how she protected Maren from being raped by their "liberators."

She had dressed Maren up to look like a retarded child. Maren was one of the very few women who escaped rape in Germany's Soviet zone. Yet Lisa was accepted to become a member of a municipal government of East Germany, hoping to bring about a new world. She and Maren were fortunate to escape East Germany in 1948, after which they immigrated to the U.S.

In 1941, Heinz had been able to immigrate to the U.S. and had taken Ruth and Jan with him. In New York Heinz found a position as the director of a private progressive school. Ruth had married and divorced. She had a child and was working as a film editor in the city. Jan, who had a history of heart trouble, was a painter. He had trained with Hans Hofmann and was continuing in the tradition of German Expressionism. When I met all the members of that family in 1952, I was awed. Heinz was living in Pennsylvania and working on a dairy farm. He was a tall, handsome man who was still on friendly terms with his ex-wives. Jan was impassioned about his painting. Lisa was learning to be a practical nurse for prematurely born babies; she was also trying her hand at painting. I think what struck me most was the manner in which their judgments were definitive, almost without appeal. How could anybody be so self-assured, especially Germans? In our small group, we had definite ideas, but we were open to discussion and contradiction. A favorite expression among radicals and New Yorkers in those days was " You're wrong! And I'll tell you why." I remember a scene in which Lisa asked Jan what he felt about one of her paintings. He proceeded to dissect it with, I thought, an uncalled-for severity, calling the composition faulty, and her color scheme askew. The method reminded me of a rigorous French explication de texte, but the tone was peremptory. It seemed to me that it was not so much a critique than it was an execution. Lisa's reaction was even more remarkable. She did not defend herself and calmly accepted Jan's opinion. It was the natural order of things. Listening to Jan talk about painting that evening was quite an event for me, too. There was no mention of the subject, its meaning, or what kind of metaphor it might be. It was about structure, disposition, conception, and vision. How was it possible to create art or speak about art outside of its social meaning and historical context? While I still believe that art is created in a historical context, that particular evening I learned that art could be talked about and appreciated *qua art*. I was not ready or tutored sufficiently to enter this form of inquiry. I always looked for meaning in paintings; the more I found the better, especially if it had social and political meaning. After the war, I had seen the Ballet Joost perform a dance called *The Green Table* which was an interpretation of the destruction wrought by war and the eternal struggles for power and dominance. To me, that was my ultimate proof that art need not be divorced from reality. Of course in the aftermath of World War II, my reality was not too hard to define. I had no idea of the multiplicity of realities and truths. I was to seek the key to these truths for a long time.

As a model, Gloria knew many painters and was more savvy about shapes and colors. Besides, she never tried to intellectualize what she saw. She simply trusted her intuitions. Her perceptions were very often remarkable, which unfortunately did not deter her from deploring her lack of verbal adeptness.

That year ended on a sad note. Eisenhower was elected President of the United States. The day after the elections, I could not find any reason to go to work. Instead I called in sick, and we wound up going to see Chaplin's latest film on Broadway, *Limelight*. But the next year, 1953, turned out to be a year that was almost my undoing.

Chapter Nineteen

Our life was becoming almost routine, what with work, parties, and therapy sessions. After three and a half years of therapy, Dr. Gold told me that I did not need him anymore except for an occasional checkup. I left his office teary-eyed. I wanted to hug him but did not dare. I was on my own. My eyes were bright, my breathing deep, and I could laugh, sing, and cry. I was on top of the world. Nothing, absolutely nothing, could go wrong now. I could do anything, and it would all turn out fine. I was healthy with a capital *H*. I was now twenty-seven years old and felt my energy to be inexhaustible. As a matter of fact, the one true result of my Reichian therapy was a liberation of my energies. I was far from knowing what I would do with them, and I was even further away from understanding what had happened in the past, such as dealing with the loss of my family during World War II. All that seemed important to my therapist was the here and now.

I was set to go on indefinitely living on cloud nine until John V. Holmes appeared in my life. Gloria had met him through a friend of Sally Sullivan, and one day in the early spring of 1953, he came to our flat with a business proposition. John was a handsome man, a curly-haired six-footer with an open face. His demeanor was intense, sincere, and serious. It would be months before he revealed an almost maniacal sort of laughter. John had a talent for inspiring trust, and besides he informed me that he was an alternate member of the national committee of the Socialist Party. He had to be one of the good guys, right?

His proposition was simple. John wanted to start an offset letter printing business, and because of his connections with various political groups, work would not be wanting. It would be a commercial enterprise dedicated to the betterment of society, but it would be profitable as well. His only problem was that his capital was limited and consisted mainly of a large light table used for layouts and negatives. He owned a desk in a loft he shared with a printer friend of his, Igal Roodenko. My role as his partner was simple. Through my good, untested credit, and the benefits accrued under my GI Bill, I could finance the cost of a small offset press, like the one I was using at Witty Brothers. I would then be my own boss and live far more comfortably than I was already living. I would be earning real money without being enslaved to the benefit of crass commercialism. I was enthusiastic. I announced to Gloria's family that I was going to be rich.

From friends and acquaintances I received an immense quantity of opinions: encouragement, warnings, and advice to seek legal counsel and exercise extreme caution. Given my former attitudes, I was at best naive, and most likely quite stupid. I did not listen to anybody, not even Gloria.

"You always foresee doom, Gloria. I trust John. I like his face and his heart is in the right place. This is the right thing to do."

And I went on to describe eloquently what we could do with the money I would earn. At one point, even before the business had started, I began to consult the real estate section of *The New York Times* to see if a house in Levittown was affordable. At the same time, I was decrying phenomena such as Levittown in American culture. Bourgeois life was not for us, yet I would have welcomed some of its amenities.

I proceeded to obtain the papers that would help me start a business. They did not include a formal partnership between John and me. Thus, the Mathis Printing Co. was founded. I resigned from Witty Brothers with all good wishes, including those of the salesman from whom I bought printing paper. I reported to our loft on West Thirty-Third Street in Manhattan and began my life as a future tycoon.

The loft contained a huge light table and a desk, like John had said. There were also a couple of presses, cabinets with fonts, and the material needed in a print shop. These belonged to Igal Roodenko, whom I did not meet until late in the morning. Igal was rarely at work before noon. He worked quite late when he was not otherwise occupied by his involvement in the War Resisters League. It always seemed to me that he worked sporadically, sitting in thought or talking on the phone, rather than bustling around the loft. With us he was rather laconic, even grumpy. I learned later that he had been a radical conscientious objector during the war and had been in federal prison in Danbury. I also discovered that he was gay in a rather shocking way. John referred to him as miss or mademoiselle. John talked to all gay men that way. He was not aware how offensive and hurtful his speech was. Among radical or liberal circles at the time, homosexuality was tolerated as a subject of merriment. There were quite a few gays strolling into that loft, among them Bayard Rustin who came quite often, generally broke, and in need of a meal. John's alleged socialism began to totally escape me. It consisted mainly of a verbal hostility to capitalism and a stated fantasy that he could either manipulate or pervert it to his profit and bring about its destruction. How this would occur escaped me, too.

The small offset press that I was to work was not there. Given our lack of funds, acquiring a new one would be impossible. Even with my GI Bill benefits, my line of credit was limited. A bank would only approve a certain amount. John had spotted a used press, fairly new, but the asking price was larger than my credit line. John sent me to negotiate for the press. He figured that my lack of experience in such matters and my relative youth would allow me to mollify the seller and negotiate an affordable price. For once, he guessed right. I remember standing by the press, admiring it, starting it, and putting on, without a doubt, a very long face full of sadness and disappointment. I stood there and talked about my financial situation until the owner took pity on me and agreed to sell the press. As future events were to prove, it would have saved me years of pain if I had failed in that endeavor.

I came back to the shop and John exclaimed: "I knew that you would put on enough theater to get what you wanted." I was flabbergasted. *Theater? Who? Me?*

It must also be noted that my experience as a pressman was quite limited. The work I did at Witty Brothers was simple enough. A two-color job was all I knew how to do, and if the registering of the colors was not absolutely precise, it hardly mattered. I taught myself what I could, but my work was not what you could call commercial quality. That would happen in the years to come, but I never reached a superior level of craftsmanship. What I did best then was to come to work early and stay late. This did not sit particularly well with Gloria. I was neglecting her. As for John, I do not know when he saw his wife and his baby daughter. When I did meet his wife, Esther, I noticed a sad, almost teary-eyed woman—and probably a very angry one. She knew John better than any of us and was well aware of his unreliability.

Despite being supportive of my efforts, Gloria began to grumble. Her needs were not being met. We were coming home from a party one Saturday night when she announced quite calmly in a matter-of-fact tone of voice: "Mathis, I want to go travel in Europe or I want to have a baby." She was not kidding.

Going to Europe was out of the question, not only because we lacked the necessary funds but because my antagonism toward France had not abated. I had absolutely no desire to return there. Occasionally I would dream about visiting my childhood friends in Paris, but was unable to understand how or why I was there. Or my dreams would take me back to Villepinte, where I would meet my father in front of our house after he had miraculously returned from Auschwitz. I would run to him, but he would turn a cold, angry face to me and refuse to either speak or acknowledge my presence despite my pleas and sobs. I'd wake up with a lump in my throat and anguish twisting my stomach into a knot. It was probably one of the ways my survivor guilt found its way into my subconscious. In 1953, survivor guilt was not yet part of the common vocabulary, and one did not speak of the Holocaust. Instead, the police action in Korea, the Cold War, the Commies with a knife at the jugular vein of the nation, Senator McCarthy's inquisitions, and the impending execution of the Rosenbergs were the only subjects worthy of note.

Deciding to have a child did not seem like a big deal. After all, we knew how children ought to be raised. Dr. Spock was also available for the minor details of daily child care. We did not ask ourselves if we were ready to accept the responsibilities of a child or if we even had the financial means to do so. Furthermore, we never questioned what kind of life an interracial child might have in a world that was eminently racist and seemingly bent on destroying itself. Our child would herald the hope for a world without hatred, a world where human beings would be judged and respected for their intrinsic values. If our society was uneasy about our child, our very special child, that was society's problem. It did not quite turn out that way.

And so, a child was conceived along with my new business venture. We were convinced then that the pains of childbirth were the invention of a sexually repressive society. That idea was fashionable among the radical and bohemian youth. There were books published and classes offered by midwives who trained expectant couples in breathing and relaxation exercises designed to guarantee an easy, natural delivery, thus avoiding the barbaric practices of conventional obstetrics. The practices involved administering anesthetics and performing episiotomies, all of which were thought to be harmful to the mother and her baby. Natural childbirth created a new obstacle for women to overcome. What if a woman failed to work through the pain? What if she tore and had to have an episiotomy? What if a midwife was not deemed safe? What if complications arose? What if nursing the baby was not feasible? What then? Well, that meant that the poor woman was just unhealthy and riddled with neuroses. Pity the poor child raised by such a mother!

We enrolled in a class for natural childbirth. I do not believe that there were more than five or six couples at the class which took place on the East Side of mid-Manhattan. I felt out of place in this posh environment. All of us eagerly followed the instructions of the midwife, breathing deeply, and then shallowly, but fast. We stretched on the floor, the men rubbing the women's back most tenderly, almost religiously. Once during these sessions on the floor, I fell asleep after working many hours. Gloria never forgave me. We eventually befriended one of the couples, Max and Martha Shamus, who struck us as an odd pair. Martha had a very strong southern accent and Max spoke New Yorkese. Both were social workers, but Max's real love was the viola di gamba, a musical instrument I had never heard of. To us, Martha seemed to be the most eccentric of the two. She told us that she came from a prominent family in Atlanta where her father was a judge. She spoke of her rebellion against her family's values. She once left us speechless when she blurted out: "I married a greasy Jew because I did not dare marry a Negro to spite my father." Another time she confessed that she enjoyed being forced to have sex with her husband. She fitted the stereotype of Southern women so well that I could almost not believe what I was hearing. I never found out what brought this couple to a natural childbirth class except, perhaps, the spirit of rebellion that dominated the sixties.

Maren and her mother helped us find a doctor who was associated with a hospital where natural childbirth, although in its experimental stages, was accepted as a safe practice for select patients. French Hospital, which was administered by nuns, was one of two hospitals in New York where a doctor could accommodate his patients with this particular practice. I have often wondered how this came about in a Catholic hospital. Of course the whole concept of natural childbirth is somewhat absurd. Women have been giving birth for millennia according to the laws of nature. In the Judeo-Christian ethos, pain associated with childbirth is God's punishment for original sin. Cultural mores in the Western world have reinforced the fear of pain and death suffered by women in childbirth. In fact, too many women have died during childbirth because of unsanitary conditions. Adrienne Rich was to write much later when the invention of forceps and the subsequent takeover of child deliveries by male doctors resulted, in just a few short months, with the death of every woman who entered a hospital to give birth. In our day, it had become routine to anesthetize women during labor and to perform cesareans sections. Research soon proved that administering an anesthetic might possibly be harmful to the infant, as was the use of forceps. The care given to the mother after childbirth, including long bed rests, proved to be debilitating. Natural childbirth was the remedy for these ills. Pain was unnecessary; after all, peasant women as well as women in primitive cultures gave birth in the morning and were back in the fields in the afternoon. Childbirth? Purely routine! Modern urban living was the culprit in the pain experienced during labor. We did not take good care of our bodies and needed to redress the damages wrought upon us by our civilization. If we could not return to the fields, exercise would restore us to health and give us a flexible musculature. Long, flexible muscles, such as those sported by the Polynesians, were the key to avoiding pain. And of course, deep breathing.

At about this same time, we became friendly with a couple living in our building. One day I noticed that a woman was speaking French to a young boy. I was intrigued. Except for going to a French movie or reading a book in French now and again, I had not sought out anyone who spoke my native tongue. In addition to my francophobia, I was determined to master the American idiom. I was also intrigued because the woman spoke French with a foreign accent. Where did she come from? The name on the mailbox read EHRLICH; it sounded German or possibly Jewish. It turned out that Hedy and Irwin were born in the same city in Poland as my father and were Jewish. Why were they speaking French to their children instead of English or Polish?

Hedy and Irvin were born in Lodz, Poland, but were not in the same social class as my father. They belonged to a small group of Jews in Poland who were assimilated into Polish society. They were university students when World War II broke out. They were fortunate and could speak an educated dialect of Polish. Unlike the vast majority of their co-religionists, they were Westernized. They did not appear to be Jewish at first sight, neither in dress nor speech. That is most likely why they survived until they were deported to Auschwitz in 1944. They belonged to the group of deportees for whom, except for Hungarians and gypsies, the Nazis had halted mass- gassing. People still died quickly, but not as indiscriminately as in 1941-1943. Hedy and Irvin did not know each other in Lodz or Auschwitz. What they did to survive, and what they endured was never discussed. Irvin's arm bore his tattooed number. If Hedy had been tattooed, it was not visible. They would only say that they had been on the death marches as Auschwitz was being evacuated, and not a day passed that they did not wake up shaking from a nightmare.

After their liberation by the Allied forces and a period of recuperation, they were sent to a camp for displaced persons. That is where they met and began to rebuild their lives. I think they were the only survivors in their families. Going back to Lodz was out of the question, because there was nothing and no one to go back to. A Soviet-occupied Poland was not a desirable place to start a new life, and the behavior of the Poles toward the Jews during the German Occupation had been far from exemplary. They opted to go to Paris to resume their university studies, something their fluency in French would permit. However, the war's aftermath had left France in dire straits. Hedy and Irwin could not find an outlet for their aspirations, so they emigrated to the United States.

When Gloria and I met them they had two children, Henri and Sylvie, both bilingual in English and French. The family had just moved to Manhattan from Patterson, New Jersey, where Irvin and two associates had founded a shop that manufactured high quality handbags. The measure of their financial success was that they could now afford to rent a bigger shop in Lower Manhattan and be closer to the stores that catered to a chic clientele. Hedy and Irvin spoke disparagingly of the two partners, both concentration camp survivors. They were uncouth, unscrupulous, and ruthless—probably the type of people who had survived by being Kapos in the camps. Still, they were skilled men. Irvin had a talent for design, and he made a good impression on people. It was he who contacted and dealt with the purchasing agents of their clients. In Hedy's words, they were people of "culture."

Gloria did not like them. She claimed that they were pretentious and snobbish. The children were eventually sent to a French Lycée in New York. Gloria saw them as white European immigrants who were easily making a fortune, for whom doors were opened, opportunities created, while she and people like her were held back and held down. Racism is a fact of life in the U.S., but I knew that for the Ehrlichs, life was not that easy. Yes, they valued the life of the mind, but that was something that had been denied to them. Years later, Hedy would resume her studies and earn a doctorate at Columbia. Meanwhile, they were both struggling with English and using their energy to create some semblance of normalcy in their daily lives. I doubt that they ever found it.

Gloria recognized that Hedy and Irwin had gone through an indescribable experience and that they had suffered in a way that she could not possibly know. But she claimed that was all over now. They were white; they could pass and blend in society. She never could. She threw that in my face, too, whenever the subject of racism came up. As I had discovered in Paris when I was living with the Leizers and their dead children, people were fond of creating a scale against which sufferings could be weighed and measured. To this day, I still find myself comparing the Holocaust to other racist experiences. Still, I know full well that somebody else's pains do not negate mine. I am grateful that I survived, as did the Ehrlichs, but I found no solace in the fact that someone suffered more or less than I did, quite the contrary. The Ehrlich's pains, as well as Gloria's pain, accentuated mine. The effect of pain being measured on some abstract scale is a denial that pain is pain. It shames the sufferer for a lack of perspective. It denies open grieving. It orders silence and impedes the process of healing. The color of my skin can't possibly let me know what racism is, even if I have felt its effect for a short time. My life could have easily been snuffed out anytime during the war, but anti-Semitism and xenophobia didn't stop after I was liberated. Now I am told, and I have been told, that this period of my life is "over and done." I can pass and be just another white man with all the privileges that status entails. Perhaps I can, but does that obliterate my memories, my consciousness? Does it mean I can choose to be deaf and blind to the continuation of human savagery? Quite the contrary is true. My gender is also seen as an impediment to understanding these issues, as if I had never felt oppression or pain.

Awaiting the arrival of our child was an exciting time for both Gloria and me. Gloria feared that she would give birth to a freak. In addition to doubting that anything good could ever happen to her, it's probable that these fears had been experienced by most women. There was also the excitement of hearing the first heartbeat, of feeling the baby's first kick in the womb, and our endless obsession with naming the baby. What a bore we must have been to our friends, but nothing comparable to the inanities uttered after the child was born.

My business life had a different kind of excitement—the kind that were provoked by my misgivings over John Holmes's behavior, as well as my naiveté and stupidity. John seldom arrived to work before noon. I thought he was drumming up business, and at times he was, but our basic problem was that we had started a business without a sufficient cash flow. John tried to raise more cash but chose an unconventional method. He began by opening several checking accounts with a minimal deposit and writing a check for cash from one account. Then he would cash it at a check-cashing service and would write another check from a different account to cover the first check. It would take several days before the checks started to bounce. With several open accounts, this carrousel can keep turning for quite a while, but it does not go on forever. So John found a man who would lend us money. He was an insurance salesman for Met Life, and in addition to the interest he expected to collect on the notes we were signing, he demanded that we buy life insurance. He did not care if we kept the insurance or not, because he would still receive his commission. The people who hired us to do work were slow to pay, and the money was eaten quickly in rents, salaries, and supplies. We were always falling behind. John devised another scheme that involved factoring accounts receivable. What that means is that at a reduced rate, a business gets paid for the work done and delivered. The full amount is then paid to the factorer, but it is almost impossible for a business to survive under these conditions. That September, I went back to work at Witty Brothers. By this time, I was thoroughly disillusioned with John's business acumen and his perpetual lies. But what I did not know was that John, in his desperate need to find money to keep the business afloat and his insane desire to ruin the capitalist system all by himself, was factoring fictitious accounts receivable. That activity could have landed us both in jail. By day I worked at Witty Brothers, and in the evening, I went to work at the shop. It was often midnight before I would get home to Gloria. She was very understanding about the situation, but our relationship began to suffer. I was so completely involved in my work that when we had decided to legalize our union that summer, I went right back to work after the ceremony at City Hall.

I was reluctant to get married; it seemed to me that I was compromising my principles, just as I had done when I married

Donna. The legalities of marriage were just too bourgeois. Two people who loved each other did not need an institutional sanction. Instead, they should strive to free themselves from the stupid conventions invented by propertied men who were afraid of liberated women. Gloria did not care for the conventions of society, but she rightly wanted a commitment that exceeded my principles. Later we joked about how we had deprived ourselves of toasters and other household gadgets by quietly getting married and without having a celebration of sorts.

Because we could not pay the rent for the printing shop, we had to move several times until the equipment wound up in a store front in Greenwich Village. Business became sporadic as did my presence at the shop. I was letting the business die out and leaving John to his own devices. By that time, he was on to new schemes. I seldom saw him.

Chapter Twenty

The big event that following year was the birth of our daughter, Monique Celia. The expected natural childbirth did not turn out as we had expected. Gloria's water broke early in the morning, and her contractions began shortly thereafter. Following the doctor's advice, we checked in to the French hospital that afternoon. I was allowed to stay with Gloria until she was taken to the labor room. I had anticipated being present at the moment of birth; it was an experience I did not want to miss. I wanted to be a partner in the process, but I was prevented from participating on the grounds that too many fathers had fainted in the delivery room. I should have had a fit, but I was intimidated by the authoritative tone of the doctor and his nurse. So, I waited in the lounge, sad, frustrated, and impotent. My wife was bringing a new life into the world, and I would not be there to see it happen. I was just sitting in a lounge, useless and with feelings of jealousy. My role in the whole process was over; it was time to walk off the stage. At three o'clock in the morning, I was sent home. My presence was superfluous and a nuisance. Three hours later, our daughter was born, and I called Gloria's family with the good news.

When I was finally able to see Gloria that afternoon, bringing with me the traditional bouquet of red roses, I found a woman triumphant with joy. She recounted all the details of Monique's birth, including the moment when the doctor feared the umbilical cord was wound around our baby's neck. Doctor Luschinsky performed an episiotomy and said in his Swiss-German accent: "Now, Gloria, you give a great big push!"

Dr. Luschinsky came into the room at this point of the tale, shook my hand and asked: "How is banana head?"

Banana head was the name he had given Monique, because her cranium had become somewhat elongated in the birth canal. Dressed in hospital garb, with a mask over my mouth, I picked up my daughter. All I could see was a crown of black hair. I thought to myself: *This baby is going to be a very special child, a very special gift to the world.*

Monique came home five days later. Gloria had a moment of panic when she realized that we were on our own with the baby. Lisa Muller, well trained in the care of prematurely born infants, came for a visit. She took charge of Monique, and we were appalled by the casual way she picked her up, turned her over on her belly, and patted her back. We also realized that the baby would not break in a thousand little pieces. Friends and family invaded our small flat for a day or two. Like most new parents, we were exhausted by all their good wishes and our lack of sleep.

Our euphoria didn't last long. The baby was still the center of our life and continued to be so in spite of the hardships that my association with John Holmes soon caused. I was at work when a collection agency called me with threats of prison. John's manipulation of the capitalist system were catching up with us. We were called to an office on Forty-second Street, where the man who had been factoring John's fictitious accounts receivable threatened to take his case to the District

Attorney if we didn't repay the money. Neither of us had any money. We agreed to repay a small sum each week, including the accrued interest. It took me years to repay that money. John soon disappeared and never paid a cent. Summons arrived at our house almost daily, and I went to court. Judgments rained on my head. My salary was garnished at Witty Brothers. Most employers would fire employees that complicated their bookkeeping, but Witty Brothers was a family affair. Still it was obvious that on my meager, depleted salary I could not provide for my family. I had to look for a second job.

Whenever I needed to find a job in New York City I made a generous use of the many newspaper ads and employment agencies. I needed a full-time job since I could not make ends meet with a part-time job. The job I eventually found was with an amusement company named Pokerino. It paid a dollar an hour, and I had a work week that was forty-eight hours long. I worked there from six P.M. to two A.M. My supervisor at Witty Brothers allowed me to check out at five-forty-five so I could report at Pokerino by six P.M. My job was very simple. I changed dollars into nickels so people who wandered in the place could roll balls into holes, hoping to make a winning poker combination. Each win brought a loud announcement, and the customer would receive a ticket. After winning several tickets, the customer would receive a stupid prize. In addition, I had to shout: "Poker in front, Shuffle in the rear!" to attract customers. Our clients, especially the regulars, did not belong to an elite class of people. To save subway fare, I walked home to Fifty-seventh Street. There were days when I could not report to my job at Witty Brothers and a few days when I was so exhausted that I slept twelve to fourteen hours like a brute.

This regime lasted until the Fourth of July. Witty Brothers had closed for the day, so we went to Central Park with a few friends. When time came for me to leave for Pokerino, Gloria broke into tears. That was the end of my career as a carnival barker and money changer. However, our financial problems were still acute. Quite often, we had to borrow five dollars from our family or friends. Our relationship was also changing. I was not home often enough, and I was constantly worried, anxious. Gloria was equally unhappy and was very involved with caring for Monique. Our basic needs were not being met, and our emotional needs were suffering as well. We had both been very poor in our lives, but now we were losing hope that we would ever extricate ourselves from the debts that John and I had incurred. These debts exceeded five thousand dollars—a huge sum in 1954. That led me to tell Lisa Muller that I was a loser. It took twelve years of our lives to become debt free. By that time, my relationship with Gloria was in shambles. We spent many years trying to repair the damage, but we failed.

The next few years were spent struggling to work our way out of debt. As soon as she could, Gloria worked as a substitute teacher in a day care center. By 1957, she had become a full-time teacher. I left my job at Witty Brothers and worked in commercial shops where the pay was better. My skills as a pressman improved. Whenever I could, I'd fill in at night in another shop. With all of our debts, it was hard to keep our heads above water. We had a tight budget that resulted all too often in arguments between us.

Once, I worked a seven-day week for twelve hours each day. I came home at the end of the week with nearly two hundred dollars in my wallet. I was so ecstatic that I walked in the apartment, throwing the bills into the air like confetti and shouting, "Money! Money!" The next day Monique became ill, and we had to pay for doctor visits and medicines. I never did that again, hoping to avoid a curse. The gods had taught me a lesson in humility.

By the summer of 1955, I had earned a week's paid vacation. But what to do with it was a dilemma. We arranged to spend that week on a commune in New Jersey. The commune survived mostly as a printing enterprise. We became the guests of Dave Dellinger and his family. Dave belonged to the War Resisters League and had been a conscientious objector in World War II and like Igal Roodenko, had served time in federal prison. He later opposed the Vietnam War and was one of the Chicago Eight prosecuted by the government for his role at the Democratic Convention of 1968. Dave was married and had children. His wife was very active in the Catholic Worker. I had known about the group which was founded by Dorothy Day and her partner, but I had never met anyone who was a member of it. I think that Dave was an atheist. Still I was amazed how respectful he and his wife were to each other. Of course they had many things in common. Both opposed war, capital punishment, prisons, racism, and the inequities fostered by the capitalist system. One was a humanist, the other believed in a Jesus abandoned long ago by the religious establishments. There was no real conflict in how they viewed the world and the human condition. I admired them. Their differences could be bridged with respect and a recognition of their common goals.

The commune consisted of four or five individual houses where individual couples lived. We were housed in a renovated, yet comfortable chicken coop. We ate with the Dellinger family, but the whole community shared one meal a day. I visited their print shop, which was very professional. It did work for nonprofit organizations, while shunning commercial work. This print shop had a purpose beyond earning money. To join the commune, you had to bring all that you possessed and believe in the work that was done. All we would bring were our debts. It was quite tempting, but only for a very short while. I was opposed to war and capital punishment, but I did not see myself as a conscientious objector. As a Holocaust survivor, I did not believe that passive resistance could stop a Hitler or a Stalin. Ghandi persuaded the British crown to leave India because the British crown was not a psychotic monster. Ghandi would have wound up in Hitler's gas chambers.

In 1956, our friends helped us find a bigger apartment on East Twelfth Street, between Second and Third Avenue. This brought us closer to Greenwich Village and Washington Square, where we liked taking Monique to the playground. It also made it easier for me to haunt the bookstores on Fourth Avenue. Gloria devoted a lot of her time and energy to Monique's education since she had been deprived of one in her childhood. That was not going to happen to her daughter. She found a special, progressive nursery school, a middle-class school, to which she obtained a scholarship. At our first parent-teacher conference we were told that Monique was a "special child." I never understood what she really meant by her assessment. She was special to us, but how special was she to other people? Interracial children were still rare in New York City; an interracial child in a middle-class private school was even rarer. Was Monique being treated as "special?" Was she understanding it and reacting accordingly? At that time, Monique proudly mispronounced her surname and announced the diversity of her parentage. In retrospect, I believe the word "special" was not meant as a flattery. It could have meant a number of things, including strange and difficult. I was reminded of it years later when my three-year-old daughter Catherine, was placed in a French *école maternelle* not knowing a single word of French, and the teacher reported: *"Elle sait ce qu'elle veut."* (She is stubborn) Nor was it flattery when a dean told me that I was the most candid person on campus.

The Museum of Modern Art had begun art classes for children. Gloria obtained a scholarship for Monique and took her there weekly. She also enrolled her in dance classes at the Henry Street Settlement House. Eventually, Gloria found a teacher to train her own voice. She was making sure that despite our poverty, our child would not be deprived access to culture. As an adult, Monique would complain that we had not given her access to her Indian or Jewish culture. We did not; at the time I would have been vehemently opposed to it. I resented the attempts of her grandparents to expose her to Christianity. We were determined to raise a new kind of person. I am happy that we raised a creative one although that is her own doing.

Marvin and Betty Mandell played a decisive role in my life. They showed up at our apartment one evening in 1958, carrying an article of the *New York Times*. As soon as I opened the door, in his usual enthusiasm, breathless way, Marvin said, "Mathis, you have to read this article. This fits you like a glove." The article described a new experimental program for adults at Brooklyn College that gave college credits for life experiences. The program also offered interdisciplinary seminars in the humanities, social sciences, natural sciences, and an education seminar for future teachers. These seminars covered all the basic requirements, but a major still had to be fulfilled in order to graduate. It was hoped that these classes would significantly reduce the time it took to graduate. Admission to the Special Baccalaureate Program was done by testing and interviews. Unlike the rest of the matriculated students who were tuition-free, the fees for this program were set at twenty dollars a credit. When I reported to an amphitheater full of people, I did not believe that I had a chance in hell. After all, I had been out of school for seventeen years and had only a high school equivalency diploma. To my great surprise, I was called back for an interview and admitted to the program. Dean Gaede was only concerned about my relative youth and adjustments thirty new students would have to make that fall. This was his program, his vision. He had persuaded the Rockefeller Foundation to fund it. His interview with me was very gentle. When I timidly asked him if I could handle a college program (I had a totally unrealistic view of what a college education required), Dean Gaede replied, "I think you should be in graduate school." What a wonderful exaggeration that was. Marvin and Betty borrowed money from their credit union for my tuition and handed me the loan book. It's a debt I can never repay.

One of the requirements I had to fulfill to attend Brooklyn College was to become a U.S. citizen. I was not yet a citizen. There had been no pressing necessity to become one and the MacCarthy years were not especially welcoming. Besides, I knew too many radical people. I was anxious about facing naturalization officers. But this time, I had a real reason to apply. After I took a test that examined my literacy and familiarity with the Constitution, the question of why I had been classified as 4p during the Korean War came up. I had served before, why had I been unable to serve later? Had the army done me any harm? I tried to explain that my main problem was one of anxiety and that I was undergoing treatment for it at the time. My two witnesses, Sally Sullivan and Renée Davis, were called in and asked to testify on the state of my mental health. They both replied: "He is the sanest man we know." Both were in therapy at the time.

When I entered Brooklyn College in the fall of 1958, I was also working at Fordham University's print shop. Travel time between Fordham and Flatbush Avenue took an average of one and three quarter hours. To get to my classes on time I had to leave work at 4:45 P.M. My immediate supervisor agreed to let me go early. George had emigrated from Bavaria in the twenties. He was a good Catholic, and his voice had retained his German intonations. He claimed that Bavarians did not buy into Naziism. Little did he know that the vast majority of SS members were Catholics from Bavaria. His favorite saying was: "Figures don't lie, but lies do figures." George gave me all the support he could during the four years I worked under him.

My first semester of college was full of angst and excitement. I was assigned to the humanities seminar led by Professor Ruth Kriesberg, the most dynamic, multitiered teacher I ever met. I was awed. She was expert in literature, the arts, philosophy, culture, and politics. She was able to tie all the disciplines together, to show their interactions. I had made up my mind that I would pursue my childhood dream and become a teacher. The arrival of Sputnik made that dream a reality. With Sputnik, the lack of science and language teachers was deplored. We had to catch up to the Soviets. In New York, the language exam for language teachers would be waived; native speakers could now become teachers. Kriesberg became my model and inspiration, helping me in other ways as well. Once I complained to her that I felt uncomfortable with my fellow students, yet I wanted to be part of the group. I felt torn. Kriesberg answered, "Instead of feeling torn by these feelings, why don't you use them as your poles. Stand on them and use them." Along with Monsieur Violle's admonition that no one could ever deprive me of what I knew, that was the most cogent advice I ever received. I asked Kriesberg to help me with my essays. She went through them with a fine tooth comb on the condition that I would rewrite them. I have used that technique all my academic life. Some debts can never be repaid often enough.

In my sophomore year, Gloria gave birth to a son. We were quite excited to have Raphaël Anthony with us. Like Monique, he was born at French Hospital. I had no more of a participatory role than I had during Monique's birth. The times still hadn't changed.

In my senior year, I had a posthumous reconciliation of sorts with my mother. My relationship with my mother had been a stormy one, but she had saved my life and my feelings toward her had softened over the years. There were a lot of issues though, that I had not resolved. There was the guilt that stemmed from her death in Auschwitz, irrational as it may have been, and the guilt I felt for being a disappointment to her. I was not the son she had expected me to be. Whenever Gloria and I argued, she would cry out that she was not my mother and that I should not visit my grievances or manias on her. She may have been right. We all carry the baggage of our past. The path to adulthood lies in how we handle that baggage and whether it energizes or paralyzes us. It is necessary to transcend it, lest we become mired in it. I had a dream one night that my mother, dressed in the elegant clothes that she had worn in a sepia photograph when she was in her early forties, was coming off a ship's gangway in New York. I was there to meet her. As we looked at each other, she put her hands on my shoulders and said in perfect English, "Mathis, you've become quite a man." Then she left. When I woke up, I understood that I had forgiven her and more importantly that I had forgiven myself. I could claim her as my own and remember her as she was and how she had struggled. That was the last time I ever dreamed of my mother. I also stopped having nightmares about the death camps. I stopped having dreams where I witnessed the death of my parents.

When I was enrolled in college, I thought I would become a secondary school teacher. That was my dream, and how in the long run I would extricate myself from poverty. In the last year of my college career, I discovered that to teach high school I would need a Master's degree or its equivalent to become certified. Brooklyn College offered a Master in French. I could continue to study there while teaching with a temporary license. I consulted with several teachers about my plans and some advised me to apply to universities outside New York City.

I did not wish to leave New York. I loved the town, and by 1962, being part of an interracial couple had become more acceptable, at least in Greenwich Village. I did not want to put up with provincial prejudice. One idiot professor opined when I told him I wanted to teach French that I was "bringing coal to Newcastle." That statement nullifies the work of all native teachers of English. However, I decided that if I did not apply I might regret it later, even if I did not enroll. I had to know what institution would admit and support a thirty-six-year-old with a wife and two children. I reasoned that only a very rich university could afford us. I applied at the most prestigious universities in the country, including, Harvard, Yale, Princeton, Columbia, and Stanford. I was convinced that the replies would be negative. I went about life as we had planned, taking the exam to get a temporary license. Six weeks after I had applied to these universities, the call came. I had fallen asleep on the couch, but Gloria shook me awake and called me to the phone.

"Hello, Mr. Szykowski. This is Mr. Carter at Stanford University. Are you in a position to accept a three-year fellowship in the Department of French and Italian?"

"Yes sir, I am."

"Professor Juilland will be in New York this Monday at the Plaza Hotel. Can you meet him there at ten A.M.?"

"Yes sir, I can."

There was no hesitation on my part. Gloria had a lot of questions and worries. She really did not want to leave New York, her aging parents, or her voice teacher. It might have been a good time to split up, but the women's liberation movement had not yet started. The Civil Rights Movement was growing, and it would not be long before women began to claim their rights.

This was in the main, a journey during which I groped for ways to heal, to understand, and grow. As I look back on the first thirty-six years of my life, I see that I have experienced a difficult childhood with many adult responsibilities. I fled Paris twice, once to avoid bombs, and the other to avoid deportation. I left the country of my birth to have a chance at a different life. I did survive, but I did not do it by myself: I had help along the way. I also had incredible luck. Surely this luck was abetted by my own will to act, but I owe immense debts of gratitude to the many people who were there to help me up when I was down. Through them, I learned to heal, and to celebrate life.

I have no regrets about the choices I made in my early life. I wanted, with others of my generation, to change a world that needed changing, and still does. The twentieth century may be remembered as the bloodiest of all centuries. We failed to change the world through political means and turned inward to change ourselves through therapy, hoping that this route would be the means to affect the world. In this we failed, too. However, for many of us, and for myself in particular, we acquired a consciousness that helped to free up our energies and lead productive lives. The last task that I had to accomplish was to understand the nature of the Holocaust and to understand, as best I could, why human beings could behave as they did. Now I believe that we are all capable, in given circumstances, to be both heroes and villains. Humanity, in its struggles for survival, appears to be trapped in unresolvable conflicts.